Presented by

Our Mission

We help Caterpillar's dealers and customers succeed through financial service excellence. As part of the Caterpillar enterprise, we will leverage our intellectual capital to deliver customer driven solutions, enhance shareholder value, and grow on our strong foundation as a caring and learning organization.

www.CatFinancial.com

NASHVILLE
AMPLIFIED

The downtown skyline at dusk

NASHVILLE
AMPLIFIED

FIONA SOLTES
with E. Thomas Wood

This book was produced in cooperation with the City of Nashville. Cherbo Publishing Group gratefully acknowledges its important contribution to *Nashville: Amplified.*

 *cherbo* publishing group, inc.

president	JACK C. CHERBO
executive vice president	ELAINE HOFFMAN
editorial director	CHRISTINA M. BEAUSANG
managing feature editor	MARGARET L. MARTIN
senior feature editor	TINA G. RUBIN
senior profiles editor	J. KELLEY YOUNGER
profiles editors	BENJAMIN PROST
	LIZA YETENEKIAN SMITH
associate editor	SYLVIA EMRICH-TOMA
proofreaders	JENNY KORNFELD
	REBECCA SAUER
profiles writers	LINDA CHASE
	SYLVIA EMRICH-TOMA
	TERRI JONISCH
	TERREN LAMP
	RODD MONTS
	KRISTINA SAUERWEIN
creative director	PERI A. HOLGUIN
senior designer	THEODORE E. YEAGER
designer	NELSON CAMPOS
senior photo editor	WALTER MLADINA
photo editor	DAVID ZANZINGER
digital color specialist	ART VASQUEZ
sales administrator	JOAN K. BAKER
client services supervisor	PATRICIA DE LEONARD
senior client services coordinator	LESLIE E. SHAW
client services coordinator	KENYA HICKS
administrative assistants	JUDY ROBITSCHEK
	BILL WAY
eastern regional manager	MARCIA WEISS
regional development manager	GLEN EDWARDS
publisher's representative	LINDA SPROEHNLE

Cherbo Publishing Group, Inc.
Encino, California 91316
© 2007 by Cherbo Publishing Group, Inc.
All rights reserved. Published 2007.

Printed in Canada
By Friesens

Subsidiary Production Office
Santa Rosa, CA, USA
888.340.6049

Library of Congress Cataloging-in-Publication data
Soltes, Fiona, and E. Thomas Wood
A pictorial guide highlighting Nashville's economic and social advantages.
Library of Congress Control Number: 2006939412
ISBN 978-1-882933-78-5

Visit the CPG Web site at www.cherbopub.com.

The information in this publication is the most recent available, has been carefully researched to ensure accuracy, and has been reviewed by the sponsor. Cherbo Publishing Group, Inc. cannot and does not guarantee either the correctness of all information furnished it or the complete absence of errors, including omissions.

Dedication:

For the many fans of Nashville—and those who don't yet know they are.

Acknowledgments:

Heartfelt thanks to every Nashvillian who has crossed my path over the last decade and a half, native or otherwise. Your charm, gentility, and welcoming spirit have truly made all the difference when it comes to defining "home." Much gratitude, also, to those who have encouraged me to be caught up in the city's optimistic attitude, and on a professional level, to those who have challenged, referred, hired, edited, and taught me, as well as graciously allowed me to add my own notes to Nashville's grand song. You are appreciated more than you know.

An exhibit at the Grand Ole Opry Museum

Left: Members of the F.A.I.T.H. Riders Motorcycle Ministry; right: live entertainment at the Wildhorse Saloon

The Skywheel at the Tennessee State Fair in Nashville

A jogger on his way up the Rose Park stairway to the Capitol Hill belvedere

TABLE OF CONTENTS

NASHVILLE TIMELINE	2
PART ONE	**8**
THE GOOD LIFE AN OVERVIEW OF NASHVILLE	
CHAPTER ONE	
ALL THIS FOR A SONG Quality of Life	10
PART TWO	**28**
TITANS OF COMMERCE NASHVILLE BUSINESS AND INDUSTRY	
CHAPTER TWO	
CULTIVATING GREAT MINDS Education	30
CHAPTER THREE	
ROCK SOLID Finance, Insurance, and Professional Services	40
CHAPTER FOUR	
VIBRANT VENTURES Health Care, Technology, and Biosciences	50
CHAPTER FIVE	
ANOTHER NASHVILLE TUNE: THE HUM OF THE PRODUCTION LINE Manufacturing, Information Technology, and Distribution	60
CHAPTER SIX	
SOUND INVESTMENTS Music, Tourism, and Entertainment	70
CHAPTER SEVEN	
BACKDROP OF A BOOM Real Estate, Development, and Construction	80
CHAPTER EIGHT	
MAKING CONNECTIONS Transportation, Telecommunications, and Energy	90
PART THREE	**100**
PORTRAITS OF SUCCESS	
PROFILES OF COMPANIES AND ORGANIZATIONS	
BIBLIOGRAPHY	206
INDEX	210
PHOTO CREDITS	216

Nashville charm, left to right: Milliners in their hat shop; fresh vegetables at Nashville Farmers Market; the legendary Ernest Tubb Record Shop

CORPORATIONS & ORGANIZATIONS PROFILED

The following organizations have made a valuable commitment to the quality of this publication. The City of Nashville gratefully acknowledges their participation in *Nashville: Amplified*.

American General Life and Accident Insurance Company	118–19
AmSouth Bank	xvi, 126
Brasfield & Gorrie	172–73
Bridgestone Americas Holding, Inc.	142–43
Caterpillar Financial Services Corporation	xvi, 112–13
Central Parking Corporation	168–69
Comdata® Corporation	116–17
Community Health Systems, Inc.	xvi, 136–37
Consumers Insurance Group, Inc.	xvi, 124–25
Cummins Filtration	146–47
Doubletree Guest Suites Nashville Airport	196–97
Earl Swensson Associates, Inc.	182
First Tennessee	xvii, 110–11
Franklin American Mortgage Company	122–23
Gaylord Opryland Resort & Convention Center	198
Gould Turner Group, P.C.	174–75
Hartmann, Inc.	148
Holland Group, The	164–65
Hospital Corporation of America	xvii, 130–33
LifeWay Christian Resources	156–57
Mars Petcare U.S.	xvii, 152–53
Metropolitan Nashville Airport Authority	202
MJM Architects	176–77
Odom's Tennessee Pride Sausage, Inc.	144–45
Quality Industries, Inc.	149
Radiology Alliance	138
Randstad USA	166–67
R. H. Boyd Publishing Corporation	xvii, 158–59
Ross Bryan Associates, Inc.—Consulting Engineers	180–81
Saint Thomas Health Services	134–35
Shirley Zeitlin and Company, Realtors®	184
Street Dixon Rick Architecture, PLC	178–79
SunTrust Bank–Nashville	114–15
Tennessee Credit Union, The	xvii, 120–21
Tractor Supply Company	192–93
Trevecca Nazarene University	106
United Methodist Publishing House, The	160
Vanderbilt University	104–05
YMCA of Middle Tennessee	188–89

Atrium of Gaylord Opryland Resort & Convention Center

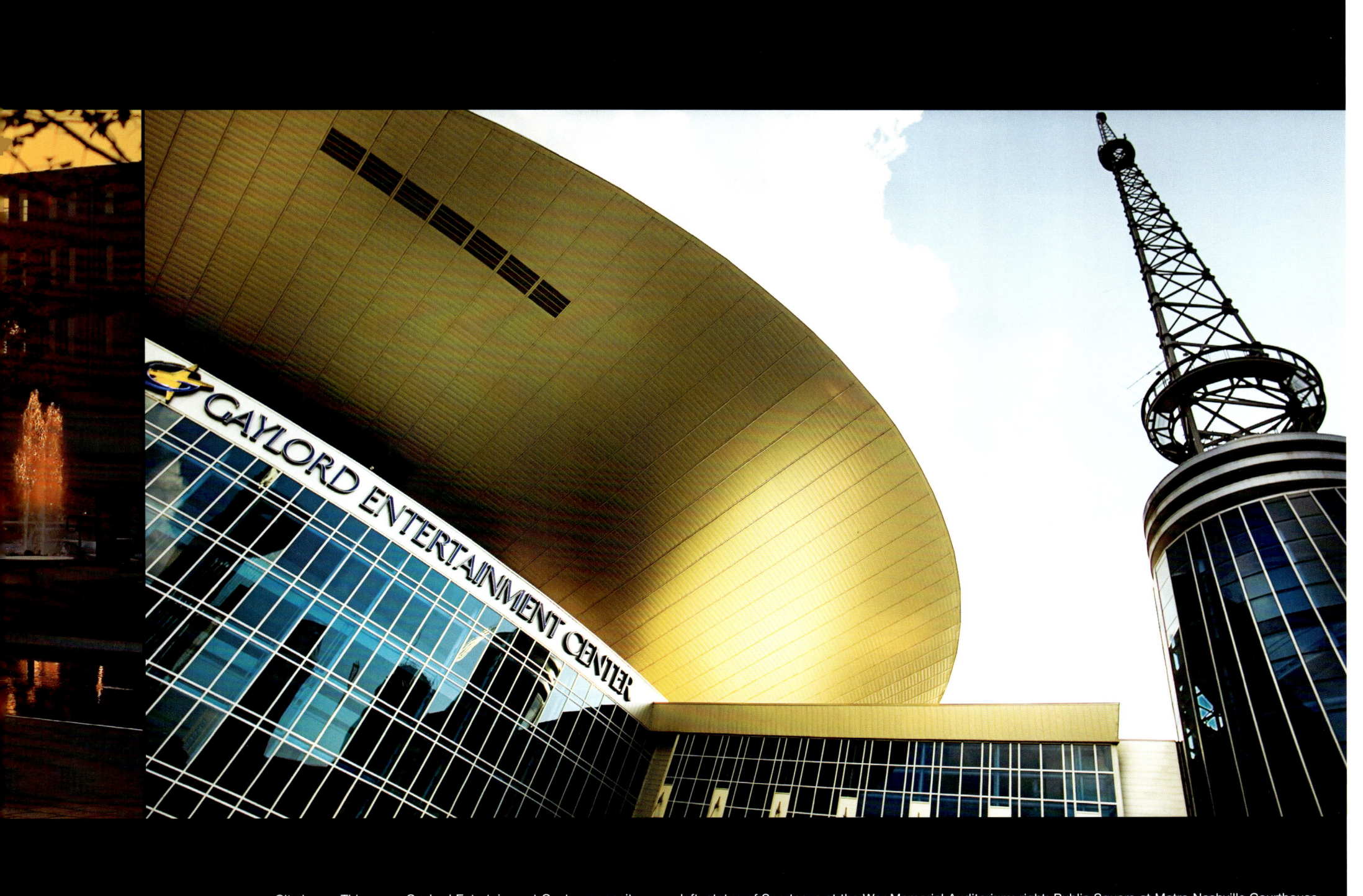

City icons: This page, Gaylord Entertainment Center; opposite page, left: statue of Spartacus at the War Memorial Auditorium; right: Public Square at Metro Nashville Courthouse

BUSINESS VISIONARIES

The following companies and organizations are recognized as innovators in their fields and have played a prominent role in this publication, as they have in the state.

American General Life and Accident Insurance Company
American General Center, Nashville, TN 37250
Contact: Donna Kowalski
Phone: 615-749-1000 / Fax: 615-749-1610
E-mail: donna_kowalski@aigag.com
Web site: www.agla.com
"We're Changing the Way Americans Think About, Purchase, and Use Life Insurance."

American General Life and Accident Insurance Company

Caterpillar Financial Services Corporation
2120 West End Avenue, Nashville, TN 37203-0001
Phone: 615-341-1000
Web site: www.catfinancial.com

Community Health Systems, Inc.
4000 Meridian Boulevard, Franklin, TN 37067
Phone: 615-465-7000
Web site: www.chs.net
"Promises Made, Promises Kept"

Consumers Insurance Group, Inc.
P.O. Box 12269, Murfreesboro, TN 37129-0046
Jimmy Clift, CEO
Bill Wheeler, President
Phone: 615-896-6133 / Fax: 615-896-0766
E-mail: bwheeler@ciusa.com
Web site: www.ciusa.com
"When You're With Us, You're Family!"

First Tennessee
511 Union Street, Suite 200, Nashville, TN 37219
Contact: Mike Edwarcs, Middle Tennessee Region President
Phone: 800-489-4040 or 615-734-6000
E-mail: allthingsfinancial@firsttennessee.com
Web site: www.firsttennessee.com
"All Things Financial"

HCA, Inc.—Hospital Corporation of America
One Park Plaza, Nashville, TN 37203
Phone: 615-344-9551
Web site: www.hcahealthcare.com

Mars Petcare, U.S.
210 Westwood Place South, Suite 400, Brentwood, TN 37027
Phone: 615-373-7774
Web site: www.mars.com

Street Dixon Rick Architecture, PLC
107 Kenner Avenue, Nashville, TN 37205
Contact: E. Baird Dixon, AIA LEED–AP, Principal, or
Stephen P. Rick, AIA LEED–AP, Principal
Phone: 615-298-2525 / Fax: 615-298-4571
E-mail: sdrarch@sdrarch.com
Web site: www.sdrarch.com

The Tennessee Credit Union
1400 8th Avenue South, Nashville, TN 37203
Contact: Michael Martin, President/CEO
Phone: 800-622-2535 / Fax: 615-242-6112
E-mail: mdmartin@ttcu.org
Web site: www.ttcu.org
"The financial choice for your life."

The refurbished Shelby Street Bridge, overlooking downtown and Riverfront Park

ABOUT THE MAYOR

In recent years, Nashville has gained increasing accolades as "the smartest place to live" and the top area for companies looking to relocate or expand. While these awards are public recognition that Nashville is a good place to live and work, the city's success reflects the efforts and hard work of its mayor—Bill Purcell.

Purcell's abilities as a consensus builder and civic booster garnered him designation in the "Mayors" category as Public Official of the Year from *Governing* magazine.

First elected as mayor of the Metropolitan Government of Nashville and Davidson County in 1999, and then reelected in 2003 with a record 84.8 percent of the vote, Purcell has proven to be a strong leader and communicator.

Since taking office, Purcell's primary focus has been on quality-of-life issues such as safety and education. Over seven years, the mayor has boosted education funding some 42 percent, from $397 million to $563 million. In fact, his efforts on education have attracted national attention as a role model for mayors. In 2006 Purcell received a grant for high-school reform from the U.S. Conference of Mayors. Nashville was one of only two cities to win this national planning grant.

Nashville's 2001 property tax increase, which helped to fund the education budget, actually coincided with an anti-tax movement in Tennessee. This victory during the state's anti-tax passion was a testament to Purcell's abilities to comprehend his constituents' priorities and his role as a master consensus builder.

Purcell's focus on quality of life included attention to the arts. In addition to increasing funding to local arts organizations, he promoted Nashville's identity as Music City, a moniker that now is recognized nationwide. Through Purcell's efforts, Metro Nashville donated land and provided financial support for the Schermerhorn Symphony Center. For these and other efforts, in 2006 Americans for the Arts honored Mayor Purcell with its National Award for Local Arts Leadership.

The mayor also has built an impressive track record of improvements to the city's infrastructure. From new sidewalks and bridges to new parks and police precincts, the work of the Purcell administration can be found in all parts of Metro Nashville. One early visible example is the renovated Shelby Street Bridge, which is now a shining icon for the city. Another example is the Public Square, a new park in the heart of the city, in front of the newly restored historic Courthouse, that will be a gathering place for Nashvillians for years to come.

From education to the arts, housing, and public safety, Bill Purcell has worked to make this new century Nashville's Century.

Nashville's War Memorial Auditorium and Square, flanking the Tennessee State Capitol

FOREWORD

Metropolitan Government of Nashville and Davidson County

Bill Purcell, Mayor

Welcome.

Nashville became a city just over 200 years ago. It grew from a small town on America's frontier into today's Metro Nashville, which ranks at the top of lists for economic development and quality of life.

Nashville: Amplified records the sounds of today's Music City. It is a diverse mix, covering music executives, health care entrepreneurs, university presidents, and religious publishers. Backing it all is a chorus of hardworking Nashvillians creating a city that is one of a kind.

Whether you live here, or visit, or want to relocate to Nashville, this book will help you know the city that we call home.

Sincerely,

Bill Purcell
Mayor

Office of the Mayor
Metropolitan Courthouse
Nashville, Tennessee 37201
Phone: 615.862.6000
Fax: 615.862.6040
mayor@nashville.gov

NASHVILLE TIMELINE

1779　　　1819　　　1828　　　1843

The Hermitage, home of U.S. president Andrew Jackson

Major General Andrew Jackson in an 1820 engraving

1779 Nashville is settled by James Robertson and John Donelson. Robertson leads a group of men who arrive on horseback Christmas Day; Donelson brings their families four months later, after traversing the Cumberland River on flatboats.

1788 Andrew Jackson becomes prosecuting attorney for the city of Nashville.

1796 Tennessee is admitted to the Union, becoming the 16th state.

1806 Nashville is chartered as a city.

1819 Andrew Jackson builds a cotton plantation in the Greek Revival style and names it the Hermitage.

1819 The city's era of frontier isolation ends when the steamboat *General Jackson* arrives from New Orleans, bringing Nashville opportunities for trade.

1821 The city opens its first school in September, exploring a new idea—public education.

1824 Singing-school teacher Allen D. Carden creates and prints *The Western Harmony* tunebook, the first music published with a Nashville imprint.

1828 Andrew Jackson is elected the seventh president of the United States, the first who does not come from aristocracy.

1833 Davidson County's first insurance business, Tennessee Marine and Fire Insurance Company, is founded.

1836 A prolific author and innovator, Nashville native Richard O. Currey is the first person to earn a doctorate to teach science at what will become the University of Tennessee.

1843 Nashville becomes the capital of Tennessee.

1850 The state's first gas utility, Nashville Gas Light Company, begins heating homes with coal from local mines. It will be the city's oldest continuously operating corporation.

1854 1855 1864 1876

Nashville and Chattanooga Railroad, 1864

1864 The Battle of Nashville, in which the Confederate army surrenders to Union forces, is the last major conflict in the western theater of the Civil War.

1866 Fisk University is founded to provide former slaves and other poverty-stricken blacks with an opportunity to receive an education.

1876 Meharry Medical College, the South's first medical school for black students, is established and eventually houses the nation's first health care program for the poor and underserved.

1881 Iroquois, a Thoroughbred sired at the Belle Meade Plantation, is the first American-born horse to win the English Derby.

1885 Sulphur Spring Bottom hosts the city's first minor league baseball game, at an enclosed wooden ballpark called Athletic Park.

1854 The Nashville and Chattanooga railroad line is completed, made possible by the efforts of Nashville businessmen, who raise the money by visiting every town along the line and asking for investments.

1855 The Hume School, Nashville's first permanent public school, opens in a three-story brick building, with 12 teachers instructing all grade levels.

1859 Construction of the Tennessee State Capitol is completed. Designed by William Strickland (who died during construction and was buried in the north façade), the capitol will be considered one of the finest examples of the Greek Revival style in America.

1869 The five-story Maxwell House Hotel, built over a 10-year period, opens and becomes a hub for Nashville's most important social and political events.

1873 Vanderbilt University is founded with a $1 million gift from shipping mogul Cornelius Vanderbilt in an attempt to heal the wounds of the Civil War. It will become one of the country's top research institutions and operate a world-renowned medical center.

1892 Steamboat captain Thomas Ryman builds the Union Gospel Tabernacle. It is renamed Ryman Auditorium in 1904 and eventually becomes the home of the *Grand Ole Opry*.

1892 A new coffee blend developed for the Maxwell House Hotel becomes an instant hit, and Maxwell House coffee is born. In 1907 President Theodore Roosevelt will inadvertently launch the company's advertising slogan when he tries it and says, "Good to the last drop."

NASHVILLE TIMELINE

1896 **1905** **1916** **1925**

Nashville's Parthenon, built for the Tennessee Centennial

1916 A devastating fire spreads rapidly through the east side of Nashville, destroying more than 600 buildings and leaving hundreds of residents homeless.

1918 Two passenger trains collide. The toll, 101 dead and 171 injured, makes this one of the deadliest rail accidents in U.S. history.

1925 The *Grand Ole Opry* begins as the *WSM Barn Dance,* a weekly country music program broadcast live from the National Life and Accident Insurance Company's radio station, WSM. It will become the oldest continuously broadcast radio program in the country and attract fans from around the world.

1896 Tennessee celebrates its 100th anniversary with an exposition held in Nashville. A full-size replica of the Parthenon is built for the event and is so popular it becomes a permanent city attraction.

1904 Citizens Savings Bank and Trust Company, which will become the nation's oldest continuously operating African-American financial institution, opens as the One-Cent Bank. Its intention is to "encourage frugality and systematic savings among our people. . . ."

1905 African-Americans in Nashville organize a highly successful boycott of segregated streetcars after city authorities decide to extend Jim Crow laws to the transportation system.

1910 The Hermitage Hotel, Nashville's first million-dollar lodging, opens and is used as headquarters for lobbyists working for and against women's suffrage.

1920 Tennessee casts the pivotal vote for the 19th Amendment to the Constitution, bringing women's suffrage to the nation. As Tennessee's capital, Nashville is headquarters for the celebration.

1933 Nashville's depressed economy gets a lift when Congress establishes the Tennessee Valley Authority (TVA) to provide the region with low-cost electricity, flood control, and economic development.

1937   1943   1957   1967

1937 William Edmondson, a Nashville sculptor, has a solo show at New York's Museum of Modern Art. He is the first African-American artist to do so.

1943 In need of a larger venue, the *Grand Ole Opry* moves to the Ryman Auditorium.

1950 Nashville is recognized as a major center of music. The moniker Music City USA catches on after WSM announcer David Cobb uses the phrase to describe the town during a broadcast.

1957 When a small group of black parents take their children to white schools, Nashville complies with the U.S. Supreme Court ruling that segregation in public schools is unconstitutional.

1957 Nashville's Dr. Dorothy Brown is the first black woman to be designated a fellow of the American College of Surgeons.

The original Country Music Hall of Fame, opened in 1967 on Music Row

1960 Sit-ins are held as part of a nonviolent movement to end racial segregation in restaurants. Many Nashville sit-in organizers will become leaders in the national Civil Rights Movement.

1963 The City of Nashville merges with Davidson County to form Metro Nashville, one of the first unions of its kind in the nation.

1967 The Country Music Hall of Fame opens, telling the history of country music through video clips, recorded music, exhibits, and live performances.

1968 Drs. Thomas Frist Sr. and Jr. and Jack C. Massey form a hospital management company, Hospital Corporation of America (HCA), to improve the quality of medical care and reduce costs. It will become the largest private operator of health care facilities in the world.

Sculptor William Edmondson, 1936

NASHVILLE TIMELINE

1974   1984   1989   1993

1974 After 31 years at the Ryman Auditorium, the *Grand Ole Opry* moves to its new home, the 4,400-seat Opry House at Opryland. Part of the old stage where performers stood at the microphone is transplanted into the new theater.

1980 The Tennessee Performing Arts Center opens, bringing top bands and musicians, touring Broadway shows, dance companies, children's theater, and even magic shows to the city.

1984 Tracy Caulkins, who swims for the Nashville Aquatic Club, wins three gold medals at the summer Olympics in Los Angeles. After this victory she retires, having set five world records and 63 American records for swimming.

1989 The first Southern Festival of Books, sponsored by the Tennessee Humanities Council, is held in Nashville and becomes a yearly event, attracting huge crowds.

1993 The top-ranked Vanderbilt University women's basketball team wins the Southeast Conference Championship and goes to the NCAA Final Four, a first for the university.

1983 The Nashville Network (TNN), a cable television station, goes on the air, presenting live *Grand Ole Opry* performances and other country music shows.

1983 Nissan trucks begin rolling off the assembly line in Smyrna, where the Japanese automaker has opened a plant that will win awards for productivity.

1998 The National Hockey League announces the 27th franchise in league history—the Nashville Predators.

Tracy Caulkins at the World Swimming Championships, 1982

1999   2004   2004   2005

1999 The Houston Oilers move to their new home—Nashville's Adelphia Coliseum—and change their name to the Tennessee Titans.

2002 Vanderbilt University Medical Center is the first major medical center to utilize the MicroTargeting Platform, a new device that assists surgeons in deep-brain stimulation of Parkinson's patients.

2004 Nashville's Gateway Bridge opens, providing the city its first clear (through-arch) span across the Cumberland River. The award-winning structure will be renamed the Korean War Veterans Memorial Bridge.

2004 The Colonial/Tudor Revival-style Belle Meade Golf Links is added to the National Register of Historic Places. It joins the metro area's 28 other historic districts, including Printers Alley and the Financial District.

2005 Nissan Motor Company announces it will move its North American headquarters and 1,300 jobs to Franklin from Los Angeles.

2006 For the second consecutive year, Nashville takes the number one spot on *Expansion Management* magazine's list of America's 50 hottest cities for business expansion and relocation.

2006 The new, 197,000-square-foot Schermerhorn Symphony Center opens. An acoustical masterpiece and the crown jewel of the city's concert halls, it houses the Nashville Symphony.

2006 Nashville celebrates 200 years of incorporation as a city, kicking off nine months of festivities with the October dedication of the new Public Square.

General Jackson Showboat passing under new Gateway Bridge

Cooling off in Rivers of Tennessee Fountains in front of River Wall, Bicentennial Mall State Park

PART ONE
THE GOOD LIFE AN OVERVIEW OF NASHVILLE

Good times are virtually guaranteed in the Music City as long as they involve people, places, or things. This page: Dense with clubs and eateries, famed lower Broadway draws an eclectic crowd. Opposite page: A band preps backstage for the *Grand Ole Opry*.

ALL THIS FOR A SONG
Quality of Life

The Nashville area is no stranger to Top 10 lists. From country music to Christian pop, Music City USA has become known far and wide for its songs, performers, and record labels. But that's not all of its chart-topping success. In June 2006, *Kiplinger's Personal Finance* magazine named Nashville number one on its list of the nation's top 50 "smart" places to live. The month before, *Forbes* magazine cited it as one of the top 10 places in America for business and careers. At the beginning of the year, *Expansion Management* magazine named it the hottest city for business relocations and expansions for the second time in a row. Before that, *Travel + Leisure* had crowned it America's friendliest city. Call it Music City, the Athens of the South, the Third Coast, or Titan Town—countless people call Nashville the best place ever to live. Culture, entertainment, history, a vibrant social scene, a bustling economic market, and a relatively low cost of living all weave together like the verses of a well-written song, making it an area like no other.

First Verse: People

Nashville, the second-largest city in Tennessee, had a population of 569,891 at the 2000 census, and the 10-county Nashville Economic Market as a whole includes just over 1.5 million people. Williamson County, southwest of the city proper, is among the nation's fastest-growing counties, and three other counties—Rutherford, Sumner, and Wilson—are among the 10 fastest growing in the state.

This page, bottom: An Asurion cell-phone servicer enjoys his work in Metro Nashville, one of the nation's fastest-growing job markets. Right and opposite page: The downtown business district is literally aglow as business and industry in the area continue to soar.

Those who move here, according to a 2005 survey by the Nashville Area Chamber of Commerce, say they do so primarily for jobs; nearly half of those surveyed were professionals age 22 to 40. Unemployment rates remain below the national average, and according to the Tennessee Department of Labor and Workforce Development, statewide employment was expected to increase by 75,800 jobs between 2005 and 2007. By 2007 things were right on target, with hiring on the upswing in virtually every sector.

Besides being intrigued by the low cost of living (less than half that of New York City and two-thirds that of Los Angeles, according to the ACCRA *Cost of Living Index)*, newcomers discover a city rife with dining and entertainment options, easy access to multiple interstate highways, and shopping. All that, and the people are just so darned nice.

For many years, the weekly *Nashville Scene* has run a "You are so Nashville if . . . ." contest. A past winner finished the sentence with "you never meant to stay here this long," and it's a joke that will bring nods of agreement from Belle Meade to Antioch. But the sentiment results from far more than economic opportunities. A spirit of optimism is evident on every corner, played out through every country music hopeful who comes to sell a song and every immigrant who comes to make a new life.

12 | THE GOOD LIFE An Overview of Nashville

Quality of Life | 13

14 | THE GOOD LIFE An Overview of Nashville

The Fourth of July is one of many excuses for Nashville youngsters to have a good time—but who needs an excuse? With American flags or without, multicultural kids like these radiate the contentment of living in a vibrant city that still has room for everyone.

The presence of immigrants can't be discounted. In the 1990s, Nashville had the highest number of new immigrant arrivals of the country's 100 largest metropolitan areas. One in seven of the city's residents is now foreign born, and the area is home to the largest concentration of Kurds outside of the Middle East. Various pockets, however, include Laotians, South Americans, Sudanese, Somalis, Mexicans, Koreans, and Thais, adding rich culture to the landscape.

And then there are the churches. Though in some cities it just *feels* like there's a church on every corner, in Nashville, it's practically true. The "buckle of the Bible Belt" is said to have more than 800 houses of worship, of myriad denominations. The Christian influence, however, is pervasive. Besides congregations, there are seminaries, Christian music companies, and major Christian publishers.

Many are surprised to find that the Music City has a variety of strong industries. One of the region's top economic drivers is health care. The Nashville Health Care Council notes, based on a 2005 study it commissioned at Middle Tennessee State University, that the local health care industry employs 94,000 people and pays total annual wages of about $6.3 billion. No surprise, considering that the area is home base for 33 major health care management companies. The economic impact of the region's health care sector is estimated at $18.3 billion per year.

16 | THE GOOD LIFE An Overview of Nashville

The music industry—it's the beat of Nashville, and it manifests around virtually every corner, in hallmarks such as (left) the Country Music Hall of Fame, (center) a B. B. King's Blues Club handbill, and (right) an impromptu street concert by John Mellencamp.

The music industry, of course, is a major player as well, with an annual impact of $6.4 billion. The Country Music Association's annual CMA Music Festival (formerly Fan Fair) drew more than 161,000 people from around the globe in 2006 alone, contributing about $19 million to the economy in just one four-day stretch.

The impact of music, however, goes far beyond dollars. The Nashville area is home to a great number of celebrities, and star sightings are not uncommon. The city embraces a "live and let live" philosophy, however. If someone is seen asking for an autograph, chances are that person is a tourist. Just about every Nashvillian knows someone in the music business, whether vocalist, songwriter, or musician—and anyone who's been to a restaurant or bar in Nashville has, no doubt, been waited on by a part-timer with big dreams.

Nashville is a place where anything can happen, and the potential for success is as real as the neighbor down the street who just landed his or her first big deal. The majority of Nashvillians may be from somewhere else, but they've bought into the idea that the city and its surrounding counties have something tangible to offer. They've been enveloped by the promise of a city on the move, one in which there's still room for everyone.

Quality of Life | 17

This page, left: From this vantage point in Bicentennial Mall State Park, Nashville is the center of the universe—and it just may be. Right and opposite page: Dawn breaks over Percy Priest Lake. Far right: A sign marks a Nashville Greenways trail linking urban neighborhoods.

Second Verse: Places

Nothing quite matches the splendor of a Middle Tennessee autumn, when the leaves range from deep reds to rich amber—unless it's a Middle Tennessee spring, when the daffodils push through the soil and the Bradford pear trees offer up bloom after glorious bloom. In between there might be a dusting of snow—or not—and by summer, the heat is on.

Much has been said about the area's temperate climate, but perhaps the best part about it is its diversity through the seasons, from crisp fall nights to languid summer days. Temperatures average just below 60 degrees annually, with lows of about 28 degrees Fahrenheit in January and highs of about 86 in June. Average humidity is 70 percent. Because of its rarity, the snow can be quite an occasion. Schools have been known to close at the prospect alone. Out-of-towners marvel at the excitement a dusting can cause, but it doesn't take long for them to join in the wonder.

White isn't the only color that can cause a stir; there's also a good bit of blue and green. The city itself straddles the Cumberland River, and Metro Nashville features 10 lakes that together attracted more than 36 million swimmers, boaters, water-skiers, and fishers in 2006. One large lake in particular, J. Percy Priest—named for a local congressman—sees five million recreational visitors annually. The region's 76 parks and playgrounds include the new Skate Park at Wave Country, and there are even about 40 golf courses. More green can be found downtown near the Tennessee State Capitol, where the 19-acre Bicentennial Mall State Park tells the state's story through a variety of monuments. Centennial Park's 132 acres, filled with sunken gardens, a lake, a band shell, and walkways, are within a few miles.

And those walkways aren't the only ones in town. In recent years, the Nashville Greenways project has been connecting neighborhoods, commercial areas, and recreational spots through a series of linear parks and trails, some of which feature paved paths along streams and rivers. There are now 29.5 miles of greenways in the city, and plans to expand the system include a bridge across the Cumberland River. The project has permanently protected 11,000 acres of plant and animal habitats and natural resources like watersheds, trees, and open land.

Stylish architecture defines Nashville. It includes (this page, below) the state capitol, a National Historic Civil Engineering Landmark; (right and opposite page, top) a statue of the goddess Athena inside Nashville's Parthenon; and the Hermitage, Andrew Jackson's home.

Nashvillians have a similarly protective attitude toward the city's diverse architecture, some of which makes the list of the most notable examples anywhere. Churches alone represent Greek Revival, Gothic Revival, neoclassicism, high Victorian Gothic, and Egyptian Revival. The Downtown Presbyterian Church is one of the best-preserved models of Egyptian Revival architecture in the country; the Cathedral of the Incarnation features a unique coffered ceiling; and Christ Church Episcopal is noted for its impressive stained glass. The state capitol, completed in 1859, is a prime example of Greek Revival style, and it's considered a highlight of the career of its designer, celebrated architect William Strickland.

Nashville architecture also includes the Parthenon, a full-size replica of the original Greek temple in Athens. At home in Centennial Park, the structure adds a special touch to the city. Built as a temporary edifice to house an international art show at the state's centennial exhibition in 1897, the building was so well liked that it was eventually reconstructed in concrete. These days, it's once again an art museum, surrounded by green space, water, walkways, gardens, and an amphitheater. Nashvillians consider it a top spot for fairs, festivals, and outdoor entertainment.

The area is rich in residential architecture, as well. The most famous examples are the numerous Southern mansions and historical sites, such as the Hermitage, the Greek Revival–style home of U.S. president Andrew Jackson; Belle Meade Plantation, another Greek Revival–style home whose grounds once housed a Thoroughbred horse farm; and Cheekwood Botanical Garden and Museum of Art, a Georgian mansion that was the residence of the Cheek family, early city entrepreneurs.

In terms of more current private residences, the city has enjoyed the recent restoration of historic districts in East Nashville and, in particular, the downtown area. A major effort is under way to turn vacant upper floors in downtown buildings into residential space. According to the Nashville Downtown Living Initiative (a task force aimed at enhancing housing offerings in the city's urban core), 57 of the original 84 target buildings are either listed on the National Register of Historic Places or are within historic districts listed on the register.

20 | THE GOOD LIFE An Overview of Nashville

Quality of Life | 21

22 | THE GOOD LIFE An Overview of Nashville

Opposite page, left: Originally a warehouse, the Quarters on Second Avenue offers dramatic downtown living. Opposite page, right, and this page, bottom: The Frist Center for the Visual Arts exhibits a Murano glass collection. This page, top: The Nashville Symphony and Chorus perform in Schermerhorn Symphony Center.

The truth is, Nashville has many properties worth saving. Thanks to its early status as a river port and railway junction, it enjoyed great success even before the Civil War. And the prosperous times ahead meant structures of grand style.

Other historical sites include Fisk University's Carl Van Vechten Gallery, a converted neo-Romanesque church housing Alfred Stieglitz's collection of Georgia O'Keeffe paintings and works by Pablo Picasso, Paul Cezanne, Pierre-Auguste Renoir, Henri Toulouse-Lautrec, and others; Travellers Rest Plantation and Museum, the Federal-style home and gardens of Judge John Overton, built in 1799; and a number of important sites related to the Civil War.

In 1806, when Nashville was incorporated, no one could have foreseen how the city would expand beyond its borders. In 1963 it became the first major city in the country to combine with its county into a fully consolidated metropolitan government. Today the emphasis is on teaming with the surrounding counties of the Nashville Economic Market, which range from agrarian Dickson County and industrial Robertson County to upscale Williamson County.

Housing prices vary greatly from county to county, but it's still possible to find a renovated Craftsman bungalow in East Nashville for under $350,000 or a new three-bedroom, single-family home in neighboring Wilson County for $200,000.

Third Verse: Things

Anyone who hasn't been to downtown Nashville since the mid 1990s isn't likely to recognize it. Arts, culture, and entertainment have come to the forefront as never before, in their variety of new venues.

First, in 1994, the Ryman Auditorium, "mother church of country music," was renovated and reopened. It had been empty for almost two decades after its *Grand Ole Opry* radio show moved to a newer entertainment complex on the outskirts of the city. Next, in 1996, came the new Nashville Arena, now known as the Gaylord Entertainment Center; and in 1999, the Nashville Stadium, later known as the Coliseum and now as LP Field. These were followed in 2001 by the new downtown Country Music Hall of Fame and the transformation of the city's historic post office into the Frist Center for the Visual Arts. Then in 2003, the Tennessee Performing Arts Center was redesigned. In 2006 Nashvillians celebrated the gala grand opening of the Schermerhorn Symphony Center, a $120 million concert hall named for the Nashville Symphony's late maestro Kenneth Schermerhorn.

Beyond the big buildings, however, the city's entertainment also includes countless music clubs and coffeehouses, with live performances virtually every night; a solid theater scene; a growing base of retail shops that eliminate the need for trips to larger cities; and a dizzying array of restaurants that prove dining out is one of the region's most popular hobbies.

The city's major arts organizations have also come into their own. The Nashville Ballet has established itself internationally as a diverse and growing entity that attracts award-winning choreographers. Nashville Children's Theatre has garnered national praise as one of the best theater companies of its kind. The Nashville Opera has also received national acclaim, and the symphony has broken international sales records with its recordings, earned Grammy nominations, toured to standing-room-only crowds, and debuted at Carnegie Hall. The Tennessee Performing Arts Center brings in the latest and hottest touring shows—such as *The Producers*, *Movin' Out*, and *Mamma Mia!*—as part of its Broadway series and even draws crowds from other regions and states. Great Performances at Vanderbilt is another top-notch draw, introducing artists of international acclaim in music and dance to local audiences.

And then there's sports. In 1997 the Nashville Predators began playing for the National Hockey League in the Gaylord Entertainment Center. Some scoffed at the idea of such a cold-weather sport in the warm-weather South, but an "icebreaker" drew 12,000 potential fans to the arena for demonstrations. A year after professional hockey made its Nashville debut, the National Football League arrived in town in the form of the Houston Oilers. The team changed its name to the Tennessee Titans, and it continues to hold home games at LP Field, downtown. The area's pro sports teams also include the Nashville Sounds (Triple A baseball), Kats (Arena Football League), and Metros (United Soccer Leagues), and motor sports take center stage at the Nashville Superspeedway.

Nashville has entertainment to beat the band. Options include (this page, left) Tootsies Orchid Lounge, a honky-tonk legend; (right) a horse and carriage ride downtown; (opposite page, left) Nashville Children's Theatre; and (right) a Tennessee Titans NFL game.

Quality of Life | 25

This page and opposite page, left: Nashville has heart, evidenced by the crowd at Christ Church Cathedral for the Blessing of the Animals. Opposite page, right: A friendly face and look-people-in-the-eye demeanor reflect Nashville's spirit of optimism.

Another team bears mention, too. It's neither a sports franchise nor a group of entertainers, but its work certainly helps fill seats in area venues—by focusing on economic development. Partnership 2010, a program of the Nashville Area Chamber of Commerce, recruits new businesses to the city and works to improve the quality of education, encourage long-term infrastructure planning, and increase personal income while facilitating sustainable growth and nurturing the industry that's already there. Bottom line, it ensures that the good life Nashvillians already enjoy keeps getting better.

Of course, there was a solid base to start with. National companies like Lay's (of Frito-Lay) and Hospital Corporation of America (HCA) first opened their doors here, and record labels like Mercury, Sony Music, and RCA all established Nashville divisions. Recent relocations to the area have run the gamut from building products manufacturer Louisiana-Pacific to automaker Nissan North America. A well-educated workforce contributes to the region's success. With 15 accredited four-year and postgraduate institutions and four accredited two-year public colleges available, the next generation is assured the resources it needs to carry the torch.

The Final Chorus: Bringing It Home

Harlan Howard, long known as the Dean of Nashville Songwriters thanks to his more than 4,000 compositions, said country music was "three chords and the truth." The city of Nashville is much the same. The comfort of a familiar song, the welcome of a friendly face, and the buildup toward a great finish are part of its landscape. As for the truth, it's evidenced in the look-people-in-the-eye demeanor of its residents, the tenacity of its industry, and the secure foundation its leaders have laid for success.

Nashville is by no means perfect. It has its challenges, just like anywhere else. But a beacon of optimism shines brightly, leading to new opportunities around every corner and new verses of history yet to be written.

U.S. Bank (left) and the BellSouth Building (right), downtown

PART TWO
TITANS OF COMMERCE NASHVILLE BUSINESS AND INDUSTRY

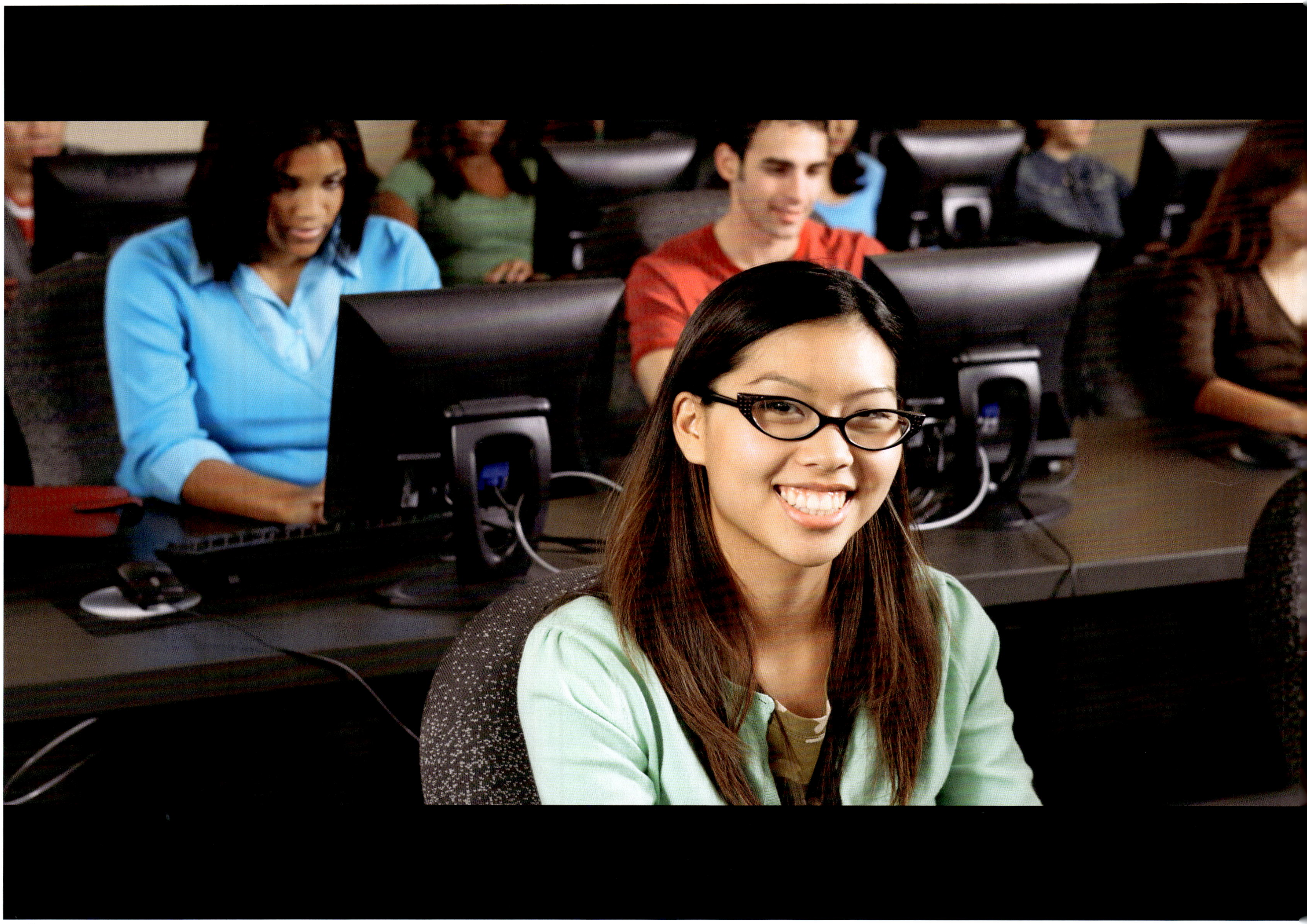

This page: Taking their place as the next generation of leaders, Vanderbilt University graduates receive their diplomas. Opposite page: Computers make note-taking easy for students in a lecture hall at one of Nashville's highly regarded colleges.

CULTIVATING GREAT MINDS
Education

Long a center of learning, Nashville had established a profusion of educational institutions by the mid-19th century, helping earn the city its classical nickname, Athens of the South. Several of the schools that flourished in Nashville's early days remain important in the life of the city today, joined by newer entities that continue the tradition of the city as a polestar of culture and education.

Vanderbilt University is at the heart of Nashville in just about any way one might construe that status. A source of high-powered human talent for employers in Nashville and far beyond; the occupant of a formidable island of real estate influencing much about the urban development of Nashville for more than a century; and a locus of civic energy and ideas, Vanderbilt is, for all intents and purposes, the gown to Nashville's town. It employs about 20,100 people, more than any other private employer in Middle Tennessee; educates 11,500 students a year; controls a $2.5 billion endowment; and attracts global attention to the city with its academic and medical programs. *U.S. News & World Report,* in its 2007 ranking of universities, places Vanderbilt as a whole and its law and medical schools in the top 18 nationally, while rating its graduate program in special education as number one in the country.

This page and opposite page, left to right: Vanderbilt University's 330-acre campus includes the internationally renowned Vanderbilt Owen Graduate School of Management; Kirkland Hall, home to administrative offices; and Wilson Hall, where psychology classes are held.

Enhancing the university's ties with the city is a high priority for Vanderbilt. Its Vanderbilt-Ingram Cancer Center reached out to Meharry Medical College to pool cancer research resources and to Church of Christ–affiliated Lipscomb University to train its nursing students. Vanderbilt trustees have promised neighbors of the campus that they will not seek further expansion of the university's physical footprint, reducing tensions that have festered for generations. And the school has become an increasingly active participant in Nashville's entrepreneurial culture. University funds and expertise have helped spawn numerous ventures, including medical companies like Pathfinder Therapeutics, which has patented an image-guided system for open-liver surgery, and for-profit education initiatives like online learning provider American Sentinel University.

Vanderbilt has given much to the community, but it is also an institution to which much has been given. A $1 million founding gift from New York shipping baron Cornelius Vanderbilt enabled the university to open its doors in 1875. In 1995, E. Bronson Ingram, patriarch of Nashville's Ingram family and then chairman of the Vanderbilt Board of Trust, concluded a capital campaign—in the last months before his death from cancer—that brought more than $557 million into university coffers. Three years later, the Ingram family donated stock worth approximately $300 million to Vanderbilt in a gift that was, at the time, the largest ever made to a U.S. institution of higher education. Such resources have made Vanderbilt part of the story of dramatic growth that has played out in Nashville and Middle Tennessee over the past quarter-century. The university's annual operating budget has been a barometer of that growth, rising from $170 million in 1982 to $2.4 billion in 2005.

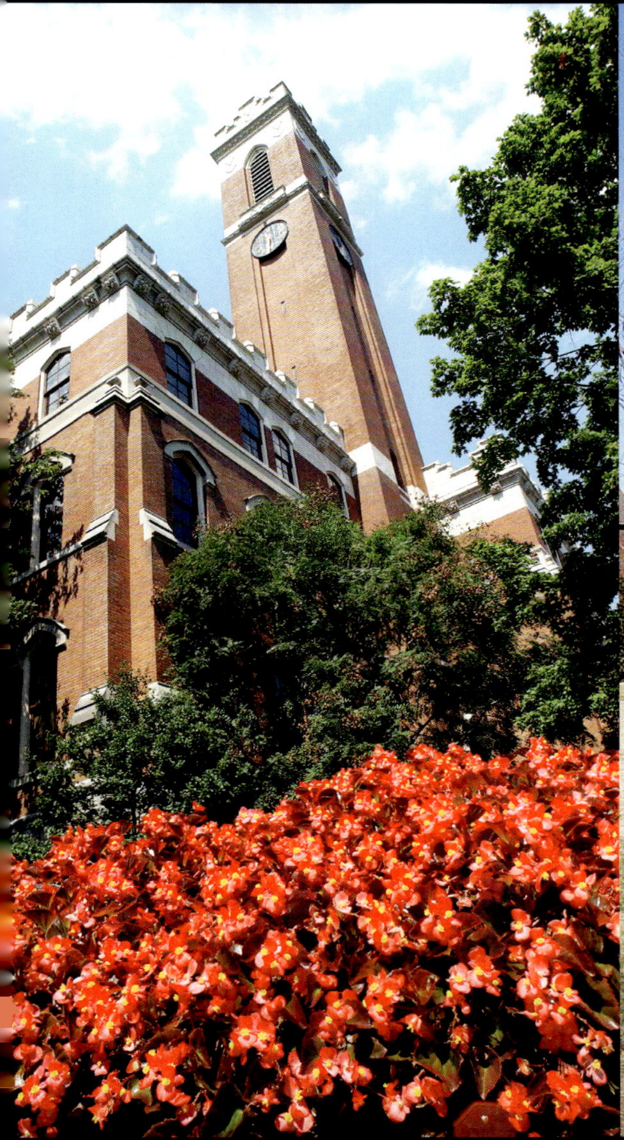

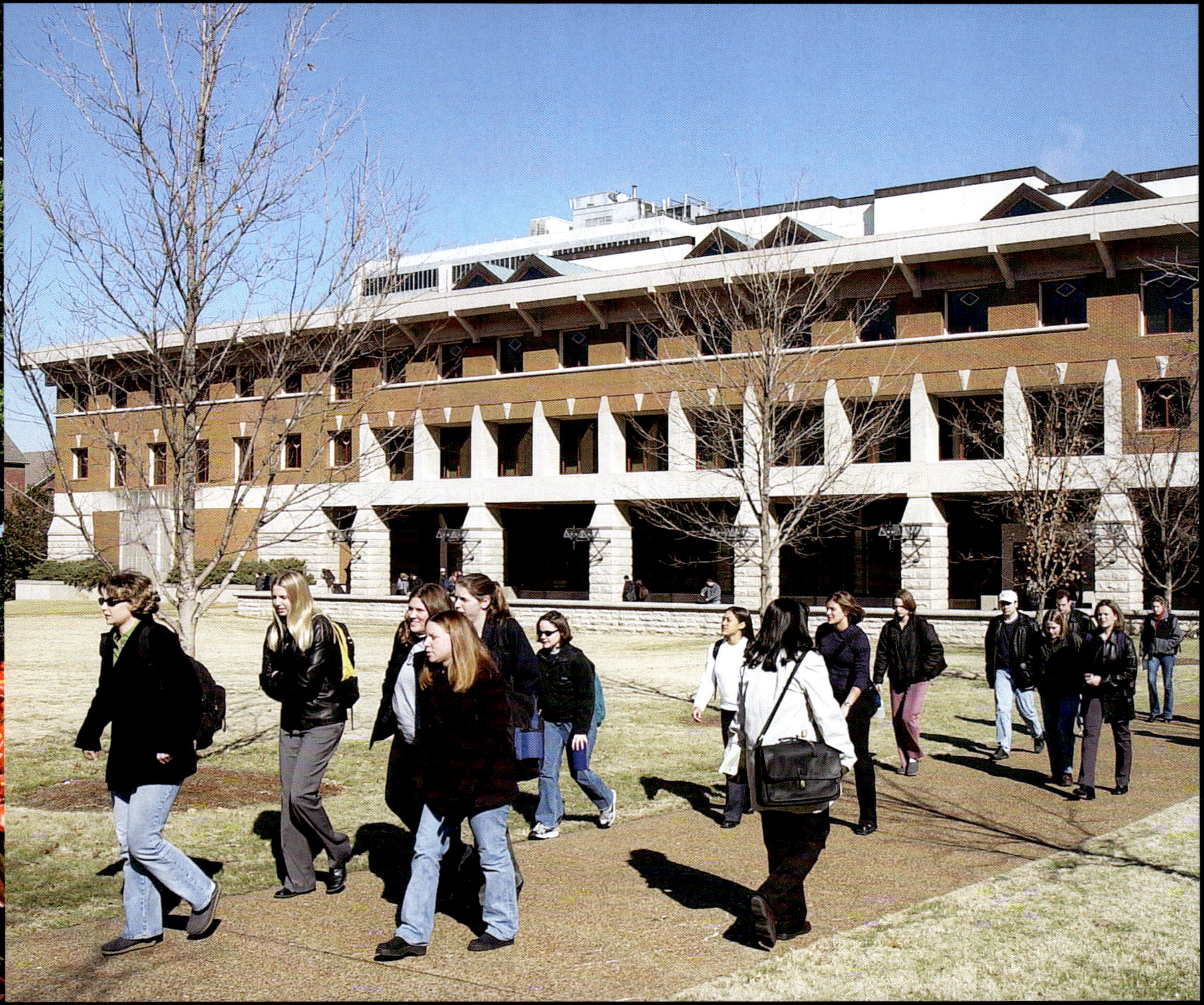

Abundant Options

Even as Vanderbilt has achieved greater wealth and clout in Nashville, other local colleges and universities have experienced their own growth spurts in recent years and have come to figure more prominently in the life of the city.

Of the region's 21 accredited four-year and postgraduate institutions of higher education, arguably the most historically significant school is Fisk University, established in 1866 as a place where newly freed slaves could get an education. Fisk, which enrolls about 825 students a year, has been made famous by the Fisk Jubilee Singers, gospel-performing students who raised funding for the university's landmark main building, now called Jubilee Hall.

Many other schools are also noteworthy. Trevecca Nazarene University, which enrolls 2,200 students in its liberal arts and preprofessional programs, offers substantial graduate programs. Belmont University, with an enrollment of nearly 4,000, is home to the nationally renowned Mike Curb College of Entertainment & Music Business and to a College of Health

Excellent colleges define the area. This page, left: Middle Tennessee University in Murfreesboro; right: a student at one of four community colleges. Opposite page, left: The Fisk Jubilee Singers, from Fisk University; right: sound mixing at Belmont University.

Sciences and Nursing that enjoys support from health care giant HCA. Both colleges are housed in state-of-the-art facilities built since 2001. Belmont's master's degree programs were rated 10th in the South on *U.S. News & World Report*'s 2007 list of best colleges, and Lipscomb University (total enrollment: 2,535 students), whose business administration programs are traditionally a pipeline of talent for local accounting firms, placed 28th in the same ranking. Historically black Tennessee State University, which educates 9,100 students a year, counts among its alumnae Olympic track champion Wilma Rudolph and television personality Oprah Winfrey. Middle Tennessee State University in Murfreesboro, with a student body of almost 23,000, is among the engines of Rutherford County's rapid growth.

Sun-belt migration patterns in the past two decades have made Nashville an infinitely more diverse locale, and the migrants include a healthy mix of highly educated professionals and skilled tradespeople. Lifelong learning and vocational education are widely available in the area at a low price through state community colleges and technology centers as well as private professional training institutes.

Nashville State Community College, one of four such colleges in the 10-county economic market, enrolls about 7,000 students annually and provides both core academic and vocational courses. It serves not only individual students but also businesses, as the college's WorkForce and Community Development Center offers employees customized education and training in categories from architectural engineering and culinary arts to accounting and psychology. Nashville State also has an alliance with the Sage Group, a Nashville-based employee-training firm serving Fortune 500 clients nationwide. Sage students can apply credits from their technology courses to an associate's degree at Nashville State.

Additional efforts to provide comprehensive training to a wide swath of students, employees, and small-business owners have resulted in state technology centers and small-business development centers in Nashville and Murfreesboro as well as in other locations in Tennessee.

This page and opposite page, left: Flash cards bring math skills home to public school students, contributing to the record gains shown in recent testing. Opposite page, right: Public high schools include award-winning Hume-Fogg Academic Magnet, downtown.

Shoring Up the System

Just over half of Metro Nashville's adults age 25 and older have attended college for at least a year. Increasing that figure and enhancing the talent pool of the greater Nashville area are critical missions of the region's public school systems, which educated almost 192,000 children at 311 public schools in the 2004–05 academic year.

Nashville is a city of the South, affected by the deficits in educational achievement that have characterized the entire region since the Civil War. The neighboring bedroom counties of Williamson and Rutherford are widely acknowledged to have some of the region's best public schools, but the city itself, which educates about 74,000 students, faces challenges. While the majority of Metro Nashville's public schools achieved the highest possible rating ("good standing") in the state's 2005–06 Adequate Yearly Progress (AYP) report, some of its high schools did not meet federal benchmarks for progress set under No Child Left Behind legislation. The Nashville Area Chamber of Commerce's Citizens Panel for a Community Report Card for 2005 gave the school system a lukewarm endorsement, citing among its reasons high school graduation rates. The state's own report card on Metro Nashville for 2005 put the graduation rate at 60.4 percent.

But there are signs of improvement in public education on numerous fronts. Between 1999 and 2006, education funding increased from $397 million to $563 million, the largest sustained increase in the system's history. The Metro school board has allocated additional staff at the high school level, and there are plans to spend $100,000 to examine successful reform strategies in other localities. A task force within the system is looking into flexible scheduling, revamping the school day, and fostering specialized learning communities within high schools. The educators can draw on examples of success within their midst, as two of the system's magnet high schools, Hume-Fogg Academic and Martin Luther King, placed in the top 50 nationally in *Newsweek*'s 2006 ranking of public schools. In 2005, KIPP Academy Nashville opened its doors as the system's first charter middle school, one of the Knowledge Is Power Program (KIPP) schools opening across the United States. The program, which features a college-prep curriculum and top-ranked teachers at its tuition-free, open-enrollment schools, has brought academic rigor and high performance to disadvantaged communities throughout the nation. Hopes are high that the KIPP model will yield similar results locally.

This page: A science project engages students at one of the area's 51 private schools, which offer excellent educational opportunities. Opposite page: Training in the computer lab of a local technical school means a better job for conscientious employees like these.

Laboratories of Leadership

Private schools have historically produced a large share of the Nashville area's business and community leaders. The 21st century has seen a dramatic expansion in educational opportunity at the area's 51 private schools, with a greater variety of high quality educational experiences available for primary and secondary learners than ever before.

Traditional boys' school Montgomery Bell Academy (MBA), for example, founded in 1867, today offers a more diverse curriculum, student body, and faculty and more financial aid than at any time in its history. Harpeth Hall, founded in 1951, is MBA's counterpart for girls in grades 5–12 and offers similar opportunities. The coeducational Ensworth School, founded in 1958, now competes with MBA, as it has added a high school on a handsome new campus in west Nashville. And the University School of Nashville, founded in 1915, today offers its K–12 students computer and science labs, a new visual arts center with studio and gallery space, and a stand-alone library.

The legacy of former governor (now senator) Lamar Alexander, who used Tennessee as a laboratory for education reform in the 1980s, is still apparent in Nashville: the city has become a hotbed for private education ventures. Nashville firms at the forefront of education reform efforts include Community Education Partners, which has made a business out of the challenge of dealing with at-risk youth in school environments; technology company Education Networks of America (ENA); and nonprofit Modern Red SchoolHouse Institute, which focuses on school improvement via customized professional development programs.

If education is the key to a successful future, Nashville has its priorities in the right place. With a clear focus on maintaining excellence and strengthening areas of weakness, leaders in academia, business, and the community are working together to ensure that the Athens of the South remains a guiding light when it comes to intellect and culture.

38 | TITANS OF COMMERCE Nashville Business and Industry

Education | 39

40 | TITANS OF COMMERCE Nashville Business and Industry

This page: The Tennessee Credit Union (top) and an insurance claims assessor (bottom) represent the excellent financial services network Nashville businesses and residents rely on. Opposite page: Designers listen intently to a client's concept presentation.

ROCK SOLID
Finance, Insurance, and Professional Services

The anxiety is over. After two decades of concern that Nashville would become a client town in the hinterlands, beyond the cares of absentee corporate owners, the financial and insurance industries are once again thriving, having reinvented their role as the engines that power Middle Tennessee's companies.

At the turn of the millennium, Nashville was bidding farewell to the last vestiges of its claim to be the Wall Street of the South. With the purchase by out-of-town interests of regional investment banks Equitable Securities Corporation in 1998 and J. C. Bradford & Company in 2000, the golden age of financial services in the city seemed to be at an end. Both firms had traced their lineage back to the depression era and had been powerhouses within and beyond the Southeast. The insurance industry that once made Nashville "the Hartford of the South" had likewise fallen prey to outside buyers.

By 2006, however, those worrisome days had vanished. In commercial and investment banking, talented veterans of the old days have started new institutions that are flourishing. The insurance sector locally bears little resemblance to its forebears but remains vibrant. And other capital-intensive financial enterprises, such as venture capital and private equity firms, now carry out the economic-engine role that the insurers once played.

Banking on Growth

The numbers don't lie: Middle Tennessee's homegrown banks are thriving. The buyouts of the 1980s–90s made several gifted bankers available for new assignments and left a substantial number of customers wondering where they ought to place their money and loyalty. The consequent flowering in the past decade of start-up bank ventures has reshaped the financial marketplace. As of mid 2005 (the latest data available), locally organized banks in the Nashville metropolitan statistical area held nearly $5.8 billion in deposits, representing 21.7 percent of the overall deposit market. A year earlier, the total for local banks had been $3.8 billion, a 16.7 percent share.

The region's largest deposit holders in 2005 were SunTrust Bank (based in Atlanta, Georgia) in the top spot, AmSouth Bank (Birmingham, Alabama) at number two, and Bank of America (Charlotte, North Carolina) in the third spot. The top seven deposit holders were all large banks based elsewhere, but the next 10 were headquartered in the Nashville area.

The merger of two of the most successful new banks, Pinnacle Financial Partners and Cavalry Bancorp, created an institution (under the Pinnacle name) with $1.83 billion in assets when it was finalized in March 2006. Among the smaller but rapidly growing banks in the area are those with a tight geographic focus, such as Lebanon's Wilson Bank & Trust, founded in 1987, which exceeded $1 billion in assets at the end of 2005; and those carving out specialized business niches, such as Franklin's Tennessee Commerce Bancorp, founded in 2000, which primarily serves businesses in the service, manufacturing, and professional sectors and has assets of more than $438 million. On a single day in April 2006, both Tennessee Commerce and another Franklin-based bank holding company, Civitas BankGroup, announced plans to list their stocks on the Nasdaq exchange.

This page, left: Nothing beats new wheels, other than the low loan rate this driver snagged. Right: First Tennessee bank anchors the city as a financial center. Opposite page, left: The Metro's growing banking market includes Fifth Third Financial Center. Right: An affordable mortgage gives a mother and her child time to play.

Specialized niches have catapulted other types of financial service companies into the limelight as well. Franklin American Mortgage Company, in Franklin, had 2005 revenues of nearly $51 million—almost seven times its figures just five years earlier. Nashville-based credit and debit card processor iPayment serves small businesses across the country, but its success is hardly small: the company's 140,000 clients generate almost $703 million in annual sales.

Investment bankers in Nashville are making a comeback parallel to that of commercial bankers, for similar reasons. The talent pool is deep, and entrepreneurs have seen opportunities in a variety of underserved sectors. Foremost among the new breed are the bankers at Avondale Partners. Several former J. C. Bradford and Equitable Securities executives founded the company in 2001, and since then, Avondale bankers have helped put together more than 60 transactions, ranging from private placements to initial public offerings, for companies in and beyond Nashville. Gen Cap America's executives engineer management buyouts of retiring owners, while those at Harpeth Capital serve smaller, middle-market companies. Financiers at Caterpillar Financial Services Corporation help customers acquire Caterpillar equipment for forestry, mining, or construction. As these varied niches might suggest, Nashville's financial infrastructure encompasses ways to access capital for every stage of business operations.

Below: Investing is once again rife with opportunity in Nashville, a boon for businesses in every sector. Right: A venture capital advisor briefs an "angel" investor on several biotechnology and health care ventures in need of early-stage capital.

Even the most embryonic concepts stand a chance of gaining the attention of investors through the structure of the Nashville Capital Network, created in 2003. Sponsored by Vanderbilt University, local industry groups, and area businesses, the network seeks to help entrepreneurs hone their ideas and to assist "angel" investors in discovering projects they want to support with early-stage capital.

At the level of true venture capital and private equity investing, numerous entities serve the Middle Tennessee marketplace. Firms such as Solidus Company and Petra Capital Partners have built winning track records with investments typically involving $2 million to $15 million. Salix Ventures invests $5 million to $7 million per company in health care services enterprises, usually splitting the funds between early and later stages. Richland Ventures is one of several local firms that will invest in slightly more mature companies in need of $5 million to $15 million in expansion capital.

Below: That mobile phone is in good hands, but just in case, it's insured by Asurion, a Nashville company that continues to expand along with the financial services industry. Left: Helmeted, happy, and backed by accident insurance, a family bikes through the park.

Still Shielding Millions

Soon after the turn of the 20th century, executives at the National Sick and Accident Insurance Company decided their company motto would be "We Shield Millions." Generations later, the city is once again home to insurers and brokers who "shield millions."

The National Life nameplate is long gone, but successor American General Life and Accident Insurance Company operates as a unit of American International Group (AIG), employing more than 900 people in Middle Tennessee and serving more than four million policyholders throughout the nation. Synaxis Group, a subsidiary of First Horizon National Corporation and the 38th-largest commercial insurance brokerage in the country, writes more than $350 million in premiums for financial services clients. And Asurion Corporation, which relocated to Nashville in 2003 and has expanded its operations considerably since arriving, serves more than 50 million mobile-telephone subscribers with handset insurance and related services, employing a staff of over 2,000 in the metro area.

Other Metro Nashville success stories in the insurance industry are North America Administrators, which manages health benefits for businesses across the country; Direct General Corporation, a financial services holding company specializing in nonstandard automobile insurance for clients across the Southeast; and Consumers Insurance Group, of Murfreesboro, which provides automobile insurance to clients in six states.

Going the Extra Mile

Benefiting from the financial ferment of 21st-century Nashville and aiding in the city's economic momentum are those who provide professional services—more than 31 percent of the workforce, as of 2005. Their institutional roots may go back a century or more, but their business horizons have broadened dramatically in recent years. Professionals in the Nashville Metro have helped their law, accounting, consulting, and architectural firms acquire national profiles and reputations for thoughtful leadership.

Ask most Nashville businesspeople about professional firms, and they may mention old-line law firms like Bass, Berry and Sims; Boult, Cummings, Conners & Berry; and Waller Lansden Dortch and Davis; or homegrown accounting firms like KraftCPAs and Lattimore Black Morgan & Cain. Ask who from the professional community has made a personal impression, however, and any number of individuals may come to mind.

Neal & Harwell's James F. Neal is not the attorney most businesspeople in town would ever hope to retain, since he specializes in white-collar criminal defense, but he's the one many would like to hear recounting his experiences. As a prosecutor, he sent Teamsters Union boss Jimmy Hoffa and Nixon-era attorney general John Mitchell to jail, and as defense counsel, he kept colorful Louisiana governor Edwin Edwards out of jail (temporarily, as things turned out). High-profile criminal and civil cases keep Neal & Harwell in the public eye today, although business and bankruptcy cases are another focus for the firm's attorneys.

This page: Attorneys at Bass, Berry and Sims are part of a culture that keeps Nashville law firms on "America's best" lists. Opposite page: Neal & Harwell's James Neal (right) is interviewed in 1964 during the jury tampering trial of Jimmy Hoffa (second from left).

Finance, Insurance, and Professional Services | 47

48 | TITANS OF COMMERCE Nashville Business and Industry

This page, left: Architects like this one are transforming residential neighborhoods. Below: Designed by Earl Swensson Associates, Children's Hospital at Vanderbilt is among the standout projects reshaping the skyline. Opposite page: Accountants uncover expenses their client had overlooked as tax time rolls around.

When Linda Rebrovick had climbed every mountain available at KPMG Consulting, this Nashville native helped engineer a 2001 spin-off that made history: the creation of systems integration and management consulting firm BearingPoint, for which she then served as executive vice president and chief marketing officer.

Among the many architects and designers who have shaped the Nashville skyline is Earl Swensson, who set up his practice—Earl Swensson Associates (ESa)—in 1961. Since those days, ESa has designed such projects as the BellSouth Tennessee headquarters, Monroe Carell Jr. Children's Hospital at Vanderbilt, and Gaylord Opryland Resort & Convention Center. Considered a leading health care facility design firm, ESa has won awards and national recognition in that category.

A number of local architects, in fact, have made the design of medical space one of their specialties, including Batey M. Gresham Jr., who established his practice in 1967. His firm, Gresham, Smith and Partners, has been the creative force behind more than two billion square feet of patient service space, as well as icons such as the Nashville International Airport and 27-story Nashville City Center. Gresham's work earned him a lifetime achievement award from the American Association of Architects in 2006. Gresham, Smith is still molding the clay: one of its latest projects is the design of the new Nissan headquarters in Franklin.

If there was ever any doubt about Nashville's ability to support business, those thoughts are long gone. Middle Tennessee's strong economic infrastructure and the remarkable people who make it so are helping local companies achieve success every day. Businesses from around the world are now eager to call Nashville home, knowing they can flourish here.

50 | TITANS OF COMMERCE Nashville Business and Industry

This page: The Vanderbilt-Ingram Cancer Center excels in Nashville's already exceptional health care network. Opposite page: A Vanderbilt LifeFlight helicopter sits atop the medical center, ready to bring critical-care patients to the Level I trauma center.

Vibrant Ventures
Health Care, Technology, and Biosciences

More than anywhere else, Nashville is the place where health care business gets done in America. Innovative local companies have developed management strategies, distribution capabilities, and advances in patient care that have met with warm receptions in the marketplace. Meanwhile, locally based medical providers offer world-class care to the people of Nashville and to many patients from across the Mid-South who seek out specialized treatment.

Health services are a major force driving the Nashville economy. Health care jobs currently employ one out of every seven workers in the region. Almost 75,000 people provide health care directly through hospitals, nursing care facilities, and ambulatory services, and nearly 20,000 more work for locally headquartered health care management companies that do business regionally or nationally. Businesses in the region's health care cluster, according to the Nashville Health Care Council, account for $8.4 billion of personal income, about 18 percent of the total personal income for Middle Tennessee residents. They also generate an estimated $459 million in state and local taxes, making up one-fifth of total tax collections in Nashville and surrounding counties.

More than 20 health care–related companies in Tennessee are publicly traded, and at least a third of them are based in Nashville. Most are hospital companies, including the country's two largest for-profit hospital operators (by number of facilities), HCA and Community Health Systems.

HCA is the largest corporate employer in the Nashville metropolitan area, with a local workforce of nearly 9,000 people. Vanderbilt University Medical Center is next, with 8,000, and then Saint Thomas Health Services, with 7,500.

A Healthy Advantage

HCA, Saint Thomas, and Vanderbilt operate the three major hospital systems centered on Nashville. Each has earned national accolades for overall excellence and leadership in medical specialties. HCA's TriStar Health System, a network of 17 general and specialty hospitals in Tennessee and Kentucky, includes Skyline Medical Center, winner of the Distinguished Hospital–Clinical Excellence Award from rating service HealthGrades in 2006. Catholic-affiliated Saint Thomas Health Services placed first in Tennessee for heart surgery and overall cardiac services in the HealthGrades ranking, while its flagship Saint Thomas Hospital received HealthGrades' Distinguished Hospital–Patient Safety and Cardiac Care Excellence awards. In *U.S. News & World Report*'s 2006 ranking of America's best hospitals, six Vanderbilt University Medical Center specialties placed in the top 25 nationally, led by kidney disease at number 12. The Vanderbilt-Ingram Cancer Center, certified as a National Cancer Institute Comprehensive Cancer Center, placed 20th nationally in the magazine's survey.

Vanderbilt's other facilities stand out as well. A Level I trauma center, comprehensive burn center, and LifeFlight helicopter ambulance system program respond to emergencies across Middle Tennessee, southern Kentucky, and northern Alabama. The university's Monroe Carell Jr. Children's Hospital, which in 2004 moved into a new, $172 million facility, offers the area's only Level IV neonatal intensive care unit and dedicated pediatric emergency department.

Nashville plays an important role in shaping the future of health care delivery as home to the Vanderbilt schools of medicine and nursing and Meharry Medical College, the nation's largest historically black institution dedicated to educating health professionals. More than 100 new physicians and 250 new nurses graduate from Vanderbilt each year, with many more taking part in advanced training and research at the university. About 150 physicians, dentists, and biomedical science experts graduate from Meharry every year. A Vanderbilt-Meharry partnership enables Meharry students to benefit from Vanderbilt's medical education strengths, and Vanderbilt students to gain experience at Metropolitan Nashville General Hospital, which Meharry operates.

The health care industry drives the economy, employing one of every seven people in fields from hospital management (opposite page) to heart surgery (this page, right). The HCA-run Skyline Medical Center (this page, left) is among many centers providing world-class care.

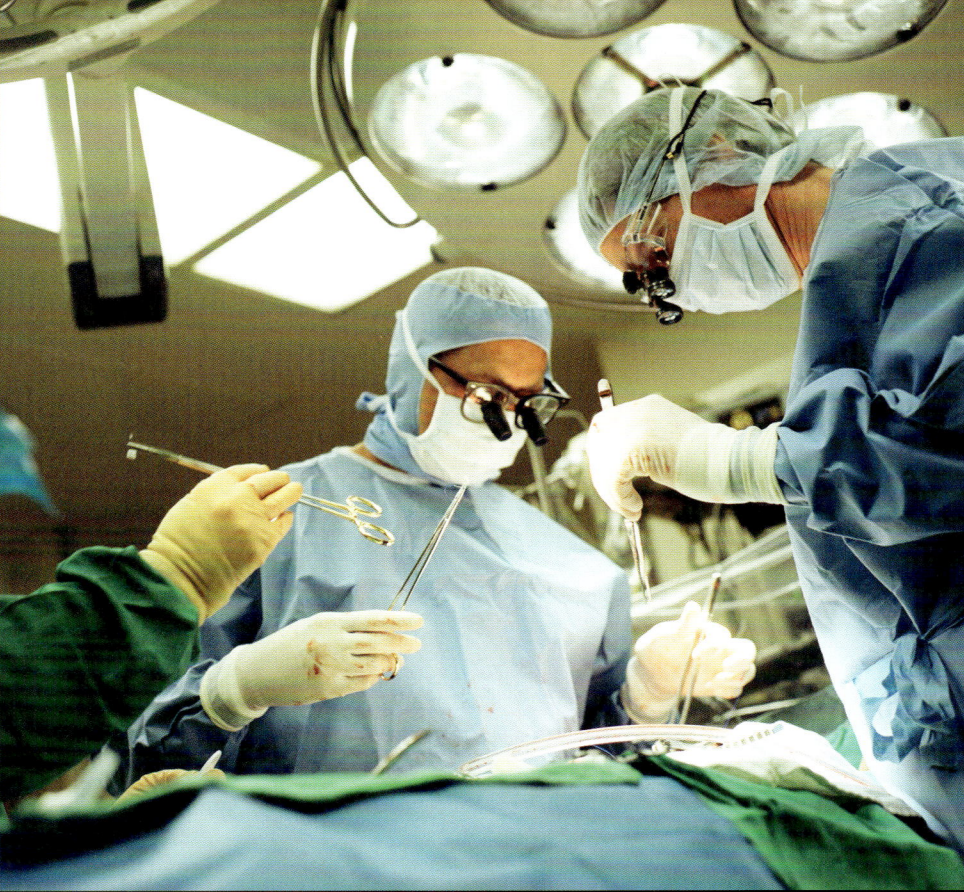

Health Care, Technology, and Biosciences | 53

Smart Business

What made Nashville a health care capital? It was a family affair, in more ways than one. Literal families do loom large on the for-profit health care scene, none more so than the Frist clan. Among the founders of HCA in 1968 were doctors Thomas F. Frist Sr. and Jr., and the chairman and CEO of the publicly held medical information company HealthStream is Robert A. Frist Jr., a grandson of the elder Dr. Frist—to mention but a few of the noteworthy Frists.

But the families that matter most in Nashville are the corporate cousins that have descended from HCA and its one-time rival, Hospital Affiliates International (HAI). HCA absorbed HAI in 1981, but by that time the two companies had nurtured a generation of health care entrepreneurs. Former HAI executive Joel Gordon, for example, essentially invented the outpatient surgery center business with his Surgical Care Affiliates, which he eventually sold to Birmingham-based HealthSouth. HCA has spun off a number of companies over the years; most recently, the national hospital networks Triad Hospitals and LifePoint Hospitals. HCA alumni have gone on to help create such major health care entities as dialysis center operator Renal Care Group (sold to German conglomerate Fresenius in early 2006) and nationwide hospital operators Psychiatric Solutions and Iasis Healthcare, to name but a few.

This page: Nashville-based health care organizations include world-renowned leaders in such services as outpatient care (left) and pharmacy operations (right). Opposite page: Meharry Medical College students consult a faculty mentor on their lab research.

It may come as a surprise, then, to learn that the largest health care company based in Nashville is not HCA and not a hospital management company. The distinction now belongs to Caremark Rx, a pharmacy benefit management company that relocated to Nashville from Birmingham, Alabama, in 2003. With almost $33 billion in 2005 revenues, Caremark finished the year $8.5 billion larger than HCA by the revenue yardstick (though HCA had the higher profits of the two). Caremark's sales expanded by 28 percent in 2005, and stock watchers predicted in early 2006 that the company still had plenty of room to grow as its industry consolidates and mail-order pharmacy arrangements become more widely adopted.

This page and opposite page, left: A researcher checks an experiment at the Cumberland Emerging Technologies Life Sciences Center. Opposite page, top right: Small but mighty, a blood-sugar monitor aids diabetes management. Bottom right: Voice-capture technology is a boon to a physician analyzing X-rays.

Caremark's business model barely existed a decade ago, and plenty of Nashville's health care companies have shared the experience of helping to build new industry niches from scratch. In the wake of Surgical Care Affiliates' success, the concept of developing outpatient surgical centers with physician investors became popular. Two local publicly traded companies, AmSurg and Symbion, mine this sector. AmSurg operates 150 outpatient centers in 32 states and saw its 2005 sales rise 17.2 percent over the previous year, to nearly $392 million. Revenues from Symbion's 22-state network of 60 facilities rose by almost 23 percent in 2005 over the year before, to nearly $266 million.

Another example is Nashville-based Healthways. The company, founded in 1981, has pioneered disease-management services that track and intervene in chronic disease cases such as diabetes, so that patients receive the care they need before their condition worsens and becomes much more expensive to treat. By mid 2006, more than 50 health insurance plans and 400 major self-insured businesses had contracted with Healthways to offer its services. A merger with California-based LifeMasters Supported Self-Care, announced in May 2006, is expected to extend services to at least another 100 employers.

On the Leading Edge

Inevitably, as 21st-century health care becomes ever more technology intensive, Nashville companies are taking a leading role in the development and implementation of tools that not only are of use to healers but are themselves healers.

Technology services for the health care industry have become a factor in the local economy. One major player is Emdeon Business Services (EBS), a Nashville-based unit of New Jersey's Emdeon Corporation that helps automate key business functions for insurers, physicians, and hospitals. EBS, which employs more than 2,600 people, most of them in Nashville, posted revenues of almost $759 million in 2005, marking a 50 percent increase in two years. Another top company is Franklin-based Spheris, which in 2005 ranked 16th on the Inc. 500 list of fastest-growing private companies and posted $209 million in 2005 revenues. Spheris uses voice-capture technology to take dictation from doctors and employs more than 5,500 people in the United States and India to get transcriptions back to the medical practices.

Nashville has developed a growing biotechnology sector in recent years and now offers a helpful infrastructure for future entrants into the field. The Cumberland Emerging Technologies Life Sciences Center in downtown Nashville is an incubator for early-stage biotech companies, while the Cool Springs Life Sciences Center in Franklin, still under development but partially operational, caters to the needs of more mature firms. The Cumberland center is a subsidiary of Cumberland Pharmaceuticals, one of whose drugs, Acetadote (acetylcysteine), has been widely adopted as a treatment for acetaminophen overdose. The Cool Springs facility is home to BioMimetic Therapeutics, whose initial public offering in May 2006 made it the first Nashville-area biotech firm to go public in recent history. BioMimetic develops orthopedic therapies that bring about the regeneration of damaged human tissue. Its first product, GEM 21S, intended for use in bone grafts and oral surgery, received regulatory approval in 2005.

This page: Carefully extracted rattlesnake venom (left) is used to produce a Brentwood biotech firm's snakebite antidote, being prepared for injection (right). Opposite page: Cell cultures provide the fundamental research that leads to medical breakthroughs.

London-based Protherics, a biotech firm that handles much of its operations from its U.S. headquarters in Brentwood, holds the distinction of being the only corporate citizen in town to have its own rattlesnake farm (located, it is a relief to report, far from Nashville in Utah), which it uses for venom production. Sheep immunized with the venom produce antibodies for the company's CroFab product, an antidote for rattlesnake bites that has become the leader in the U.S. antivenom market. Another Protherics product, CytoFab, treats severe sepsis. Advanced clinical trials for the latter are scheduled for 2007 in conjunction with pharmaceutical giant AstraZeneca.

Supporting all of the creativity that emerges from the health care sector locally is a network of entrepreneurs, investors, and industry veterans. There are abundant opportunities to raise private capital in Nashville to support business concepts involving health care, and the history of the industry is replete with examples of knowledgeable investors who have repeatedly plowed their winnings back into new local ventures. Likewise, health care in Nashville has a long history of cross-fertilization with academe, most notably in the close ties between Vanderbilt University Medical Center faculty and the numerous health care companies they founded or on whose boards they sit. Few would deny that the overall environment for health-care business innovation in Nashville has never been more favorable than it is today.

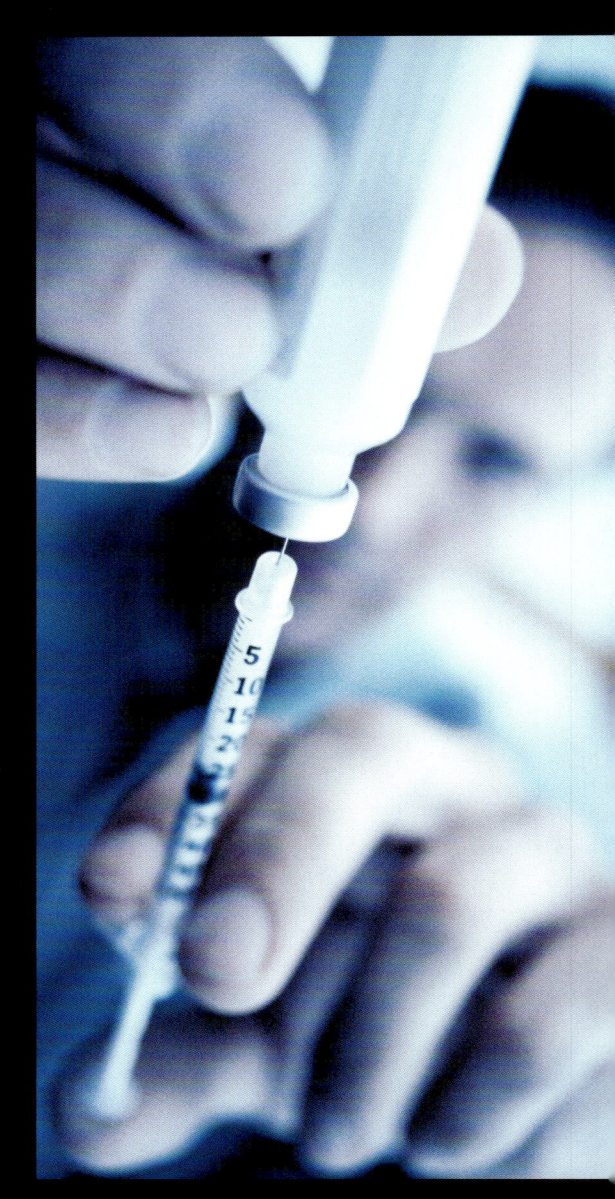

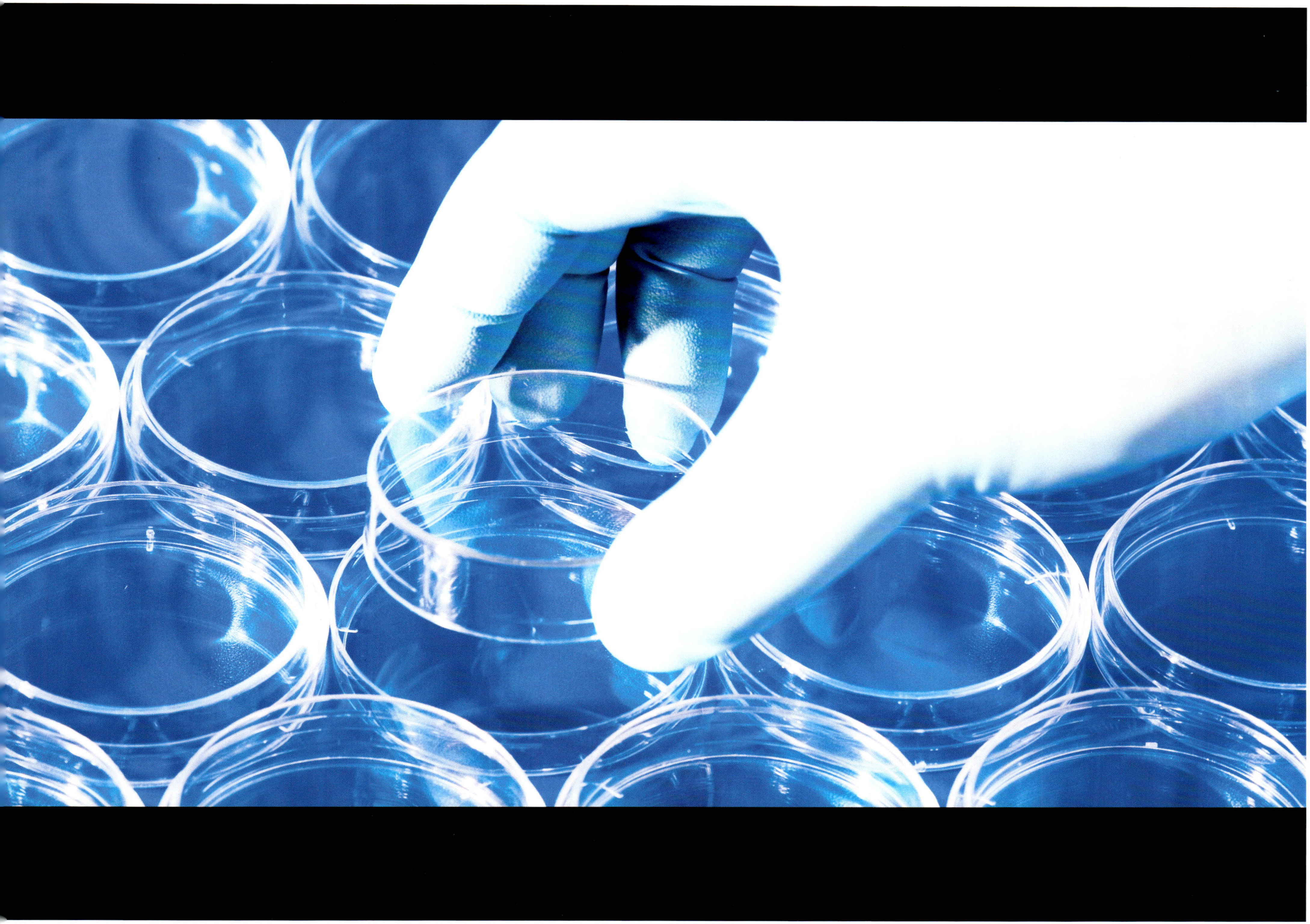

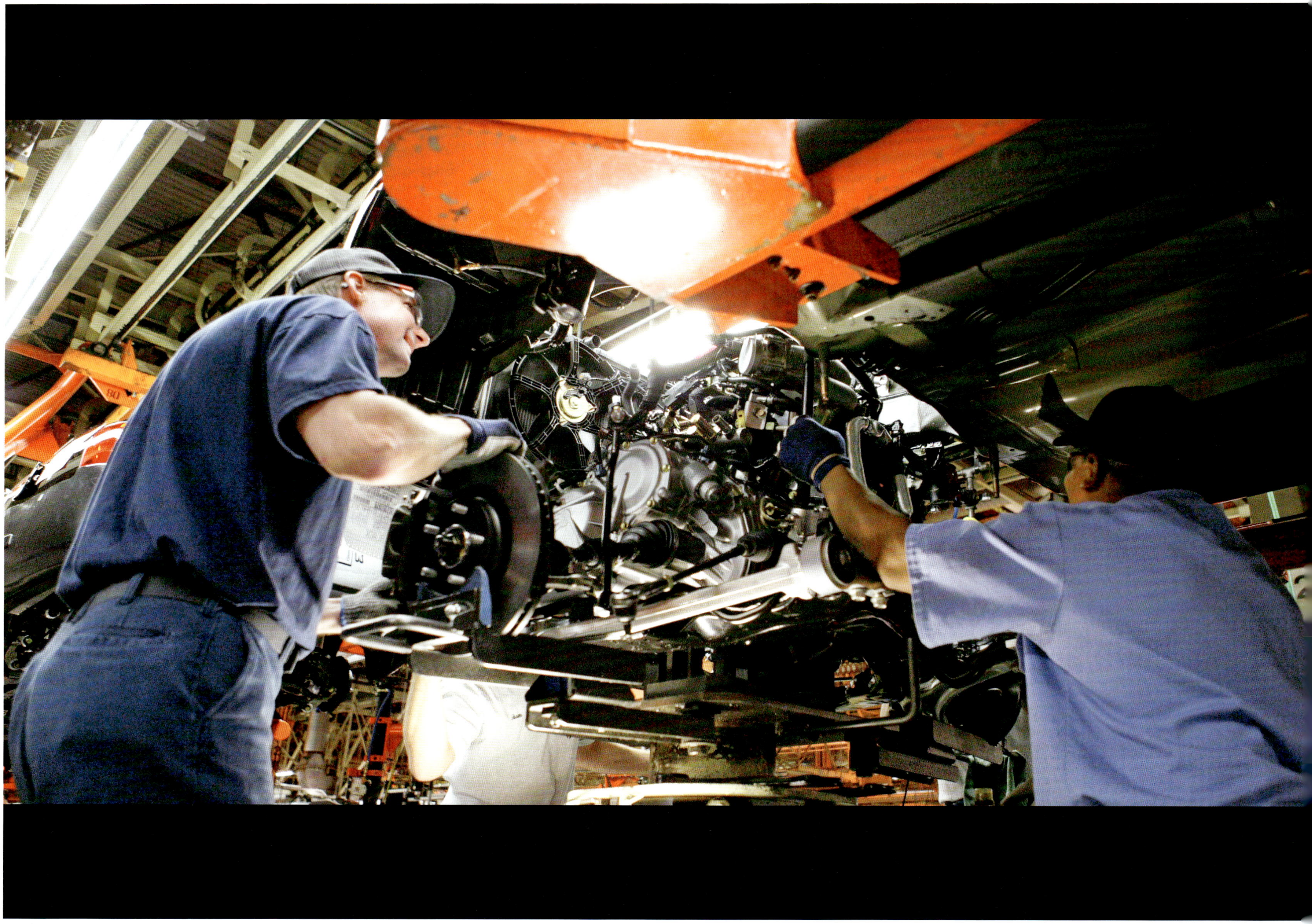

Nissan's classy midsize sedan, the Altima (this page), is among the vehicles made in the company's plant (opposite page) in Smyrna. Tennessee auto, component, and tire makers lead the state's manufacturing economy with a hefty 33 percent of the jobs.

ANOTHER NASHVILLE TUNE: THE HUM OF THE PRODUCTION LINE

Manufacturing, Information Technology, and Distribution

Middle Tennesseans are among the lucky ones. In an era of national concern about the future of manufacturing enterprises and jobs, the Nashville area is one place where those fears are decidedly muted. Everyone now understands that globalization can mean the end of American jobs that migrated a generation ago, in many cases, from the northern United States to the southern, and that those jobs may keep walking all the way to China—if cheap labor is all that matters to the manufacturer. Fortunately, the Greater Nashville area is home to many industries that need something more: easy access to distribution channels out of a central and well-served geographic location, a low-cost business environment, and a critical mass of skilled and educated workers. Nashville enjoys a clear edge in those categories. And according to the University of Tennessee's Center of Business and Economic Research, between 2003 and 2005 Nashville added manufacturing jobs at a rate of 3.18 percent. That figure may seem small, but to put it in perspective, Nashville was the only metro area in the state to add manufacturing jobs in that period.

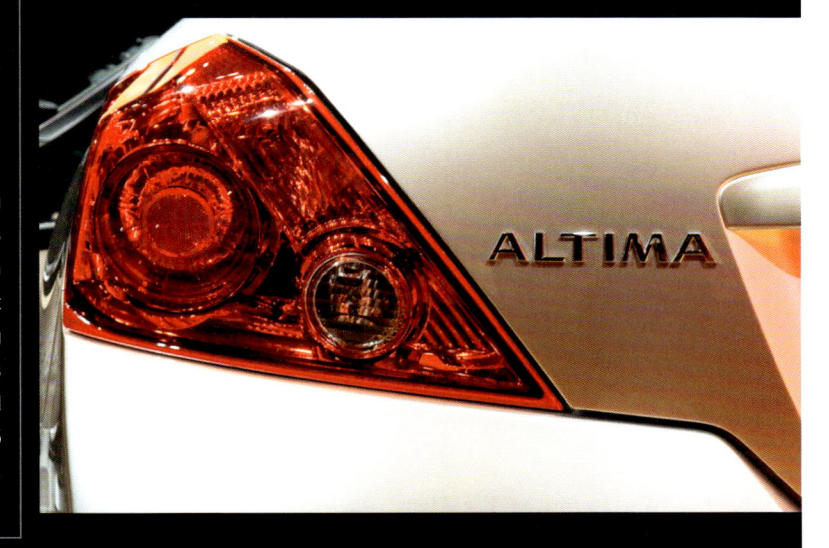

Further proof of the city's success is reflected in the contributions that two large automobile plants lured here in the 1980s—Nissan and Saturn—continue to make to the economy, and by the legacies of many corporate investments less dramatic than those of Nissan and Saturn but no less significant in their aggregate impact.

Nashville manufacturers keep the nation's economy humming and work flowing with goods such as (both pages, left to right) an Electrolux Home Products kitchen range; Louisiana-Pacific Corporation oriented strand board (OSB) sheathing; Vought Aircraft Industries wings (shown in the process of alignment for attachment); and Robert Bosch Corporation brake systems.

Economic Engines

Nashville is no Motor City. But the importance of auto-industry employers to Middle Tennessee's economy has been significant ever since Nissan arrived, and it has just become greater since Nissan "arrived" again. The first arrival came in 1980, when Nissan North America chose sleepy Smyrna, not far from Metro Nashville's southwestern boundary, as the site of what became a 5.4 million-square-foot, 6,700-employee plant producing more than half a million cars every year. The second "arrival" came in November 2005, when the automaker announced it would relocate its North American headquarters to Cool Springs, in Williamson County, from Gardena, a Los Angeles–area city that had been its home since 1960. Each move had a transforming impact on the Midstate, and between the brackets of Nissan's moves have been corporate developments that were huge in their own right. Japan's Bridgestone Corporation bought a troubled, 800-employee Firestone Tire plant in La Vergne in 1988 and turned it into what is now the site of 4,900 tire-manufacturing jobs as well as Bridgestone's main U.S. office. In 1985 General Motors chose the village of Spring Hill as the site for its most ambitious project in a generation, the creation of a car called Saturn, constructing a plant that now employs nearly 4,000 people.

Nashville had a foothold in auto manufacturing as early as 1956, when Ford Motor Company built a glass plant out near the Gothic hulk of the now empty Tennessee State Penitentiary. Ford now owns the two million-square-foot plant again after spinning it out to Visteon Corporation in 2000.

All that transpired between the Nissan arrivals has affected the economy of the entire region. Component manufacturers have followed the automakers to Tennessee from around the world. Among them are Mahle Tennex North America, a unit of Germany's Mahle International that produces automotive filters in Murfreesboro; Italy's Teksid Aluminum Foundry, which casts aluminum components in Dickson; and Japanese metal-stamping specialist Unipres, which has a facility in Portland (Tennessee).

Investment in Nashville has continued in other manufacturing sectors as well. The world's number-one producer of oriented strand board (OSB) siding, Louisiana-Pacific Corporation, moved its headquarters to Nashville from Portland, Oregon, in 2004. That same year, industrial and environmental filter maker Clarcor announced that it, too, would pull up roots and head to Middle Tennessee. Williamson County's gain was Rockford, Illinois' loss as Clarcor set up its new headquarters in Franklin and began expanding. Fifteen years earlier, in 1989, Cummins Filtration moved from Cookeville to Nashville, where it established global headquarters and solidified its position as one of the world's leading makers of filters and exhaust systems for diesel engines.

The area's manufacturing industry includes companies that run the gamut of industrial sectors. Northwest of Nashville in Ashland City, the flagship plant of A. O. Smith Water Products Company, which has been producing water heaters since 1946, employs about 1,800 workers—more than any other non-automotive manufacturer in the area. Vought Aircraft Industries, a fixture next to Nashville International Airport since 1939, employs 965 people who turn out wings and tail sections for both civilian and military purposes. Whirlpool Corporation's facility in La Vergne has a workforce of 850 people, who manufacture such products as room air conditioners and built-in refrigerators. Electrolux Home Products, the leading employer in Robertson County, manufactures electric and gas ranges at its Springfield plant, where it employs 750 people.

While it may not be as large as those corporate titans, one Nashville icon has long been a fixture on the global stage—literally: Gibson Guitar Corp. Crafting the instruments for some of the world's best performers since it was founded in 1894, Gibson is now growing at a rate of 26 percent annually, with revenues in the vicinity of $300 million. The passing of time has only motivated the company, which is tuning up to move ahead of the competition. In 2002 Gibson introduced the first digital electric guitar, which *USA Today* deemed a technological departure as remarkable as the first all-electric guitars that debuted in the 1930s. In 2005 Gibson bought naming rights to the world-renowned amphitheater at Universal CityWalk in Los Angeles.

A Center of the Word, Holy and Otherwise

Nashville has been producing printed pages, as well as words to fill them, for most of its nearly 230 years. In the 19th century, the city emerged as the locus of much of the nation's religious publishing. It carries on that role today. Thomas Nelson, one of the world's most prolific printers of Bibles and related study materials, with a line of more than 3,400 products, employs over 200 people in Nashville and recorded $253 million in 2006 revenues. (Gideons International, which fans out across the world to distribute the Good Book, also makes its home in Nashville.) The United Methodist Publishing House is also based in Nashville, as is its counterpart, LifeWay Christian Resources of the Southern Baptist Convention. United Methodist Publishing House, founded in 1789, today sees annual sales of more than $110 million; LifeWay,

Opposite page, left: Gibson helps put the music in Music City, as one performer can attest. Opposite page, right: A press check helps maintain a Nashville publisher's reputation for excellence. This page: Uplifting books, in high demand throughout the region, line the shelves of this Christian bookstore.

a nonprofit publisher established in 1891, records sales totaling $428.5 million yearly. R. H. Boyd Publishing Corporation, founded by freed slave Richard Henry Boyd in 1896 and still run by his descendants, is known around the world as a leading publisher of contemporary religious materials oriented toward African-American readers.

Mainstream book publishing thrives in Nashville as well. Cumberland House Publishing, which saw sales of $9.4 million and turned out 54 titles in 2005, is one of several midsize publishers in the area. Others include Thomas Nelson subsidiary Rutledge Hill Press, publisher of H. Jackson Brown Jr.'s well-known *Life's Little Instruction Book* and related titles, and contract publishers Providence Publishing Corporation and Favorite Recipes Press.

National media outlets based in the Nashville area include Publishing Group of America (producer of the weekly newspaper supplement *American Profile*), American Hometown Publishing, Journal Communications, and business information specialist M. Lee Smith Publishers.

Technology Magnet

Information technology powers today's economy, and in Nashville, it also provides employment. According to the University of Tennessee study quoted earlier, Nashville's IT sector accounts for 2.7 percent of the area's jobs—a higher share than that of any other city in the state.

On the computer side of the industry, Dell has made itself at home in Nashville and nearby Lebanon since 1999, when the company located some of its assembly operations and call center functions there. Dell's latest expansion in the area is expected to provide jobs for up to 1,000 people, bringing its local workforce to about 4,500 in 2007. Dell competitor Gateway established its own assembly plant—the only such facility it has in the United States—in La Vergne in late 2006, bringing 300 more IT jobs to town. Gateway shares its new space with Taiwan-based Quanta Computer Corporation, a key Gateway supplier that employs another 230 people locally.

Innumerable Nashville companies provide IT services, from Web site development and wireless network design to data recovery and e-commerce consulting. One of the early firms to open for business in the area, Digital Dog, has created hundreds of Web sites since its inception in 1994, winning recognition for its use of cutting-edge design and technology. Another IT company, Beacon Technologies, began providing computer and Internet services and video teleconferencing systems in 1998; from 2003 to 2004, its revenues shot up more than 58 percent.

Rated a Five-Star Logistics Metro by *Expansion Management* magazine, Nashville delivers. This page: Trucks stand ready to take to the interstates. Opposite page, left: Loading a cargo plane begins at dawn for this worker at Nashville International Airport's all-cargo complex. Opposite page, right: Goods designated for the Gulf Coast head down the Cumberland River on a barge.

Nashville's appeal to high-tech companies stems in part from the excellent support they find here. Several organizations, starting with the Nashville Technology Council, pull members of the tech community together and provide plentiful opportunities to network and learn. Local universities, of which the Metro has many, are also bastions of tech knowledge waiting to be accessed. Belmont University and Nashville State Community College, for example, both have technology centers. Vanderbilt University covers a great deal of ground with three special offerings: an engineering management program, an office of technology transfer, and a center for doing business on the Internet. A myriad of private schools and companies also focus on educating future tech pros and serving as community resources.

Made for Trade

With its competitive location and excellent infrastructure, Nashville has long been a center of distribution. A Class 1 railroad and two short-line carriers connect overland with the nation's busiest markets and ports, and more than 70 major trucking companies take to the highways day and night. About 30 commercial barge firms operate large fleets on the Cumberland River, and 16 air cargo companies land and take off around the clock.

All this support has earned Nashville a reputation as one of the nation's top distribution centers and designation as a foreign-trade zone (FTZ), which means that customs duty is eliminated on products that pass through the zone. As part of the U.S. Department of Commerce agreement for the zones, foreign companies with local branches can even assign a location outside the FTZ as a "subzone," which allows them to assemble or repackage their products at one of their own buildings, still free of tariff.

At least 20 of the nation's top retailers, manufacturers, and freight forwarders have distribution centers in Middle Tennessee. Those employing the largest workforces are United Parcel Service (Nashville), with 2,500 employees; Ingram Book Group (La Vergne), 2,050; Gap (Gallatin), 1,450; Thomas Nelson, (Nashville), 1,200; and Borders Group (La Vergne), 1,000. Others in the Nashville Metro include grocery supplier Performance Food Group, prerecorded media producer Cinram, and children's clothing maker Oshkosh B'Gosh.

Manufacturing, Information Technology, and Distribution | 67

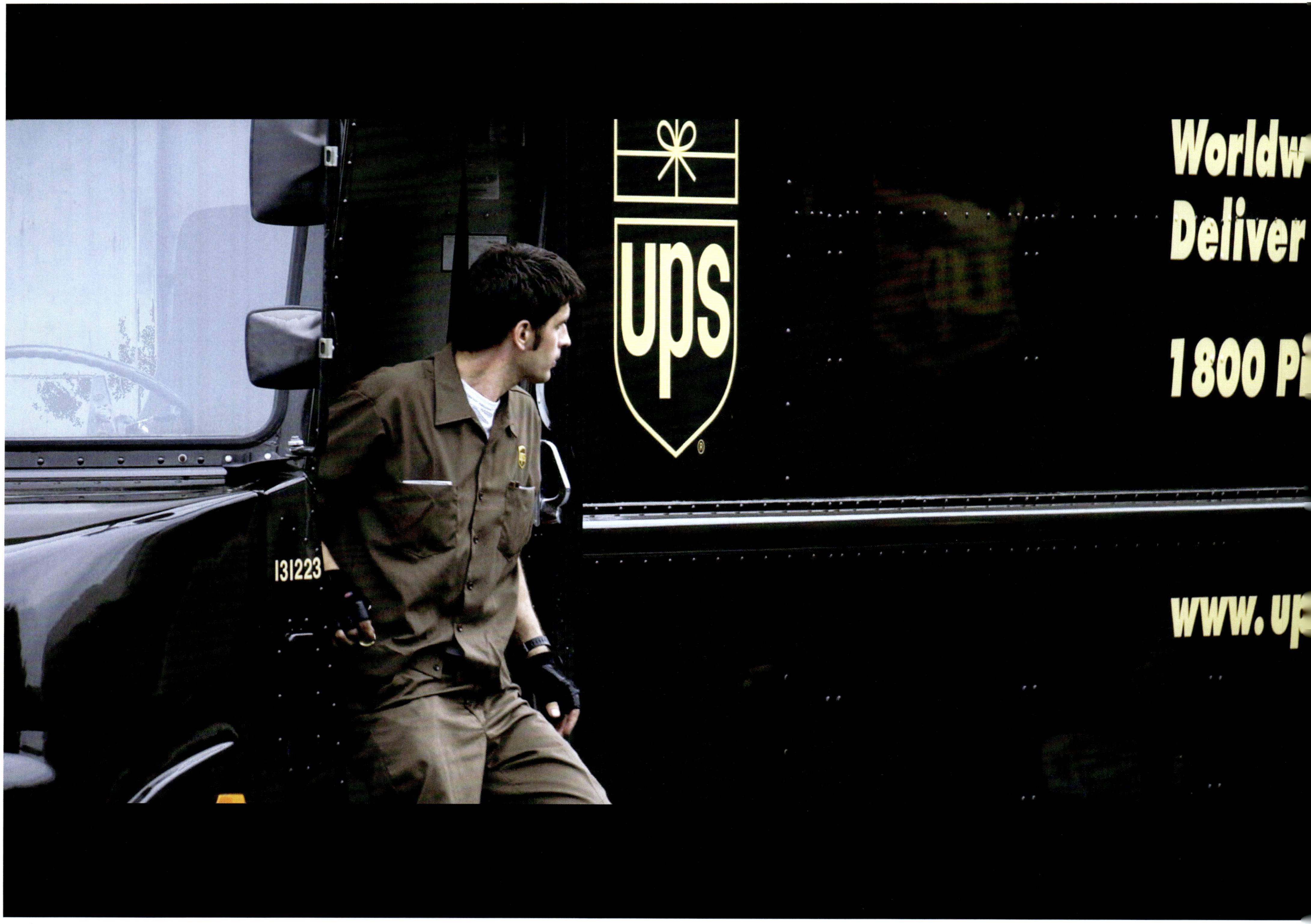
ups
131223
Worldw
Deliver
1800 P
www.up

This page: Inventory management is critical at the distribution center of a leading U.S. wholesaler. Opposite page: A UPS driver stops to pick up packages en route to the company's Nashville center, which employs 2,500 people—the area's largest distribution workforce.

Ingram Book Group, a division of Nashville-based Ingram Industries headquartered in La Vergne, is one of the dominant book wholesalers in the United States. The division distributes 175 million books and audiotapes annually to more than 30,000 bookstores, and it posted sales of more than $289 million in 2005 (the latest data available). Ingram Entertainment Holdings, also based in La Vergne but run independently from Ingram Industries, is among the nation's largest independent DVD, video, and computer game wholesalers. The company delivers about 106 million products annually to 10,000 retailers, recording revenues of $839 million. According to *Forbes* magazine, Ingram Entertainment is also the top U.S. distributor of DVD hardware and software.

Another distributor with Nashville roots and a nationwide presence is Brentwood's Ozburn-Hessey Logistics, which has been providing storage and delivery services since 1951. The company has grown dramatically in recent years, acquiring logistics centers across the country, including global freight-forwarding firm Barthco International. Ozburn-Hessey can now compete for contracts on which it might previously have settled for a subcontracting role.

Middle Tennesseans are indeed fortunate, and not just because of their region's geography and business climate. Foresight and smart investment have kept the manufacturing industry viable here, while in other cities and states it has fared less well. The continued stability of Nashville's producers and distributors will be a key advantage in the region's economic future.

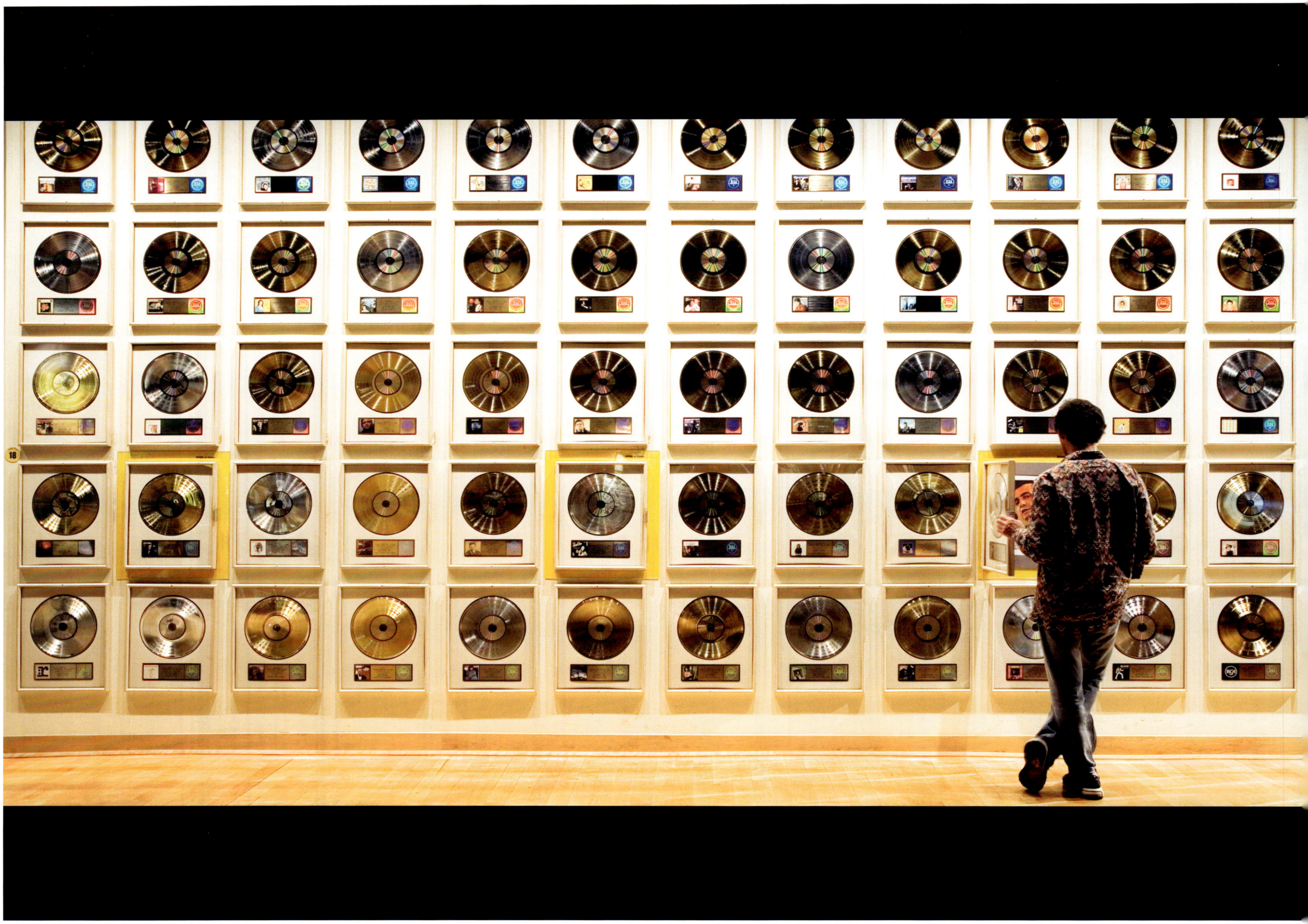

A musical consciousness encompassing every genre gives the city its global identity. This page: Bluegrass entertainers The Grascals perform at the Nashville Music Classic festival at Smiley Hollow, in Ridgetop. Opposite page: A fan opens an album on the Gold Records Wall of the Country Music Hall of Fame and Museum.

SOUND INVESTMENTS
Music, Tourism, and Entertainment

First of all, the city is at peace with whatever anyone in the great wide world thinks it is all about. Strangers passing through town over the years, such as filmmaker Robert Altman in the 1970s and essayist V. S. Naipaul in the 1980s, have either caricatured the culture of the Music City or produced overwrought analyses of Nashville's tuneful anthropology. The Nashville of old, less sure of its identity, used to cringe at this form of scrutiny, and people outside the music business tended to flee from any association with the country scene.

Today's Nashville, by contrast, is happy to be viewed through whatever lens anyone chooses to use, as long as people know where it is on the map. The music industry, its ally the tourism industry, and the ever-diversifying general entertainment sector are sources of pride to Nashville residents, who now understand well the dynamic impact those industries have on the local economy. Visitors and newcomers who arrive with images of a cornpone capital on their minds soon learn the Music City is about more than country and more than music.

This page, left: Bar glasses are all set for Nashville's lively nightlife. This page, right: Lighting and decor make the difference during a show at the Wildhorse Saloon. Opposite page: Sound technicians listen to the mix at one of the area's 180 recording studios.

Granted, many outsiders will always think of Patsy Cline or Hank Williams Sr. when they hear the word "Nashville." That's fine, but think Kid Rock, or John Kay of Steppenwolf, or rapper Young Buck. Think of the Gospel Music Association, or the Fisk Jubilee Singers, or classical music label Naxos. Think of the Hard Rock Café downtown, an emblem of Nashville's truly amplified side, within the riverfront nightlife district that draws visitors for cigars and martinis as much as for line dancing at the Wildhorse Saloon. Nashville is big enough for them all.

Music to Their Ears

The Nashville that tourists see represents only one facet of the entertainment industry's economic presence. A 2006 study prepared by Belmont University for the Nashville Area Chamber of Commerce put hard numbers to a business sector whose scale had not been fully quantified before. The report's bottom-line figure, placing the total economic impact of the music industry in the Nashville area at $6.38 billion a year, confirmed the music business's central role in the city's prosperity. Nearly $4 billion of that amount comes from the direct and secondary impact of spending by music-related enterprises, ranging from performers and record labels to trade groups, performing-rights organizations, music industry media outlets, management and booking services, and professionals such as lawyers and accountants who specialize in the industry. Another $2.42 billion comes from spending by tourists in Nashville.

Music, Tourism, and Entertainment | 73

This page and opposite page, left to right: Likenesses of Sara Evans and Kenny Chesney advertise TV network Great American Country on the Gaylord Entertainment Center tower; diners overlook indoor gardens at the Gaylord Opryland Resort & Convention Center; the NHL Predators take the ice at Gaylord Entertainment Center.

The Belmont survey found that there are approximately 5,000 working union musicians, 180 recording studios, 130 music publishers, 80 record labels, and 27 entertainment publications in Nashville. It calculated that more than 19,000 area jobs are directly related to the making of music, generating some $722 million in salary and wages annually. In annual payroll and number of employees, these figures put the music industry roughly on a par with, and possibly ahead of, auto manufacturing or commercial banking among the drivers of economic growth in Middle Tennessee, as indicated by a comparison of census data. Taking into account the indirect creation of jobs attributable to music industry activity, Belmont pegs the industry's total employment impact at more than 54,000 jobs. Music-related economic activity also contributes more than $75 million in taxes to local and state governments each year.

Some 10.5 million people visit Nashville in a typical year, with more than a third coming for the city's music and music-related attractions, the study reported. Of the other two thirds, many are on their way to conventions and other group events. Gaylord Entertainment's massive Opryland hotel complex, on the east side of the city, is the hub of Nashville's convention trade. Situated on 172 acres, with 2,881 guest rooms and 600,000 square feet of meeting and exhibit space, the Opryland is the nation's fourth-largest hotel, ranked by total meeting space. Its annual revenues increased by 47 percent in 2006.

Downtown Nashville has a convention center, but it is too small to handle many of the mega conventions on which the city's convention and visitors bureau would like to bid. A movement within the business community to push for the building of a new downtown convention facility began to gather steam in 2006. Early plans under discussion have involved funding the new center in ways that would put little or no public money at risk, but the boosters will have to present solid facts and figures if they want to gain broad public support for another big project downtown.

There is widespread belief among Nashvillians that out-of-towners convinced city officials to hand over excessive incentive packages to lure National Hockey League and National Football League franchises in the 1990s, and Metro Nashville has, in fact, paid out far more to build and maintain the Nashville Predators' home, Gaylord Entertainment Center, and the Tennessee Titans' LP Field than it has recouped in tax revenues from them. Supporters argue that pro sports have brought the city a payoff by raising its national visibility and have generated an economic impact that exceeds the city's annual subsidy.

This page and opposite page, left: Pro sports include the Firestone Indy 200 at the Nashville SuperSpeedway and the annual Iroquois Steeplechase at Percy Warner Park. Opposite page, center: Nashville's oldest surviving recording studio, from 1957, helped establish the Nashville Sound. Opposite page, right: Country music dynamos Bomshel record for locally owned Curb Records.

That debate aside, Nashville has definitely got game. The Predators, returning to the ice in 2005 after losing the prior season to the NHL strike, defied prophets of doom by posting their best attendance figures since the 2001–02 season. The Titans have struggled on the field in recent years but retain an obsessive legion of fans. The minor league Nashville Sounds, AAA baseball affiliate of the Milwaukee Brewers, are slated to occupy a new riverfront stadium in 2008 located at the other end of the Shelby Street Pedestrian Bridge from the Titans' stadium. LP Field also hosts the annual collegiate Music City Bowl, a face-off between teams from the Southeast Conference and the Atlantic Coast Conference, while Gaylord Entertainment Center has been the site of a number of college basketball tournaments.

Other sporting events in the area range from NASCAR racing at the Nashville SuperSpeedway to horse racing at Percy Warner Park. The Iroquois Steeplechase, a major horse racing event in the social calendar, is held at the park each May. There is also a significant race for humans: the annual Country Music Marathon takes about 22,000 participants through the city in April. The Nashville Sports Council, which seeks to attract and promote events that will benefit the city, notes the sports sector brought $34 million to the local economy in 2005–06, the fourth year it has broken the $30 million mark.

A Country Consciousness

Whatever else Nashville has to offer, the brand of the city is country music. Those who love the genre consider Nashville a place of pilgrimage and refer to downtown's Ryman Auditorium, early home of the *Grand Ole Opry*, as the Mother Church. The Ryman, owned by Gaylord Entertainment, drew 425,000 visitors for tours in 2005, while the nearby Country Music Hall of Fame and Museum attracted nearly 300,000. The two facilities are focal points for a culture and industry with a rich heritage and a global reach, as demonstrated when the Country Music Association's annual CMA Awards were held in New York's Madison Square Garden in November 2005, drawing 36 million viewers to a live, prime-time television broadcast.

Country music has been a business in Nashville ever since 1925, when the National Life and Accident Insurance Company put a hillbilly music show on the radio station it owned, WSM, in an effort to sell more insurance policies. The insurance company changed hands long ago, but WSM still carries the show, which became the *Grand Ole Opry* in December 1927. Now the nation's longest-running live radio program, the *Opry* is broadcast from Gaylord's Grand Ole Opry House, next to the Opryland hotel—though it returns for sessions at the Ryman a few times each year.

Music Row, a business neighborhood that is home to a large concentration of the city's music industry enterprises, originated with shrewd real estate investments by entrepreneurs such as producer Owen Bradley and guitar virtuoso Chet Atkins in the 1950s. Today this stretch of 16th and 17th avenues south, dubbed Music Square East and West, is the seat of power for the recording and publishing conglomerates that dominate the production and marketing of country music.

Consolidation at national and international levels has reduced the number of players in this field, as in so many other industrial sectors. The world's four major music conglomerates—EMI, Sony BMG, Universal Music Group, and Warner Music Group—maintain outposts in Nashville under a bewildering array of labels. Local units of the "Big Four" produced all but one of the 10 best-selling country albums of 2005, and that one came from a Disney-owned label based in Nashville, Lyric Street Records. Sony BMG accounted for four of the top 10 through its BNA Records, Arista Nashville, and Epic Records labels, while Universal's Mercury Nashville and DreamWorks Nashville labels accounted for three other top sellers, with Warner Bros. Nashville and EMI's Capitol Nashville Records posting one each.

Many small record companies thrive under the radar of the global behemoths, the classic example being Oh Boy Records, which singer-songwriter John Prine founded in the early 1980s. The company has since taken under wing other musical wordsmiths, including Todd Snider and the legendary Kris Kristofferson. Only one locally owned record label, however, has the market clout to produce gold and platinum hits regularly. Curb Records, which former California lieutenant governor Mike Curb transplanted to Nashville in 1992, is one of the largest independent record firms in the world, with a roster that includes Tim McGraw, LeAnn Rimes, and Lee Greenwood.

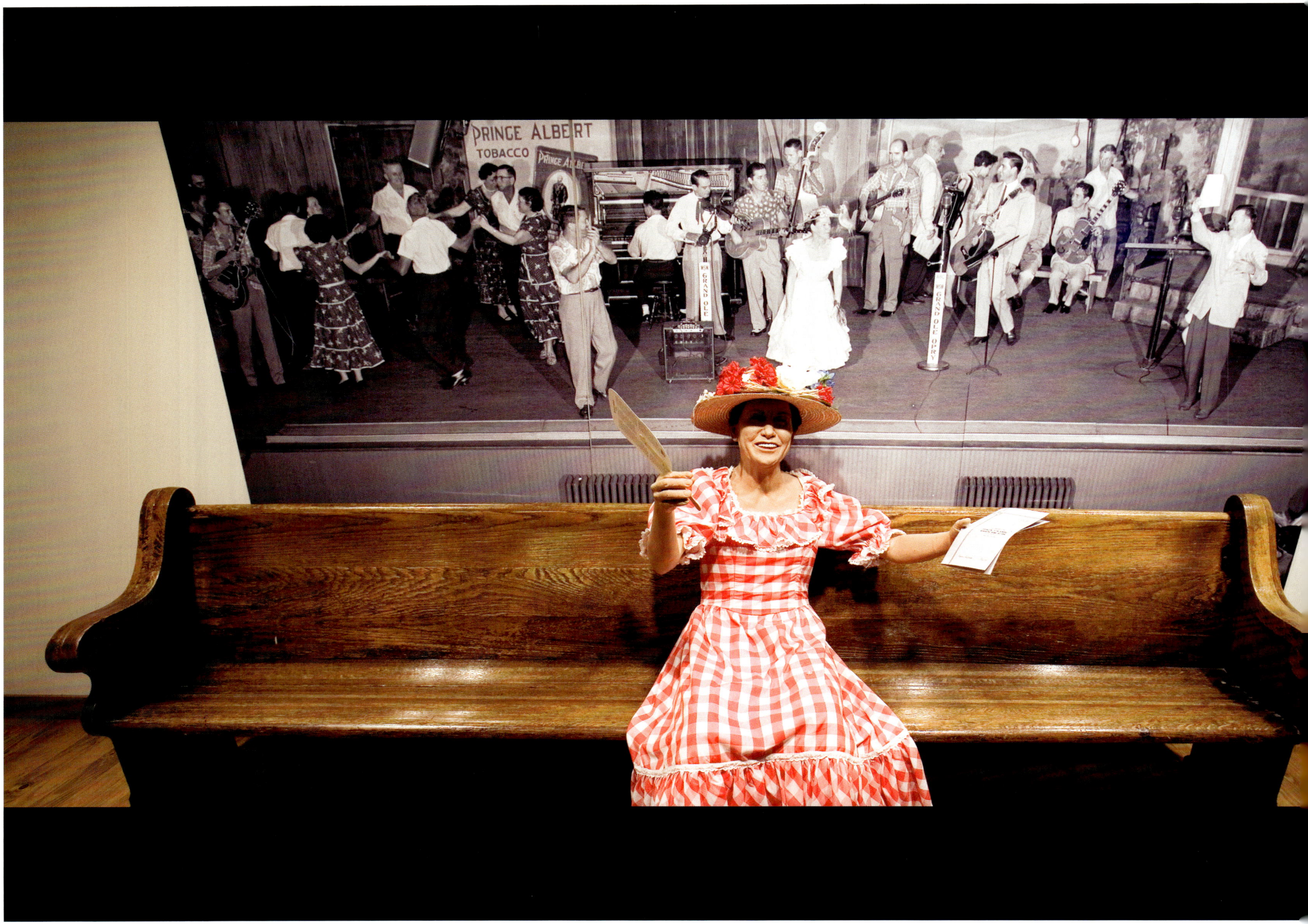
PRINCE ALBERT
TOBACCO
GRAND OLE OPRY

This page: With hundreds of recording studios, publishing offices, and radio stations, Music Row is considered the heart of the industry. Opposite page: A wax statue of Minnie Pearl, country comedy's favorite character, takes a breather at the Grand Ole Opry Museum.

Behind the Scenes

The country scene provides less steady work for music and film production facilities in Nashville than it once did, as technologies that make home recording easier have cut into the business of recording studios, while high-end music video production often happens on one coast or the other. On the other hand, recording artists from well beyond the country crowd beat a path to some of Nashville's premier recording venues, such as Blackbird Studio, whose clients have included not only the Dixie Chicks and Gretchen Wilson but also R. Kelly, the Red Hot Chili Peppers, and Smashmouth. On the video side, Film House has become the undisputed leader among independent video producers in Nashville, with a national clientele for its specialty of producing television commercials to promote radio stations.

Vital to the entertainment industry are the myriad print outlets, ranging from trade magazines to supermarket tabloids, that tell Music Row insiders and the wider world what's happening musically in Nashville. *Billboard* magazine's Nashville bureau and *Music Row* magazine are trusted sources for getting the scoop on industry doings. *Country Weekly*, owned by the publisher of the *National Enquirer*, has a newsstand circulation of more than 400,000 copies a week.

"Chicken Little" moments are part of the heritage of Music Row. Every few years, it seems, collective anxiety sets in as some of the record labels decide to move decision-making functions to one of the coasts, or sales of country music go through a slump, or the rise of digital media leads to new concerns over copyright protection. On these occasions, the worries of Music Row have tended to be exaggerated in the broader community, which historically has had limited understanding of how the music industry really works. The sky has never fallen yet, and it is an indicator of the maturing relationship between the music world and the rest of Nashville that these episodes have become fewer and less dramatic as the years have gone by. The Row is part of the Nashville business community now, fully appreciated as one of the cornerstone industries that make the city hum.

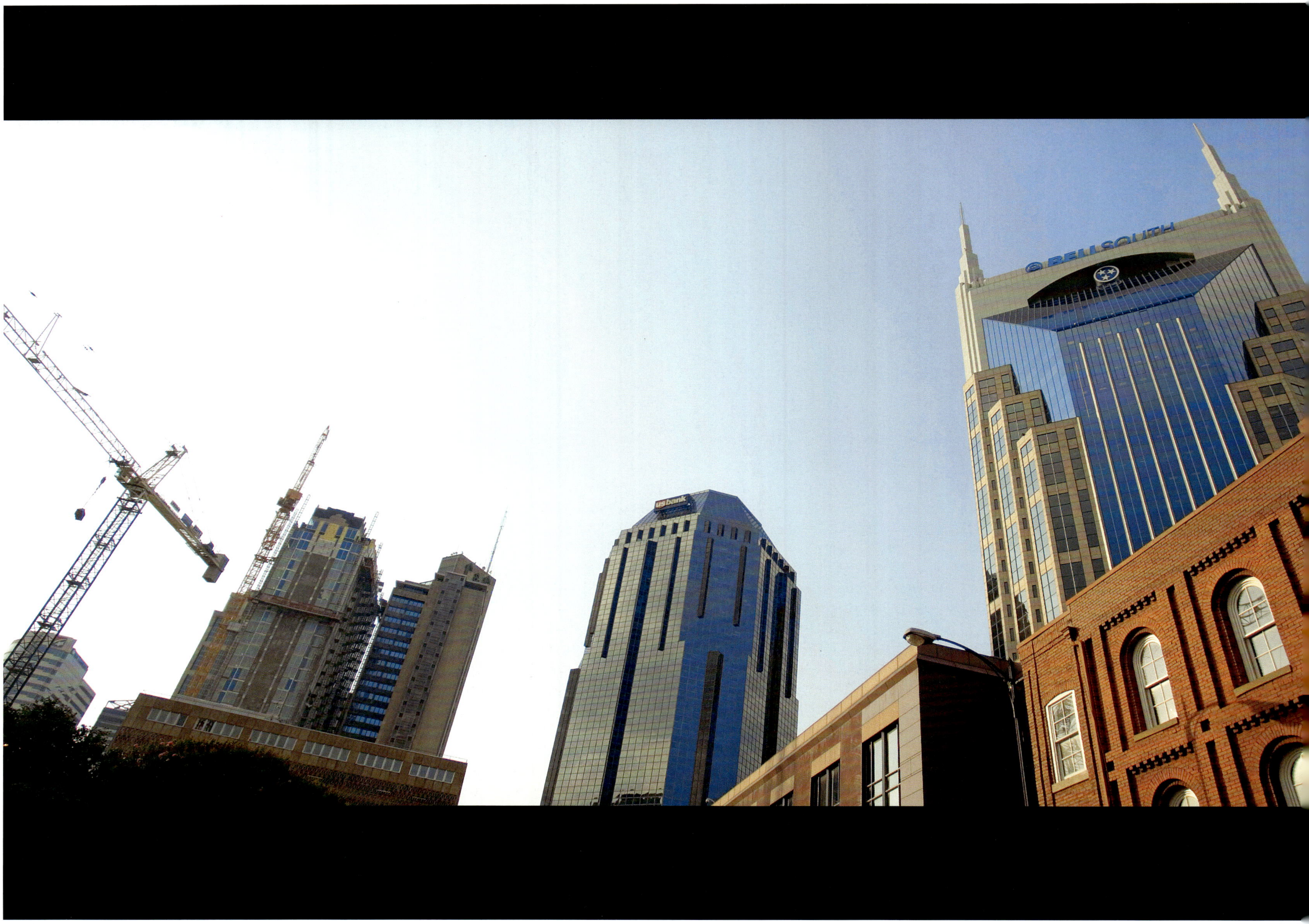
BELLSOUTH
usbank

This page: Custom homes like this Rogan Allen model in Green Hills are transforming desirable neighborhoods into masterpieces. Opposite page: Omnipresent cranes hint at the changes coming to downtown as commercial construction continues unabated.

BACKDROP OF A BOOM
Real Estate, Development, and Construction

A reshaped urban skyline, high-end real estate development in areas long left stagnant, knockdowns and sumptuous reconstructions of homes in the most desirable neighborhoods, and cranes everywhere—these are the outward signs of that sometimes intangible phenomenon, civic growth. The story of Nashville in the early 21st century involves all these elements and more.

Residential real estate has enjoyed a prolonged boom in Nashville and surrounding counties, but not at the fevered pitch found in some parts of the United States in this decade. The median home price in the Greater Nashville metropolitan area in the second quarter of 2006 was $177,900, up 11.4 percent from the same period a year earlier.

Certain hot spots, though, are seeing a dramatic rise in property values. As the Green Hills neighborhood has transitioned from modest affluence to something far grander, its last rental duplexes and cramped Cape Cod bungalows are falling to the wrecking ball, to be replaced by top-flight custom homes. Builder Rogan Allen has transformed the character of entire streets in Green Hills over the past few years, while other neighborhoods have their own agents of change at work, focusing on a narrow geographic area where they can buy, bulldoze, and build several properties simultaneously. In Belle Meade, the traditional preserve of Nashville's old money and the epicenter of one of the nation's wealthiest zip codes (37205), what was a mansion to prior generations is increasingly just not enough house for today's owners; the wreckers are busy there as well.

New amenities are fueling the reemergence of downtown as a center of activity. This page, left: Alabama business leaders visit the new main library's Civil Rights Collection. This page, right: The Schermerhorn Symphony Center now graces SoBro. Opposite page: The Shelby Street Bridge adds a vital pedestrian corridor.

Historically, the primary choice many home buyers faced in the Nashville market was whether to buy in Area 2 or elsewhere. Area 2 encompasses a broad suburban swath of southwestern Davidson County, including the stately early-20th-century homes of the Whitland/West End/Richland area, the opulent mansions of Belle Meade, and the leafy expanses of Green Hills, Forest Hills, and Oak Hill, with their combination of large postwar ranch houses and newer luxury homes. Area 2 has certainly lost none of its cachet: on a typical spring weekend in 2006, there were 117 sales listings in the zone priced at $1 million or more, with a top price of $6.9 million.

Yet the numbers tell a new story about which areas are most desirable to buyers. In Brentwood, just over the Williamson County line from Metro Nashville, the median home price was $343,549. Throughout the counties surrounding Nashville/Davidson County, prices rose substantially during the year, with the greatest increases seen in Wilson County, to the east (up 17 percent), and Sumner County, to the northeast (up 13 percent).

A Continuing Renaissance

Downtown Nashville is abloom. The past dozen years have seen a beautiful new main library taking the place of a failed shopping mall, the new Country Music Hall of Fame and Museum rising in what had been a decaying industrial area south of Broadway, and many more developments. The unveiling in 2006 of an entirely reinvented Public Square and the new Schermerhorn Symphony Center have put in place two more amenities that make downtown the place to be. The Nashville Sounds baseball park, scheduled to rise in 2008 in the shadow of the pedestrianized Shelby Street Bridge, will mark a further enhancement.

In addition to the new attractions, one landmark commercial project epitomizes downtown's revival as a business center: 13-story SunTrust Plaza. On the rise next to the Ryman Auditorium, it will encompass 338,000 square feet of office space when it is completed in December 2007. Nashville commercial developer Eakin Partners signed SunTrust Bank as the anchor tenant. Local firms Brasfield & Gorrie and Hastings Architecture Associates are handling, respectively, the general contracting and design of the the structure.

Of all that is happening in the residential, commercial, and industrial sectors of Nashville real estate, no phenomenon is more dramatic than the flowering of urban residential development. A decade ago, only a few hardy pioneers lived downtown. By the second quarter of 2006, almost 3,500 housing units were available or under construction in the area.

Entrepreneur Tony Giarratana is responsible for some of the highest-profile developments in the district. Overcoming much local skepticism, in 1998 he topped out the $35 million Cumberland—a 24-story apartment tower on Church Street, the former main artery of commercial Nashville that had fallen on hard times. Occupancy has remained steadily high there, and Giarratana has since had plenty of company among downtown developers. His 31-story, $70 million Viridian condo tower, also on the now revived Church Street, opened in October 2006. The building marks a symbolic change in the Nashville skyline: Viridian will match the height of the neighboring Life and Casualty Tower, which was hailed as the tallest building in the South when it opened in 1957. And Giarratana has received development and tax-increment financing approval on a 55-story, $200 million condominium development a half-block down Church Street from Viridian, to be known as Signature Tower.

Other high-rise condo projects are under way in the Gulch area, where 12th Avenue South meets the railroad lines running through downtown, and in SoBro, the newly redeveloped area south of Broadway near the Cumberland

This page: Stylish homes in the area include Craftsman bungalows like this one, with its added Tudor-style details, in Belle Meade. Opposite page: High-profile urban housing developments such as the Icon (left), in the Gulch, and the Row at 31st (right), in West End Park, are redefining city living.

The Commercial Sector

A thriving local economy in recent years has led to an upsurge in the development of new office and industrial properties, while vacancy rates for existing space keep trending downward. In the office market, the area's overall vacancy rate was 13.9 percent at the end of 2004, 12.2 percent at year-end 2005, and 8.3 percent at the end of 2006. Class A office construction is under way on a large scale in Cool Springs and several other hot spots.

In the past decade or so, a structural change has cushioned Nashville's commercial real estate economy from the cyclical swings that caused turmoil locally as recently as the early 1990s. Real estate investment trusts (REITs) from across the country now own a large portion of the city's class A commercial property. Investment risks are now largely spread among REIT shareholders rather than local banks. Middle Tennessee does have two sector-specific REITs of its own: Healthcare Realty Trust, which employs 215 people and saw revenues of more that $254 million in 2005 (latest data available), and National Health Realty, which shares employees with affiliated nursing home chain National HealthCare Corporation and generated $19.8 million in 2005 revenue. Still, out-of-town players dominate the office and industrial property markets.

River. On a smaller scale but in large numbers, developers are converting old industrial and office space into living quarters throughout the downtown area. Multifamily home developments are also flourishing. A good example is Row 8.9n (so named because its row houses are between 8th and 9th avenues North), across from the Farmer's Market. The development has been praised nationally as an innovative fusion of affordable and upscale urban housing.

Parallel to the rediscovery of downtown, East Nashville has been experiencing a rebirth over the past 15 years. From the mayor to young marrieds and members of the city's gay community, residents across the river from downtown have realized the potential of neighborhoods that long suffered from neglect. The residential and retail cluster centered on the Five Points area is Nashville's hipster magnet today. Some of the city's trendiest coffeehouses, bars, and restaurants are there, patronized by singles and young professionals who have settled into the rehabbed late-Victorian homes of the surrounding area.

This page, top: Decreasing vacancy rates and a thriving economy are bringing record commercial construction. This page, bottom: A rendering shows Nissan North America's future headquarters in Cool Springs. Opposite page: A Franklin suburb, Cool Springs accounts for more than half of Williamson County's vacant office space.

The most important of those REITs is North Carolina–based Crescent Resources, primary developer of the Cool Springs office park in Williamson County. Where livestock roamed 20 years ago, Crescent and others have created a burgeoning network of office buildings, hotels, and retail establishments. Soon to become part of that network is Nissan Motor Co.'s North American base, which is being moved to Middle Tennessee from the Los Angeles area. Nissan's 1,300 employees are temporarily ensconced in the BellSouth Tower downtown, but construction is under way on the company's headquarters building, slated for completion in 2008.

Within Nashville proper, hometown developer Alex S. Palmer & Company has cleared a midtown site for West End Summit, an intended office complex. Other major participants in the property scene prosper by owning or managing many smaller properties. Such is the case with longtime association-management powerhouse Ghertner & Company, for example, and such well-known office/retail players as H. G. Hill Realty Company and Brookside Properties.

Momentum in Building

Commercial construction accounted for the majority of the record $1.9 billion in building permits issued by Metro Nashville in 2006. With permit issuances so far in the first quarter of 2007 running at an average of almost $6 million per business day, odds are that the record will tumble again this year.

Census estimates tallied almost 3,000 construction companies in the seven-county Nashville statistical area as of 2002, generating $1.36 billion in annual payrolls and employing nearly 35,000 workers. Selling homes and leasing out commercial space keep plenty of people busy in Nashville as well: the area's 1,154 real estate–related businesses, as recorded by the Census Bureau, employed 6,485 people in 2002.

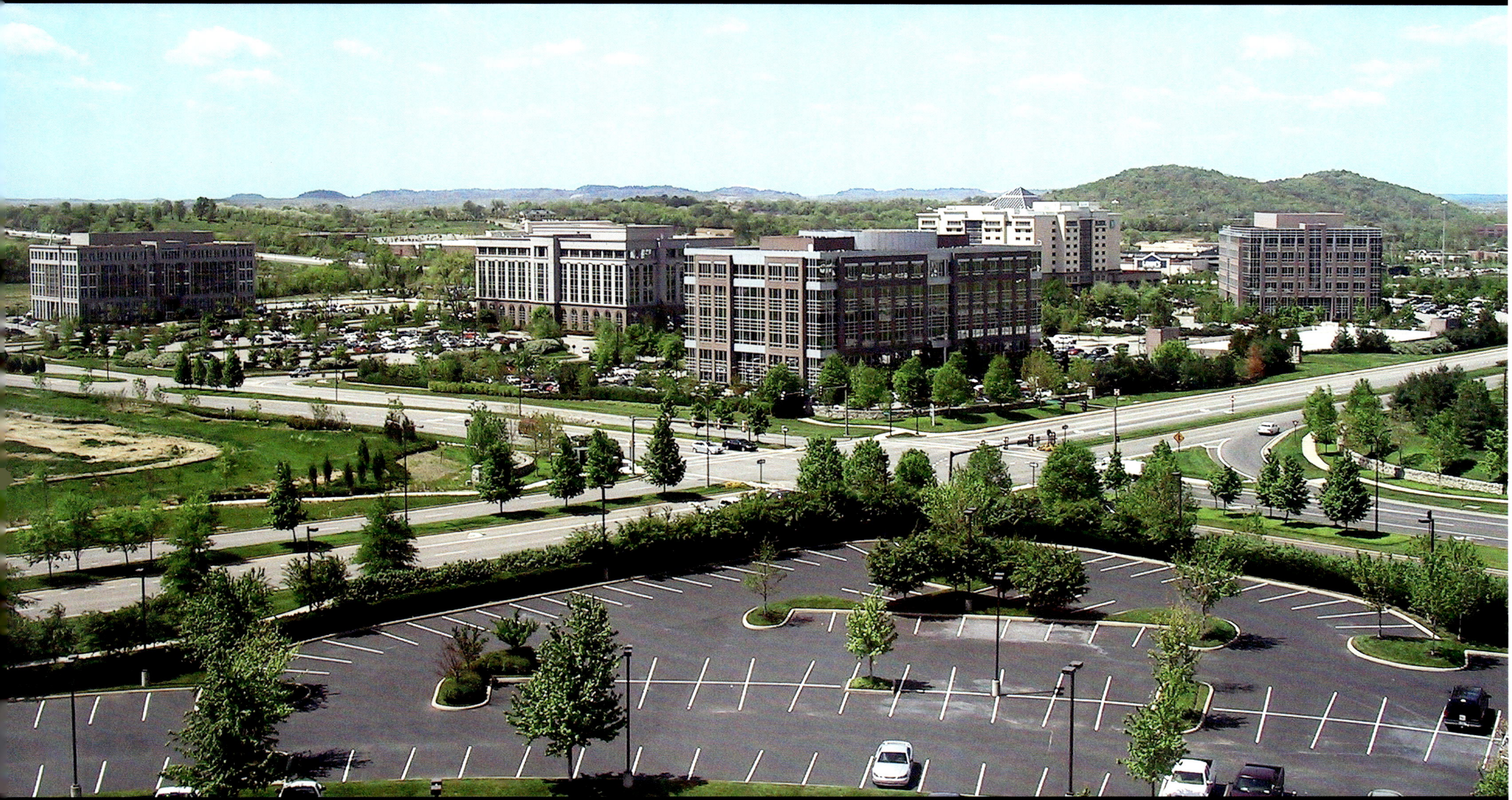

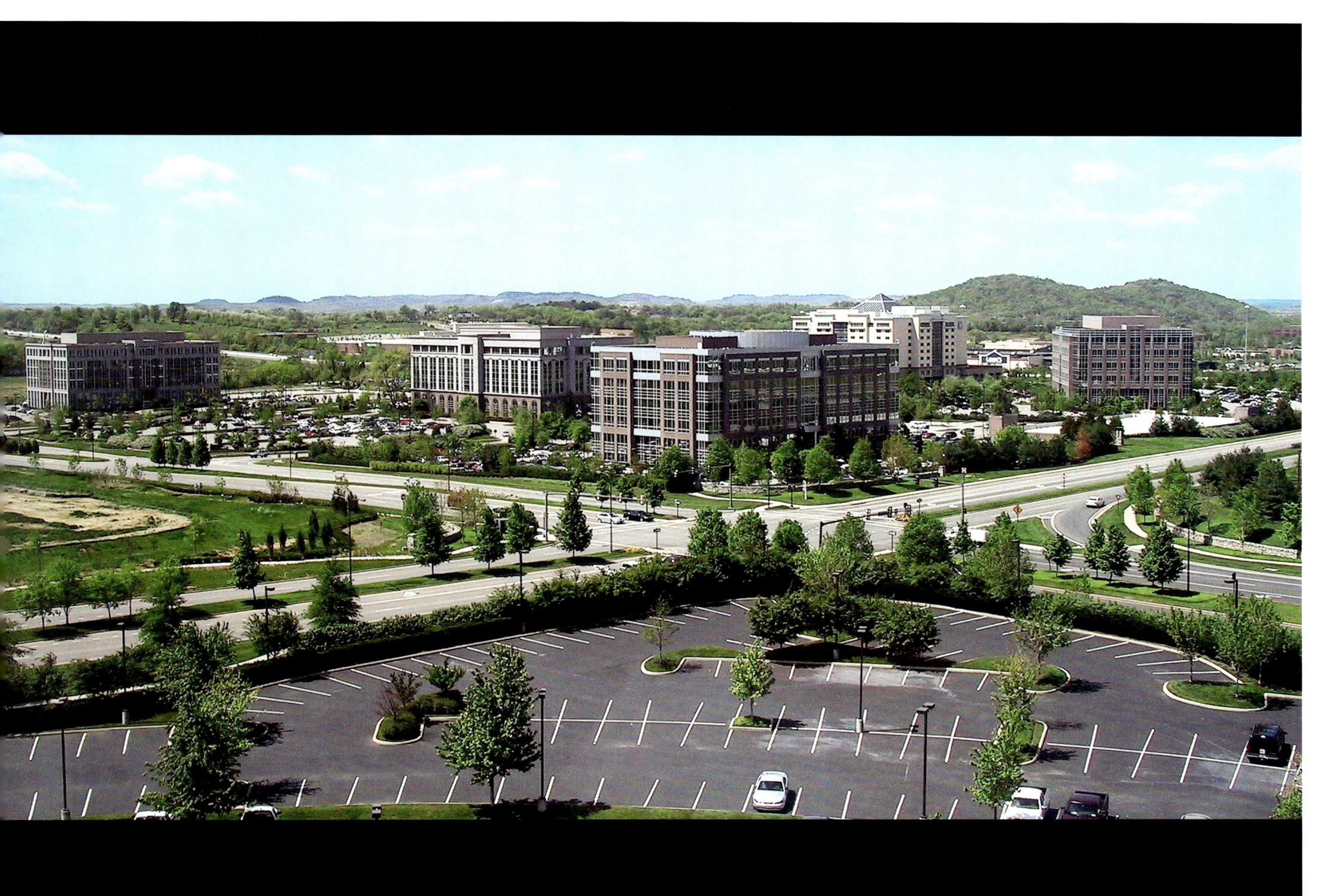

88 | TITANS OF COMMERCE Nashville Business and Industry

This page, left: Trendy multifamily housing adds appeal to restored East Nashville. Right: The Sarah Cannon Research Institute, built by Batten & Shaw, is among the city's recent commercial projects. Opposite page: Signature Tower, soon to be the area's tallest building, is shown in a composite of Nashville's projected development.

Nashville is home to five construction firms that record more than $50 million in annual sales, including hospital constructor Batten & Shaw, multifamily housing specialist Construction Enterprises, road building firm Highways, full-service firm RCR Building Corporation, and the area's largest construction company, 82-year-old Hardaway Construction Corporation, which actually posts revenues in excess of $140 million.

These and numerous other commercial builders in Metro Nashville work for clients across the United States, but they rarely lack for work at home. According to broker Colliers Turley Martin Tucker, the Nashville market had more than a million square feet of new office space under construction as 2007 began. Another million square feet of new industrial space is set to be built during the year in six major projects. Outpacing those categories by far, however, is new retail space. With 2.5 million square feet under construction or planned for construction, it's rare to drive anywhere in the area without passing earthmovers and cranes at work on a shopping or mixed-use development.

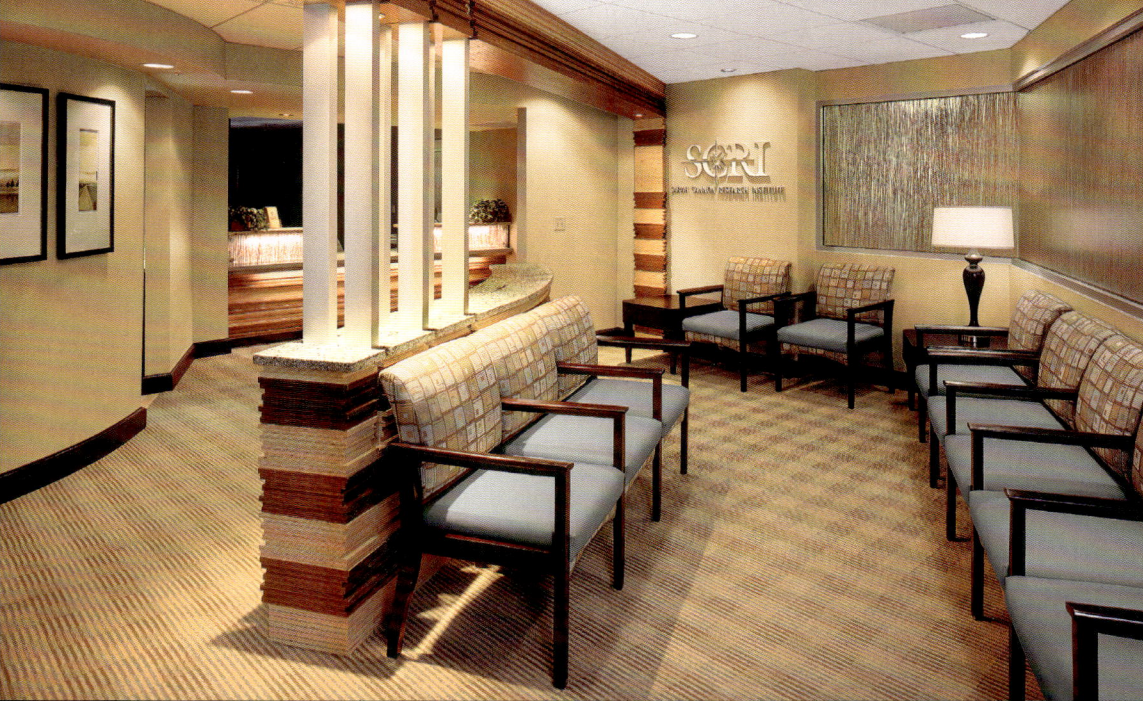

All signs indicate that Middle Tennessee's building boom will continue in the near future. Growth presents challenges to neighborhoods and communities, especially in such fields as education, infrastructure, and environmental impact. It will be up to Greater Nashville's leaders and citizens to continue steering the growth in directions that benefit the community as a whole.

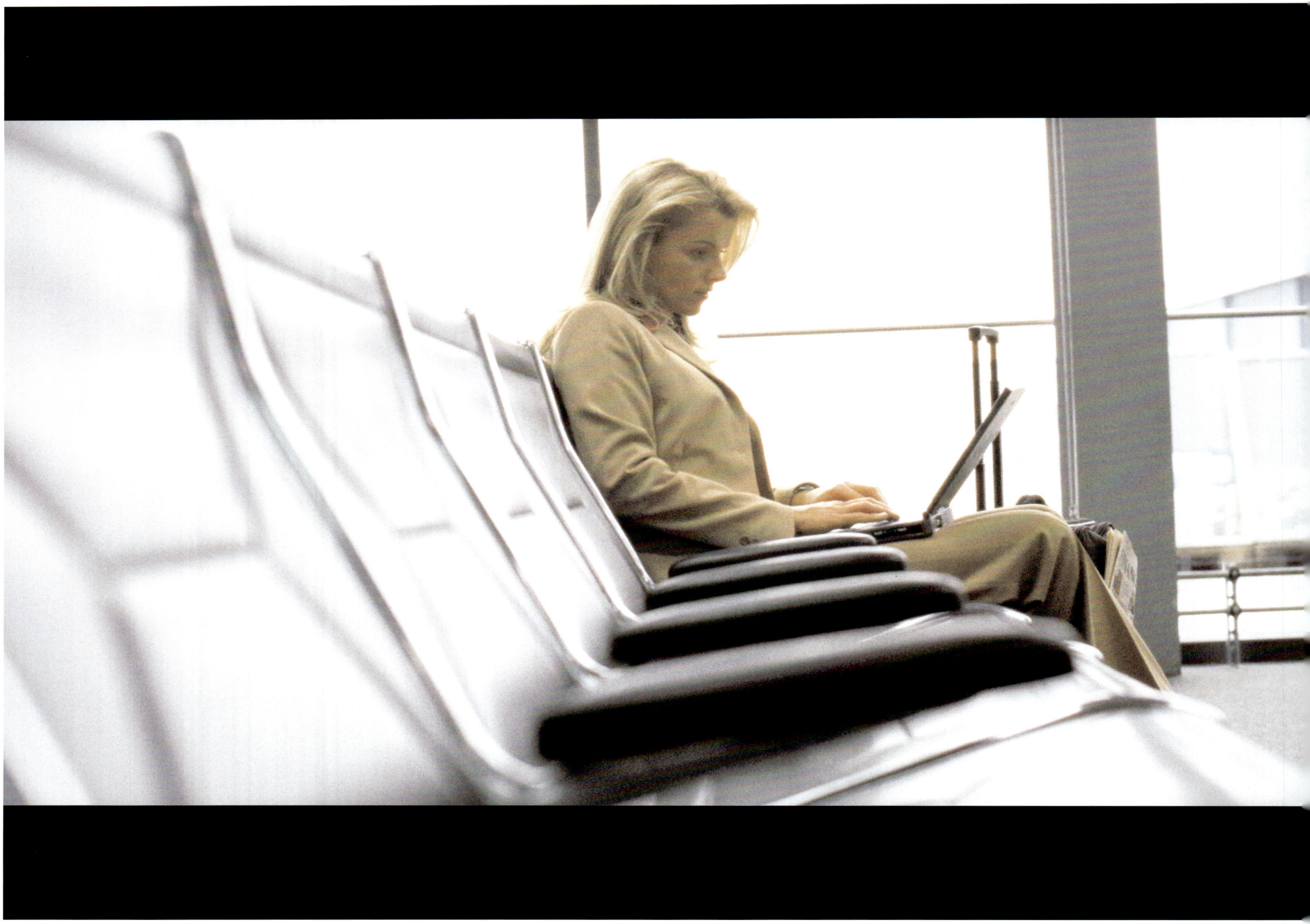

This page: Dell computers are unloaded from a China Airlines Boeing 747 at Nashville International Airport's all-cargo complex. Opposite page: Nashville's wireless network, easily accessible from the airport, makes it easy to do business on the road.

MAKING CONNECTIONS
Transportation, Telecommunications, and Energy

Nashville's recent success in luring corporate relocations and major investment has much to do with the fact that people and goods can get to and from the area so easily by so many modes of transportation. City and business leaders have always done a yeoman's job of capitalizing on Nashville's natural advantages, enabling the city to prosper over the centuries as a river town, a rail town, a place where the interstate highways meet, and a center for air travel. Completing today's infrastructure are wired and wireless telecommunications and energy systems designed to keep Nashville moving forward.

Travelers and cargo reach much of the country quickly by air from Nashville International Airport. Known as BNA since its establishment as Berry Field in 1937, Nashville International plays a vital role in the local economy, contributing 56,000 jobs and $1.3 billion in annual wages to the local economy. The 16 scheduled airlines that serve BNA carry more than 9.5 million passengers a year on an average of 400 daily flights. A total of 89 destinations are served, 49 of them with non-stop flights. Atlanta and Chicago are about an hour and a half away by air; New York, under two and a half hours; and Los Angeles, about four hours.

This page: Live sounds of Music City welcome travelers at Nashville International Airport. Opposite page, left: Traffic shoots into the city on I-65, one of four area interstates. Opposite page, right: The *Music City Star,* Nashville's new commuter rail line, stops for passengers at Riverfront Station downtown.

Nashville International sits on more than 4,500 acres, providing four runways of up to 11,000 feet. Its 820,000-square-foot passenger terminal has 61 air carrier gates and 78 commuter aircraft parking positions. The air cargo facilities at BNA handle nearly 74,000 tons of goods annually, with international shipments the fastest-growing subsector of its cargo trade.

The Metropolitan Nashville Airport Authority (MNAA) operates the main airport as well as the general aviation facility, John C. Tune Airport, in west Nashville, without tapping into local property taxes. User fees and other revenues fund its budget. In late 2006, the MNAA launched a five-year renovation of the BNA terminal that will add shops and restaurants and facilitate the check-in process.

By Land and Sea

Nashville is a major hub in the nation's Interstate Highway System. Interstates 65 (north-south), 40 (east-west), and 24 (northwest-southeast) pass through the city, while the I-440 and Downtown Loop connectors span its center. State Route 840, an outer loop linking four counties, is now open for most of its planned distance, with only a stretch west of the city still to be completed. More than 75 percent of U.S. markets can be reached within a one-day's drive of Nashville.

Traffic congestion has become as much an issue in Middle Tennessee as it is in most urbanized areas in America. Federal transportation statistics indicate that drivers in the metro area logged an aggregate 44.5 million miles in 2005, or nearly half the distance to Venus. Staggering as that figure may appear, it is perhaps even more alarming to note that the number was only 30.2 million in 2003. Nashville's rapid growth means more slowdowns on area roads, but efforts to improve the situation are under way. In summer 2006, commuter rail service debuted on a 32-mile run between Lebanon and downtown Nashville known as the East Corridor. Long-range plans call for a rail network spanning nine counties. Dedicated buses and shuttles operated by the Metro Transit Authority take riders from the rail terminus at Riverfront Park to locations around downtown and midtown.

Long before the advent of the interstate system, Nashville was a place where rail met river. The successors of the steamboats and steam locomotives that carried out much of the city's 19th-century commerce are the tugboats of waterway shippers like Nashville-based Ingram Barge Company and the boxcars of nationwide freight railway CSX. Ingram Barge ships commodities throughout the river systems of the eastern United States, accounting for much of the Cumberland River's traffic. According to U.S. Army Corps of Engineers statistics, in 2004 (the latest data available) almost 13 million tons of commodities floated to Nashville, and about 4.8 million tons left the area to head back up the Cumberland. More than half the loads on the incoming barges were coal; the rest comprised building materials. The outbound barges carried limestone, gypsum, sand, and scrap metals. CSX, whose rail network extends 22,000 miles, runs 90 trains a day through Nashville's Radnor Yard. That makes Radnor—an intermodal hub for the Southeast—one of CSX's busiest stations.

94 | TITANS OF COMMERCE Nashville Business and Industry

This page, left: Sophisticated telecommunications make Nashville an attractive location for call centers like this one. This page, right: With satellite TV's myriad offerings, a family finds a program to watch together. Opposite page: CSX cars at multimodal Radnor Yard and one of many barges on the Cumberland River help Nashville earn its reputation as a five-star logistics metro.

Switched On

The establishment of several large call-center and back-office operations in recent years is one tangible sign of the city's robust telecommunications infrastructure. Pharmacy benefit manager Caremark Rx began setting up a call center in 2005 that, when fully staffed in 2008, will employ 600 people. T-Mobile provides jobs for about 850 workers at a Nashville call center, and Dell Computer has more than 1,500 people on the payroll at its local technical support facility. Nashville and the seven surrounding counties have a single local calling area. With more than 144,000 miles of fiber-optic transmission lines in the region, as well as synchronous optical network (SONET) ring technology to ensure continuity and reliability, the city is able to provide whatever telecom services a business might need.

About 10 main telephone companies compete for corporate customers in voice, data, and broadband Internet services. The traditional monopoly of Comcast on residential broadband and cable television was broken as BellSouth's DSL service, sold in tandem with DirecTV, began to penetrate more neighborhoods, and Dish TV from Echostar became available. Nashville has made strides in providing wireless Internet capability more widely. The city's public library system implemented free wireless Internet access at all branches in 2006, and paid wireless access is available at Nashville International Airport.

Transportation, Telecommunications, and Energy | 95

This page: Nashville Electric Service, whose meter is shown, and other area utilities buy power from the ultrareliable Tennessee Valley Authority. Opposite page: A downtown substation helps distribute electricity along 17,000 miles of transmission lines.

Middle Tennessee historically has enjoyed lower utility rates than some other regions of the country—but these days, Nashvillians feel the pinch of rising energy prices along with everyone else. A powerful advantage, however, is that the Tennessee Valley Authority's (TVA's) hydroelectric power assures the region of an abundant flow. The government-owned Nashville Electric Service (NES) serves more than 320,000 customers in Metropolitan Nashville and minor portions of adjacent counties, while user-owned Middle Tennessee Electric Membership Corporation distributes power to about 168,034 members in Cannon, Rutherford, Williamson, and Wilson counties. Both utilities purchase all of their power from TVA, although long-discussed federal regulatory changes might unshackle them from TVA and allow them to explore new sources of electricity.

NES has made concerted efforts to increase the reliability of its power supply. In bad weather, its customers have endured occasional outages—an average of three per year, for about an hour each, according to NES. Since 2002, however, the company has spent about $14 million a year on an accelerated tree-trimming program intended to remove limbs that might fall across wires during storms. In the five years since the program began, power outages have dropped by 19 percent for NES customers. Middle Tennessee Electric has always had a rigorous tree-trimming policy.

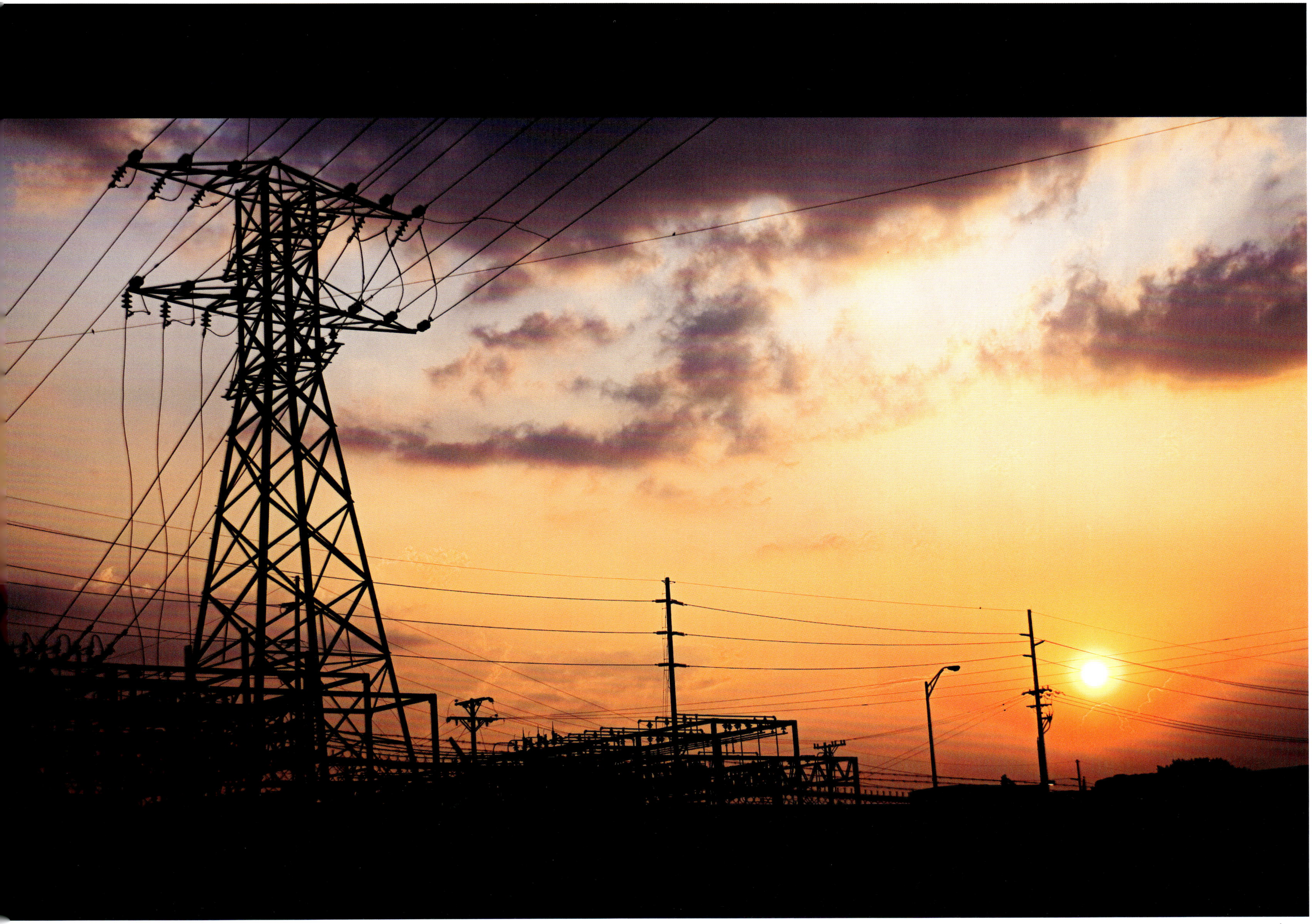

This page, left: The TVA invests billions to ensure that Cumberland Fossil Plant, the top electricity producer in its system, generates clean energy. Opposite page: Natural gas, the least expensive and cleanest fossil fuel, goes from storage facility to stovetop.

Natural gas is the heating mode of choice in most Nashville homes, and many families use gas-powered appliances as well. Nashville Gas, owned by Piedmont Gas Company of North Carolina, furnishes natural gas to 150,000 customers in the area and portions of eight surrounding counties, while Texas-based Atmos Energy, a southeastern regional utility, serves about 110,000 in Williamson, Rutherford, and Maury counties. Nashville Gas is thought to be the oldest continuously operating business in Nashville, tracing its roots back to 1849, when it was founded as the Nashville Gas and Light Company.

Building and improving the city's infrastructure has been key to the region's economic success and remains a priority today. The wholehearted support of government, business, and the community assures that Middle Tennessee will, indeed, continue to move forward.

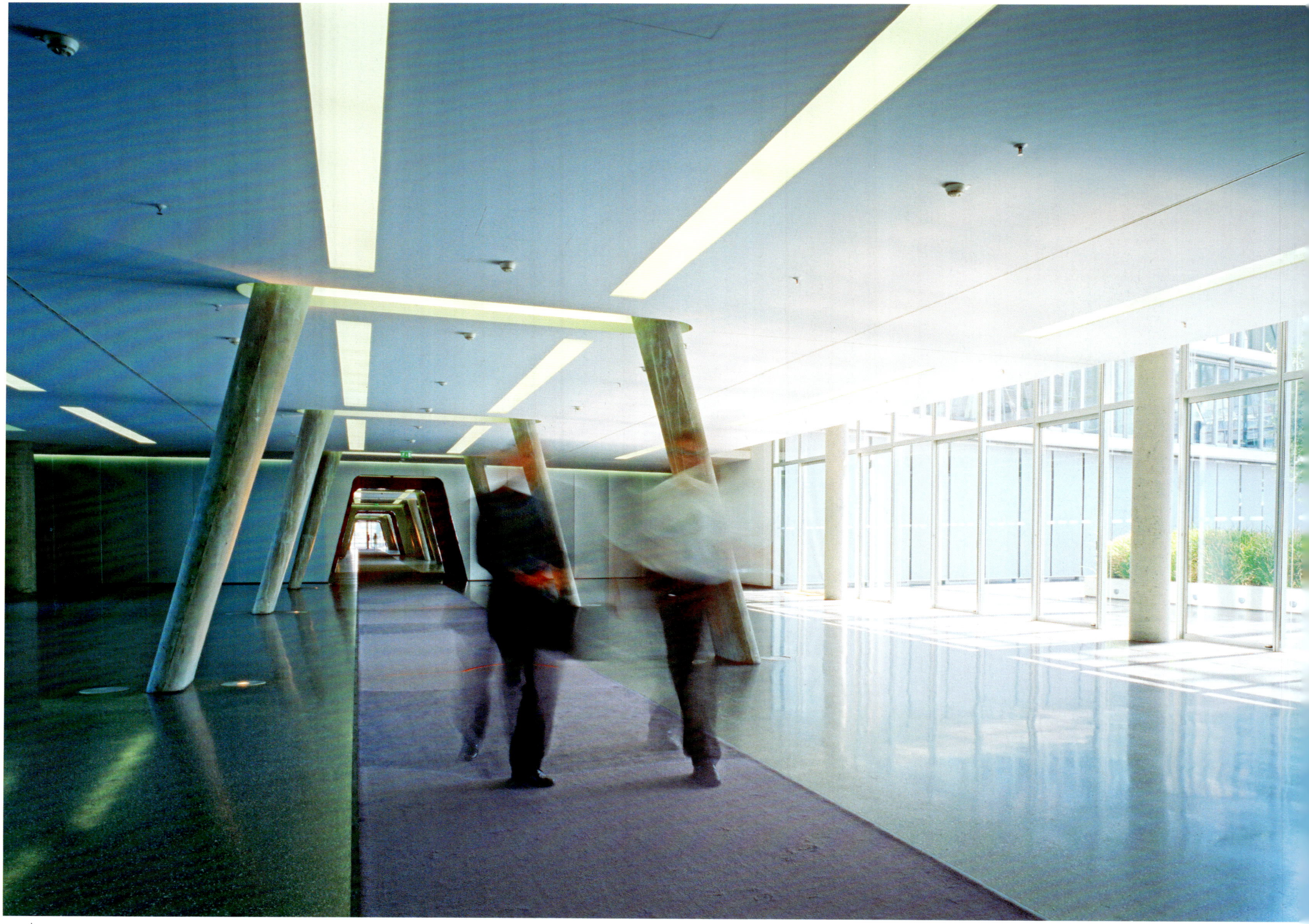

PART THREE
PORTRAITS OF SUCCESS:
PROFILES OF COMPANIES AND ORGANIZATIONS

Education
Trevecca Nazarene University, 106
Vanderbilt University, 104–05

Financial and Insurance Services
American General Life and Accident Insurance Company, 118–19
AmSouth Bank, 126
Caterpillar Financial Services Corporation, 112–13
Comdata® Corporation, 116–17
Consumers Insurance Group, Inc., 124–25
First Tennessee, 110–11
Franklin American Mortgage Company, 122–23
SunTrust Bank–Nashville, 114–15
Tennessee Credit Union, The, 120–21

Health Care and Biotechnology
Community Health Systems, Inc., 136–37
Hospital Corporation of America, 130–33
Radiology Alliance, 138
Saint Thomas Health Services, 134–35

Manufacturing and Distribution
Bridgestone Americas Holding, Inc., 142–43
Cummins Filtration, 146–47
Hartmann, Inc., 148
Odom's Tennessee Pride Sausage, Inc., 144–45
Quality Industries, Inc., 149

Pet Care
Mars Petcare U.S., 152–53

Printing and Publishing
LifeWay Christian Resources, 156–57
R. H. Boyd Publishing Corporation, 158–59
United Methodist Publishing House, The, 160

Professional and Business Services
Central Parking Corporation, 168–69
Holland Group, The, 164–65
Randstad USA, 166–67

Real Estate, Development, and Construction Services
Brasfield & Gorrie, 172–73
Earl Swensson Associates, Inc., 182
Gould Turner Group, P.C., 174–75
MJM Architects, 176–77
Ross Bryan Associates, Inc.— Consulting Engineers, 180–81
Shirley Zeitlin and Company, Realtors®, 184
Street Dixon Rick Architecture, PLC, 178–79

Recreation and Youth Services
YMCA of Middle Tennessee, 188–89

Retail and Sales
Tractor Supply Company, 192–93

Tourism and Hospitality
Doubletree Guest Suites Nashville Airport, 196–97
Gaylord Opryland Resort & Convention Center, 198

Transportations Services
Metropolitan Nashville Airport Authority, 202

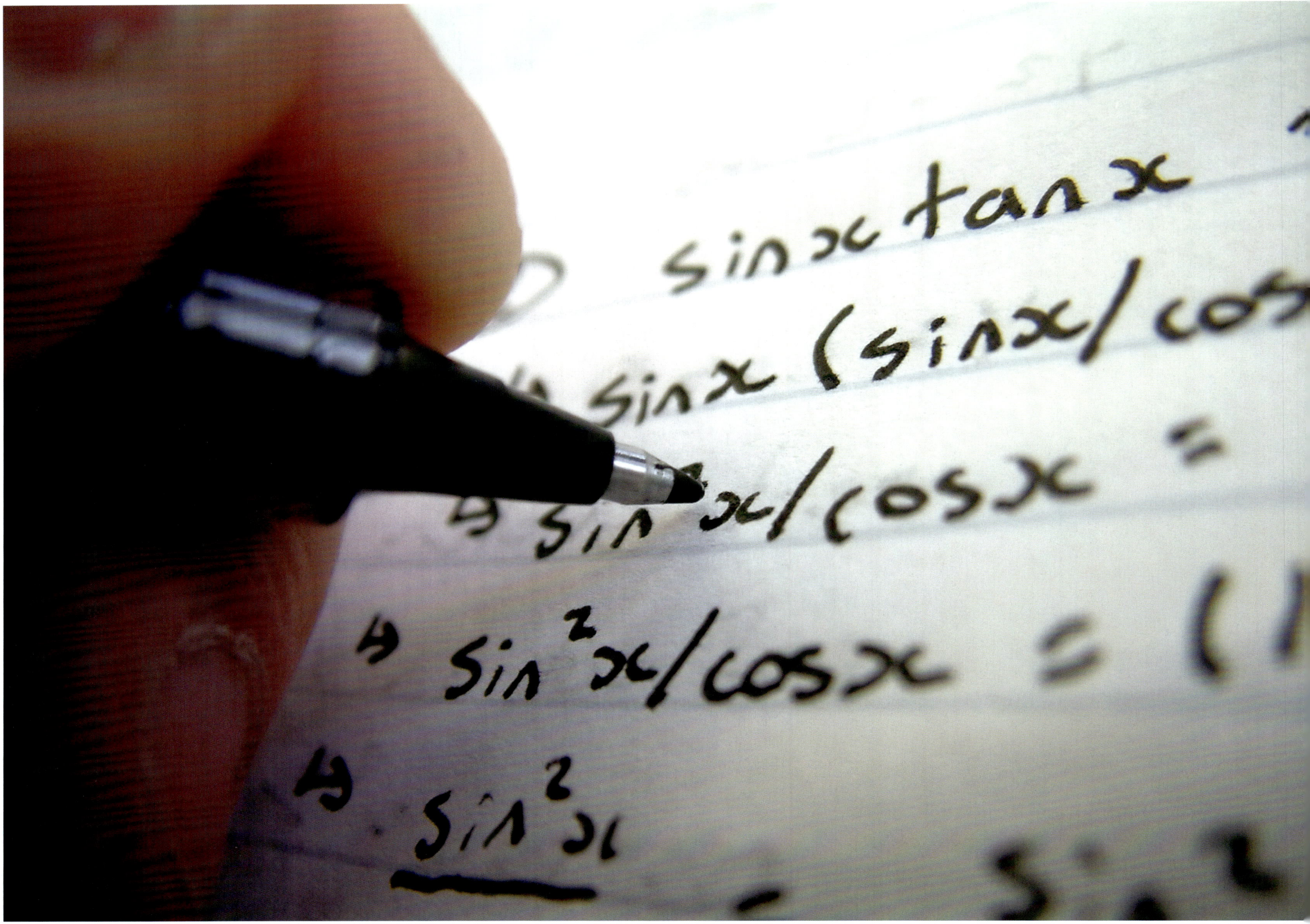
sinx tanx
sinx (sinx/cos
sin²x/cosx =
sin²x/cosx =

PROFILES OF COMPANIES AND ORGANIZATIONS
Education

Vanderbilt University

This world-class university makes a difference in the lives of its students, faculty, and staff; affects its city and the world through the work of its 10 prestigious schools and colleges; provides outstanding health care at its medical center; and continually increases the frontiers of knowledge through its research centers and institutes.

Right: Victorian-style Benson Science Hall stands in a grove of Vanderbilt University's oldest and most majestic trees, which were small and young when the hall was built in 1880. Back then, machine and forge shops and steam boilers for the new campus heating plant were in the basement; classrooms and laboratories for botany, geology, and engineering were on upper floors. Today Benson Science Hall houses the College of Arts and Science's English and history departments.

Vanderbilt University is internationally recognized as one of the premier research and teaching universities, and its undergraduate, graduate, and professional programs rank among the finest in the world. The university's students—approximately 6,400 undergraduates and 5,100 graduate and professional students—and more than 2,600 full-time faculty and 17,500 staff members work together to support multidisciplinary study, research, and public service. Vanderbilt is the largest private employer in Middle Tennessee and the second-largest private employer based in the state.

Vanderbilt's academics comprise interdisciplinary programs and centers, as well as 10 schools and colleges: the College of Arts and Science, Graduate School, Blair School of Music, Divinity School, School of Engineering, Law School, School of Medicine, School of Nursing, Owen Graduate School of Management, and Peabody College of education and human development. Peabody, which has the number one special-education program in the nation according to *U.S.News & World Report*, has also had its entire graduate program of education and human development ranked in the *U.S.News* top 10 since 1995.

Visit Vanderbilt

With so much to offer in the way of public lectures and forums, shopping, art and music, dining, and architecture, Vanderbilt launched its Visit Vanderbilt initiative in the summer of 2006 in order to draw an increasing number of visitors to the unique, historic campus.

Easy to access from any part of Nashville, Vanderbilt is a playground for the heart and mind, open to those with a curious nature and an appreciation for beauty and learning. On campus, public art celebrates themes ranging from children's play to the pursuit of knowledge. A world-class concert hall is lauded by architects and music-lovers alike. An array of galleries shows works by students as well as nationally celebrated artists. And tickets to Southeastern Conference football, tennis, soccer, basketball, baseball, and more are available year-round. The 330-acre campus is truly an oasis for all in the middle of the vibrant city of Nashville.

The Medical Center

The Vanderbilt University Medical Center (VUMC) is driven by discovery and the immediate incorporation of new knowledge into innovation in patient care and physician and nurse education. Vanderbilt provides health care services through (among other entities) its hospitals and clinics, which include Vanderbilt University Hospital, the Vanderbilt Clinic, and the Monroe Carell Jr. Children's Hospital at Vanderbilt.

In 2005 *U.S.News* again named VUMC among the nation's elite in its annual list of the 50 best hospitals. The rankings were based on several factors including reputation among board-certified physicians, nursing care, mortality statistics, and medical technology. VUMC ranks among the top 50 in seven specialties: kidney disease; ear, nose, and throat; urology; respiratory disorders; cancer; hormonal disorders; and gynecology. VUMC is home to the region's only Level I trauma center, Level IV neonatal intensive care unit, and the state's only comprehensive organ transplant program and comprehensive adult and pediatric burn center.

VUMC's commitment to research leads to much of its cutting-edge knowledge in so many areas of medicine. Of 123 medical schools, Vanderbilt ranked 15th in funding from the National Institutes of Health (NIH) in 2004. The same year, eight Vanderbilt medical school programs ranked in the top 10 for NIH funding. In addition, two Vanderbilt medical school faculty members have won a Nobel Prize: Earl Sutherland Jr. (1971) and Stanley Cohen (1986).

The Vanderbilt Vision

Vanderbilt was founded in 1873 with a gift of one million dollars from Commodore Cornelius Vanderbilt, the rail and shipping magnate. He sought to strengthen the ties between the North and South after the Civil War. From the beginning, the school was a full-fledged university, with not only liberal arts and sciences beyond the bachelor's degree level, but also with professional schools. The original 75-acre campus expanded over the years as the university added schools and programs.

In 1949, Vanderbilt University was invited to join the exclusive Association of American Universities, a recognition that led the university to begin measuring itself against national standards. In 1963, the university's 90th anniversary, Vanderbilt was ranked among the top 20 private universities in the country for the first time.

Vanderbilt continues to offer students a gateway to greatness, attracting some of the best and brightest scholars in the country and from around the world. Vanderbilt graduates can be found everywhere, doing everything—serving as elected federal officials, ruling from the judge's bench, starting businesses and running major corporations, discovering cures in laboratories, writing and performing for the stage and screen, healing the sick, and educating students of all ages.

Vanderbilt Goals and Values

Vanderbilt University is committed to leading the quest for new knowledge through scholarship, disseminating that knowledge through teaching and outreach, and promoting creative experimentation with ideas and concepts. The institution proudly places the highest value on intellectual freedom and fiercely supports open inquiry, quality, compassion, and excellence in all endeavors.

Top left: The white-domed Faye and Joe Wyatt Center for Education, with its Corinthian columns, dominates the Peabody College campus. The Wyatt Center is one of the nation's most advanced learning environments, with enhanced computer classrooms, videoconferencing and multimedia seminar rooms, satellite downlink and broadcast capabilities, and video-editing suites. Bottom left: When Vanderbilt opened for classes in October 1875, this building housed classrooms, labs, the administrative offices for all departments except law and medicine, and the library. Kirkland Hall, with its trademark clock tower, now houses Vanderbilt memorabilia, as well as the offices of the chancellor and general officers, several deans, and other university administrators.

A community-centered consciousness and a grounding in faith shape students' experiences at this Christian university, which offers a wide array of bachelor's, master's, and associate's degree programs and a doctorate in education, along with intercollegiate sports, social activities, and the opportunity to serve, locally and globally.

Above left: In 1905 Trevecca College, which later became Trevecca Nazarene University, was located on 4th Avenue in Nashville, on the site that is now occupied by the Ryman Auditorium, the home of the Grand Ole Opry®. Above right: Trevecca's Waggoner Library, with its two-story rotunda/reading area, provides students with an attractive and comfortable place to study.

When J. O. McClurkan, a Cumberland Presbyterian minister, founded the Bible Training School in 1901, his goal was to educate people who wanted careers in Christian ministry. During the ensuing 106 years as that school grew and became Trevecca Nazarene University, successive administrations expanded McClurkan's original goal so that Trevecca's programs would meet the needs of a diverse student population—traditional undergraduates, adult degree-completion students, and people seeking graduate education—for a variety of careers and professions.

Bachelor's degree programs, including nursing, digital graphics, and music business were added, as were master's programs in education, religion, counseling, library and information science, and allied health (physician assistant).

Trevecca's academic programs reflect its desire to respond to the cultural and economic needs of Middle Tennessee. The university's degree-completion program for adults, which began in 1987, was the first program of its type in Middle Tennessee. The music business program, graduate business management programs, and an internship program were added to strengthen the region's workforce. Known within educational circles in Tennessee for the quality of its teacher preparation programs, Trevecca also added a doctoral degree in education in 1999 to increase its service to educators and state schools.

Located only minutes from downtown Nashville, Trevecca is home to more than 2,200 students who want to study and learn in an urban setting, a caring environment, and a place where a Christian worldview is valued. That worldview emphasizes community, and the larger Trevecca community offers students many opportunities to serve. These opportunities can take place in one of the parts of the greater Trevecca community, which includes Trevecca Healthcare Center, Trevecca Community Church of the Nazarene, and Trevecca Towers Retirement Center. Students are also encouraged to participate in activities that allow them to serve the neighborhoods surrounding the campus. Trevecca students lead after-school activities for neighborhood children, work in other programs of the neighborhood, host an annual Angel Tree party in December, and learn how to be contributing members of a larger community.

Trevecca's motto, *Esse Quam Videri*—To be rather than to seem—expresses the university's emphasis on authenticity and integrity in all things. This emphasis is a significant feature of a Trevecca education, through which students are challenged to use their training and skills to serve and lead in their chosen careers and professions.

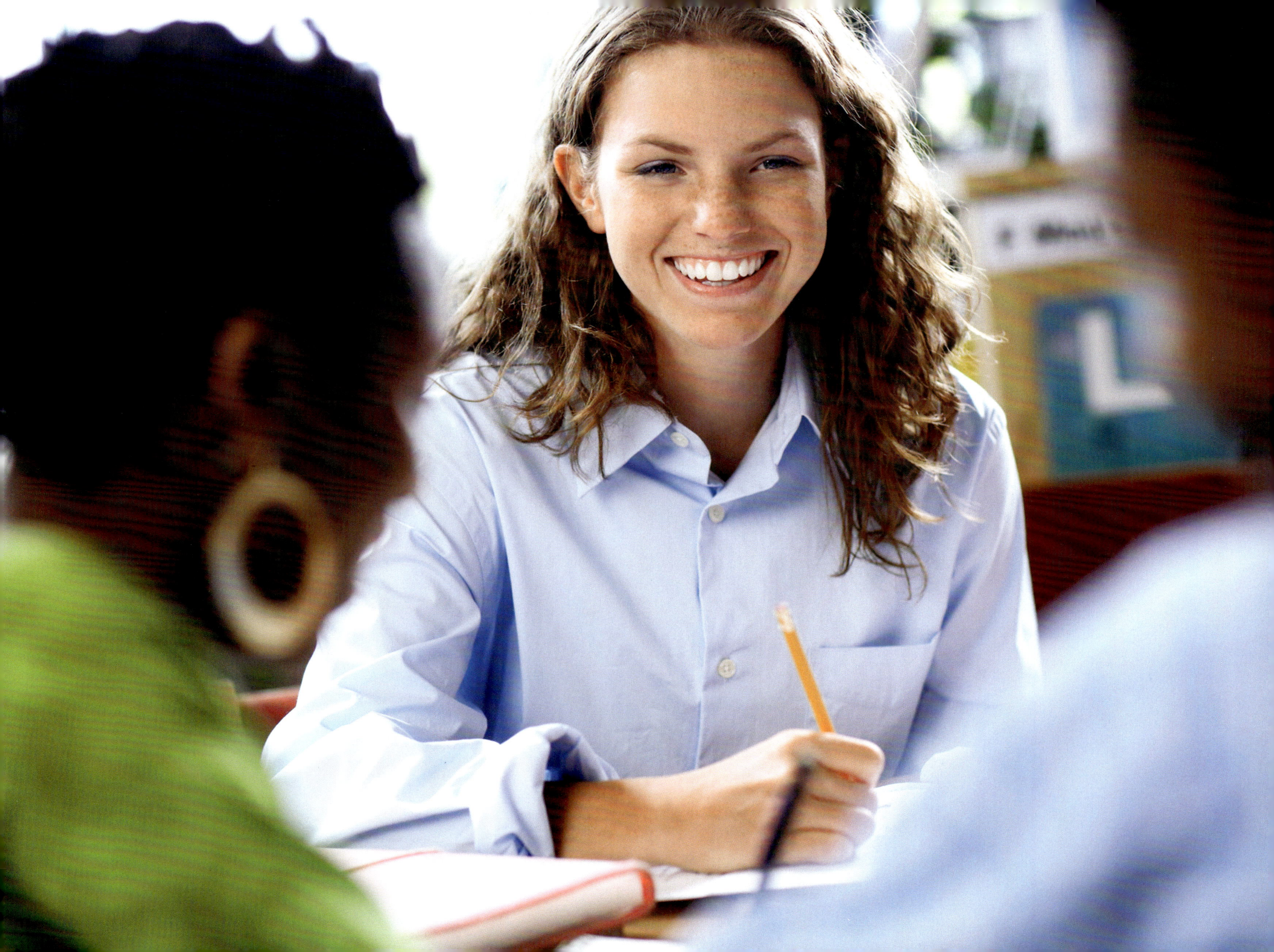
L

108 | PORTRAITS OF SUCCESS Profiles of Companies and Organizations

PROFILES OF COMPANIES AND ORGANIZATIONS
Financial and Insurance Services

This Tennessee-headquartered institution provides comprehensive financial services and has earned one of the highest customer-retention rates of any bank in the nation. It also is recognized as a leader in its communities and as one of the nation's best places to work.

Above: With employees, community representatives, and "Working Money," First Tennessee celebrates the opening of a financial center. Right: The bank is a sponsor of the NHL's Nashville Predators; here, mascot Gnash shows how to open a Predators account.

First Tennessee is the only major bank headquartered in Tennessee and is known for customer-retention ratings that are tops in the industry, for leadership in community involvement, and as one of the nation's best places to work. The company's family-friendly policies and its commitment to employees as its most important resource have brought it national and statewide recognition, from *Working Mother*, *AARP*, *Fortune*, and others that have named the company an employer of choice.

"First Tennessee offers homegrown customer service with national financial expertise," says Mike Edwards, president of First Tennessee for the Middle Tennessee region. "We live and work here, just like our customers, and we have a stake in the growth and livelihood of our communities just as they do."

The bank's national expertise is gained from being a part of one of the nation's 30 largest financial services companies. First Tennessee's parent company—First Horizon National Corporation (FHN)—operates in more than 40 states. FHN includes, in addition to First Tennessee: First Horizon Home Loans, which, according to *Inside Mortgage Finance* magazine, is among the top 20 of all mortgage-servicing companies by servicing volume in dollars; and FTN Financial, which is one of the nation's top underwriters in government agency securities.

First Tennessee is the leading bank in Tennessee by deposit market share and operates more than 40 financial centers in Middle Tennessee.

As a result of a multiyear strategic growth plan initiated in 2003, the bank doubled its Middle Tennessee presence in three years. The combination of this expansion and an equally aggressive community-involvement commitment that provides more than $800,000 to more than 150 nonprofit organizations each year, plus sponsorships of many of the region's prominent events and sports teams, has made First Tennessee a recognized leader in its community.

First Tennessee's history began in 1864 with the establishment of First National Bank of Memphis. Its statewide expansion began in 1926 when it merged with rival Central-State National of Memphis—the first in a series of mergers that eventually would bring the modern-day First Tennessee to a position of dominance in serving the banking customers of Tennessee. In 1964 the bank celebrated its 100th anniversary with a flag-raising ceremony on the plaza of its new 23-story office building at Madison Avenue and Third Street in Memphis. The building remains the bank's headquarters to this day. The name First Tennessee Bank was adopted on January 1, 1977. With an expanding presence in Knoxville; Chattanooga; northeast Tennessee's Tri-Cities of Kingsport, Johnson City, and Bristol; and Middle Tennessee, the bank began its climb to become the state leader in retail and commercial banking market share.

In 2003, First Tennessee adopted a new vision statement: "Our Vision— A premier national financial services company, dedicated to creating the highest levels of value, producing long-term levels of industry-leading profitability and growth." The statement is supported by a declaration of six core values: "employees first, exceptional teamwork, individual accountability, absolute determination, knowing our customers, and doing the right thing."

The 2001 acquisition of Synaxis Group, headquartered in Nashville, added commercial insurance to First Tennessee's comprehensive services. Offering risk management for financial services clients, Synaxis is ranked by *Business Insurance* magazine among the 50 largest commercial insurance brokerages in the United States by premiums served.

After this acquisition, the company began a national expansion strategy for its mortgage division, First Tennessee Mortgage Services, Inc., which today ranges from coast to coast. Under the First Horizon brand name outside of Tennessee, First Tennessee continues to grow, including establishing a banking presence in targeted geographic areas such as northern Virginia; Dallas–Fort Worth, Texas; Atlanta, Georgia; and Greensboro, North Carolina.

The name of the parent company was changed from First Tennessee National Corporation to First Horizon National Corporation (NYSE:FHN) in 2004 to reflect the company's expanding national image. Across the United States, FHN has a workforce of more than 12,000. Its employees provide high quality services in banking, insurance, investments, mortgage, credit, and financial planning, supported by the most advanced technologies.

Above left: First Tennessee celebrates the opening of each new financial center by hosting a neighborhood celebration. Above right: First Tennessee's "Working Money" spreads the word about the bank's free checking accounts.

Caterpillar Financial Services Corporation

As global markets demand more Caterpillar machines for building roads, housing, power plants, centers of industry, and other infrastructure, this company, an arm of the Fortune 100 equipment maker, enables such development through customer-friendly finance and leasing services.

Above: Caterpillar Financial Services Corporation implements 6 Sigma, a fact-based, data-driven decision-making process that has led to unprecedented success. Above right: Cat Financial's headquarters is on West End Avenue, across from Vanderbilt University.

On August 12, 1981, Caterpillar Inc. (Cat) enacted a business strategy that has paid huge dividends for the company and its customers: The earthmoving equipment manufacturer formed Caterpillar Leasing Company in Peoria, Illinois, with seven employees who leased lift trucks to U.S. customers. In 1983, experiencing unprecedented success, the leasing company became Caterpillar Financial Services Corporation, which began financing and leasing all kinds of Cat construction equipment.

The company moved to Nashville in 1991. Celebrating 25 years in business, Cat Financial today provides financing alternatives for Caterpillar machinery and engines, Solar® gas turbines, marine vessels, and other equipment. It also extends loans to customers and dealers.

In February 2000, Caterpillar's Financial Products Division moved into new headquarters on West End Avenue near downtown Nashville. Cat Financial, Cat Insurance, Cat Redistribution, and Cat Power Ventures Corporation form Caterpillar's Financial Products Division. All four companies, with 1,590 employees worldwide, provide financial services and support to Caterpillar customers in 42 countries throughout the Americas, Asia, Australia, Europe, and the Middle East.

Cat Financial offers customers full service after they buy new or used Cat equipment. Cat Insurance protects every piece of Cat equipment at every stage of its life, from marine transit to extended coverage. Cat Redistribution and Cat Financial experts sell and finance used equipment online at www.CatUsed.com or at auction. Cat Power Ventures develops, funds, and operates independent power plants that use Caterpillar engines and Solar gas turbines. In 2005, Cat Financial reported more than $25 billion in assets, a direct result of customer focus and 6 Sigma processes—fact-based, data-driven decision-making processes that have led to unprecedented success.

General and heavy construction, forestry, mining, waste, and marine markets, among others, look to Caterpillar for the right equipment. Cat Financial attunes itself to their needs; instead of uniform financing for these markets, Cat Financial creates financing packages that fit each customer's needs and position them for success. That may involve helping them meet cash flow requirements, freeing bank lines for other purchases, or arranging a variable payment schedule. The new Cat AccessAccount℠ helps customers obtain instant credit through U.S. dealerships to buy parts, obtain service, and rent equipment.

A typical customer would finance or lease a Cat machine and insure it with coverage bought from Cat Insurance. Finance and leasing options include installment loans, finance and operating leases, working capital loans, and government lease-purchase plans. Caterpillar's worldwide network of dealerships works with Cat Financial to build business relationships by giving customers fast and efficient service.

Cat Financial's tenet of business excellence permeates the company, having helped it win the 1999 Tennessee Quality Excellence Award with Global Excellence Commendation and the 2003 Malcolm Baldrige National Quality Award for its U.S. operations. Today foreign Cat Financial offices use the Baldrige criteria in their operations.

Cat Financial employees serve their communities through annual monetary and volunteer support for United Way, Junior Achievement, Second Harvest Food Bank, the Juvenile Diabetes Research Foundation, and other good causes. Employees live by Caterpillar's "Values in Action" principle of caring for others in their workplace and world.

Above left: Developers worldwide depend on Caterpillar machines, and they depend on Cat Financial to help them lease, buy, and insure those machines. Above right: Cat Financial won the 2003 Malcolm Baldrige National Quality Award, one of the nation's top business honors.

Financial and Insurance Services | 113

This long-time Nashville bank provides consumer, commercial, corporate, and institutional clients with deposit, credit, trust, investment, and other services, offering 'big bank' products at the local community level.

Right: The new headquarters for SunTrust Bank–Nashville, a part of SunTrust Banks, Inc., will be in SunTrust Plaza, shown in this rendering. The complex—located on Commerce Street, between 4th and 5th Avenues, in downtown Nashville—is projected for completion in December 2007.

THE SUNTRUST MISSION
Help people and institutions prosper.

Provide financial services that meet the needs, exceed the expectations, and enhance the lives of our colleagues, clients, communities, and ultimately our shareholders.

"Seeing beyond money" is a theme that summarizes the promise of SunTrust Banks, Inc. and expresses the company's uniqueness to its clients. For SunTrust, "seeing beyond money" means always doing what is best for its clients.

SunTrust Banks delivers on its client promise as one of the nation's largest commercial banking organizations. Headquartered in Atlanta, Georgia, SunTrust Banks operates primarily in the Southeast as well as in selected markets nationally. With such a broad geographic reach and its extensive product offering, SunTrust Banks is uniquely capable of serving a wide range of consumer, commercial, corporate, and institutional clients with deposit, credit, trust, and investment services.

The growth of SunTrust Bank–Nashville, part of SunTrust Banks, Inc., began many years ago, in the days when Davidson County had a population of 114,000, and the most popular method of transportation was the streetcar. A trio of entrepreneurs, Frank Farris, Walter Diehl, and Charles Sykes, set out to prove that Nashville needed another bank. They organized the enterprise and first opened the doors of the bank in downtown Nashville on July 18, 1927, as Third National Bank—the predecessor of SunTrust Bank–Nashville. What began as a bank with just $720,000 in assets has grown in some 80 years to become Nashville's largest commercial banking institution based on deposits.

In January 1948, the bank's president, Frank Farris, announced plans for establishing branch offices, and the first branch was opened in West Nashville in April 1948. Today the bank's branch network has expanded to 59 locations in the greater Nashville area to serve the needs of customers. In 1964 Third National Bank CEO Sam Fleming and president John W. Clay announced the purchase of the Nashville Trust Company. (Nashville Trust later became Nashville City Bank, with Third National Bank retaining only the trust business.) Shortly after the merger, the National Life and Accident Insurance Company asked Third National Bank to join in the formation of a holding company, which brought additional business opportunities for both companies.

As expansion continued, on March 28, 1968, senior chairman of the board Walter Diehl cut the ribbon for the opening of a new 21-story headquarters for the bank. The soaring bronze tower was built on the site of Nashville's famous Maxwell House Hotel, which was destroyed by fire on Christmas Day, 1961. December 1986 brought the announcement from Third National Bank chairman of the board Charles J. Kane and president John W. Clay Jr. that the bank would be merging with SunTrust Banks. By 1995 all of the bank's branches in Nashville carried the SunTrust name.

SunTrust highlights and honors include:

- a ranking for SunTrust Mortgage of highest in customer satisfaction among home mortgage service providers, according to a study by J. D. Power and Associates;

- a Community Reinvestment Act (CRA) rating of "outstanding," the highest rating, from the Federal Reserve Bank of Atlanta in its 2005 examination of the bank;

- a ranking of 24th on *DiversityInc* magazine's list of Top 50 Companies for Diversity;

- a ranking among the top 100 in *Fortune* magazine's annual survey of the Best Companies for Minorities; and

- the Secretary of Labor's New Freedom Initiative Award for exemplary and innovative efforts in furthering the employment and workplace environment for people with disabilities.

SunTrust Bank–Nashville's new headquarters will be in the 13-story SunTrust Plaza, projected for opening in December 2007. Located on Nashville's Commerce Street, between 4th and 5th Avenues, SunTrust Plaza is next to the historic Ryman Auditorium. With SunTrust's deep roots in the music industry, it is fitting for its Nashville headquarters to be located next to the "Mother Church" of country music.

A hallmark of SunTrust's success and a key element in its future is its local market orientation. Experience has shown that no one knows the unique needs of each community better than those who live and work there. Delivery of "big bank" products and services at the local level is the way the SunTrust model works. Nashville's president and CEO, Robert E. McNeilly III, is charged with supporting the company's overall initiatives by identifying opportunities and achieving lending, investment, and service goals to ensure that the company is making the right moves in the right places.

SunTrust and its employees are committed to the Nashville community. Both the bank and its employees are giving of their time and money. Charitable contributions are made to United Way, and employees serve as volunteers building houses with Nashville Area Habitat for Humanity and working with social service providers, schools, and other groups to continually strengthen the Nashville community.

Left: The SunTrust logo includes a sunburst design and the familiar SunTrust name; warm yellow, orange, and red symbolize SunTrust as approachable and inviting, while blue communicates solidity, strength, trust, and integrity.

A leading provider of electronic payment and information systems for the transportation and retail industries, Comdata Corporation enables more than $38 billion in credit card, gift card, fuel, and other transactions annually.

Necessity, "the mother of invention," is the starting point for many companies that become highly successful. Comdata® Corporation is one of these. Founded in 1969 with the purpose of providing a computerized dispatching service for household moving companies, Comdata was soon led by its activities to its true calling.

At that time, trucking companies faced a widespread logistics challenge: getting purchase authorizations, cash, and payroll checks to a workforce that was constantly on the move. In turn, truck drivers needed company approvals and funds for fuel, repairs, and settlements while they were traveling. Comdata made it possible for trucking companies to supply drivers with what they needed and in the process launched the Comdata® Card—a payment solution that helps drive an industry.

Today, Comdata serves more than 20,000 customers and processes transactions that touch every part of the economy. The company's more-than 1,600 employees help organizations of all kinds manage critical business issues. From payroll to controlled spending to stored value solutions, Comdata provides innovative tools to create success for businesses, their customers, and their employees.

Moving Money and Information

For nearly four decades, Comdata has been in the forefront of payment innovations. Its integrated financial solutions are changing the way companies manage data, pay their employees, process merchant transactions, and manage spending on key business purchases, from fuel to travel. Also a pioneer in the concept of stored value, Comdata has fundamentally changed the retail industry through its gift card solutions. Comdata's specialty is providing custom-designed solutions that improve efficiency and reduce costs for the industries it serves.

- Transportation: Comdata offers complete business solutions that help over-the-road, private, and commercial fleets improve efficiency and profitability, including controlled spending, payroll and electronic funds distribution services, regulatory compliance, and receivables financing solutions.
- Retail: Comdata's solutions help retailers handle their most important transactions with services such as Comdata's gift card and loyalty programs, payroll and electronic funds distribution, and payment processing.
- Aviation: Comdata's suite of solutions helps businesses control their general aviation-related expenses, including fuel, catering, ground transportation, and travel. It also provides payment processing and private-label card services to fixed-base operators that serve its general aviation clients.
- Construction: Construction managers can gain precise control over expenses and better manage project costs using Comdata's controlled spending, payroll and electronic funds distribution services, and custom payment network solutions.
- Government: Comdata's range of financial services helps government agencies save money, increase efficiency, and gain control over

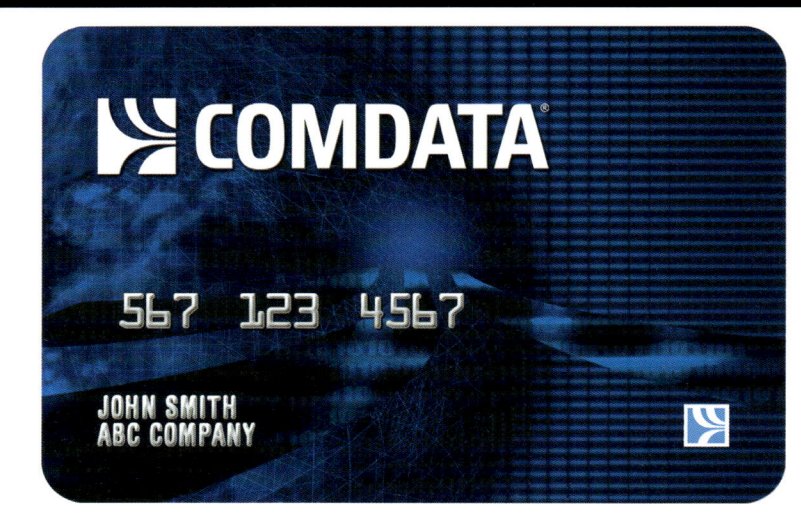

Right: The Comdata® Card consolidates key business transactions—managing purchases, payroll, fuel, and more—on a single card and single data point.

important processes. Government agencies can purchase fuel on a tax-exempt basis, manage employees' business purchases, and improve WIC/EBT benefits with a card-based payment program.

- Restaurant and hospitality: Comdata provides this industry with a suite of solutions for building stronger customer relationships, consolidating card processing, and eliminating the expense of payroll checks.

Comdata International Retail Services focuses on transactions outside of the country, including Internet-based virtual gift cards.

Comdata's rich history includes the support of many charitable organizations within the community. The company participates in Big Brothers of Nashville; First Steps, Inc.; the Salvation Army; United Way; Ronald McDonald House; and many other organizations that assist children, families, and individuals in need. Comdata's outstanding employee benefits for women, including child care and tuition cost reimbursement, earned it the YWCA of Nashville and Middle Tennessee 2002 Academy for Women of Achievement corporate award.

Since 1995, Comdata has been a wholly owned subsidiary of Ceridian Corporation, a multibillion-dollar information services and human resources management company headquartered in Minneapolis, Minnesota.

A History of Innovation

1969—Comdata is founded by C. W. Harter and Robert Whitney.

1972—The company is the first to offer paper-based funds transfer specialized for the trucking industry with, initially, 100 acceptance locations.

1981—Comdata introduces the Blue Card, offering card-based electronic data capture and information management services to the long-haul trucking industry.

1987—Comdata Card serves more than 100,000 drivers and their companies.

1989—Comdata branches into paperless fuel tax reporting, driver log auditing, and governmental compliance reporting when it acquires Dallas-based Transceiver. The company moves from its small facility in Nashville to a new, state-of-the-art headquarters in Brentwood, Tennessee.

1995—Comdata becomes the owner of truck stop point-of-sale and automated fueling terminals when it acquires Nashville-based Trendar.

1999—Comdata card integrates the Maestro® debit network into its services, allowing cardholders to use company-authorized and personal funds to buy personal items, goods, and services.

2000—Comdata introduces the MasterCard® Corporate Fleet Card, the first credit card in the nation with debit capabilities. The company distributes 150,000 cards initially. Stored Value Systems (SVS) becomes a wholly owned Comdata subsidiary.

2001—Comdata expands into Canada when it signs an agreement with Petro-Canada. SVS becomes the first cash card provider to offer foreign currency conversion at the point of sale.

2002—Comdata acquires an interest in Salt Lake City–based Gift Card Solutions and launches the company's International Retail Services division.

2003—Comdata Card combines purchasing, fleet, fuel, travel and entertainment, and payroll on one employee card.

2005—Comdata broadens its role as a provider of business-to-business electronic payment services by acquiring New York–based Tranvia, Inc., a merchant processor of credit, debit, pre-pay, and e-commerce transactions.

2006—Comdata purchases the remaining interest in Gift Card Solutions.

Left: Comdata Corporation's headquarters is just outside of Nashville in Brentwood, Tennessee. The company's gift card and stored value operations are headquartered in Louisville, Kentucky. Comdata also has a presence in more than 21 countries worldwide and employs more than 1,600 associates. Above right: Since 1969, Comdata has been a pioneer in payment solutions. Companies use Comdata to centralize key business transactions in real-time data environments, including card-based corporate security, controlled spending for business purchases, employee payroll, and business-centered funds disbursement. The company is also a leading supplier of gift cards in the retail industry.

Financial and Insurance Services | 117

American General Life and Accident Insurance Company

This Nashville insurer is changing the way Americans think about, purchase, and use life insurance. The company is committed to serving the needs of today's 'middle market' with a personal touch, and its overall approach has earned it more than three million customers nationwide and stellar ratings from prominent industry authorities.

Right: The headquarters of American General Life and Accident Insurance Company (AGLA) is forward-looking in its modern architecture and in what it represents—insuring the nation's vast, and often underrepresented, "middle market" with convenient, personalized, comprehensive, and reliable financial programs. The 320,000-square-foot building is set on a spacious campus located in Davidson County, in southern metropolitan Nashville.

At American General Life and Accident Insurance Company (AGLA), people make the difference. This company's cornerstone has been and always will be excellent customer service with a personal touch. Its agents devote their careers to establishing customer relationships as they sell and service the company's life, health, and annuity products. AGLA is known for financial strength and for making insurance easier to understand.

Product and Marketing Innovation

AGLA is changing the way Americans think about, purchase, and use life insurance. Its new "Quality of Life . . . Insurance" offers customers life insurance protection and the important flexibility to receive benefits during their lifetime for critical, chronic, or terminal illness. It can also build cash value for retirement or other needs.

Through marketing partnerships with employers and associations, AGLA offers small-business employees or association members unique, innovative life insurance, retirement savings, and other financial solutions.

Nashville Roots

AGLA has been in Nashville for more than 100 years. It incorporated on February 28, 1900, as the National Sick and Accident Association of Nashville. In 1968 it became a wholly owned subsidiary of NLT Corporation (NLT). That year, American General Corporation (AGC) of Houston, Texas, acquired another Nashville insurance company, Life and Casualty Insurance Company of Tennessee (L&C). In 1982 AGC acquired NLT and its subsidiaries, and then consolidated its insurance subsidiary—The National Life and Accident Insurance Company—with L&C. AGLA adopted its current name in 1984.

Equitable Life of McLean, Virginia, was merged into AGLA in 1988. Gulf Life Insurance Company followed in 1995. AGLA then acquired the Independent Life and Accident Insurance Company and Home Beneficial Insurance Company in 1997. In 2001 AGLA and its parent, American General Corporation, were acquired by

American International Group, Inc. (AIG), one of the world's international insurance and financial services leaders.

Today more than 800 employees work in AGLA's 320,000-square-foot headquarters campus in southern metropolitan Nashville (Davidson County). The company's 150,000-square-foot records facility is located nearby.

Technology Leadership and Financial Stability

A technology leader, AGLA pioneered SmartPad®—a system using a handheld computer notebook with pen entry—for use by insurance agents. The user-friendly system is capable of generating immediate receipts for insurance transactions, electronically completing applications and customer-service forms, and automatically sending records to a central system each night. In 1997 AGLA was awarded the Computerworld Smithsonian Technology Award for SmartPad. The Nashville home office also uses imaging technology to expedite the processing and tracking of insurance transactions and to provide quality customer service.

Overall, the insurance industry's prominent independent ratings agencies continue to recognize American General Life and Accident Insurance Company's growth and insurer financial strength.

Customer Orientation and Community Involvement

AGLA is committed to serving its more than three million customers across the country. It operates more than 200 offices nationwide, with more than 3,000 sales and service agents. Dedicated customer service teams staff the home office in Nashville.

Altogether they provide customer service that is both personal and professional. AGLA also distributes products and provides opportunities for more than 1,200 independent agents.

At AGLA, helping people reach their greatest potential never stops. The thousands of caring and dedicated people at AGLA consider this a way of life, volunteering to improve their communities.

Employees support nonprofit organizations and youth programs by volunteering, serving as board members, donating money, and sponsoring good causes. They donate time and talent to such nonprofits as the American Heart Association, the Bethlehem Centers of Nashville, the Boy Scouts and Girl Scouts of America, Junior Achievement, the Juvenile Diabetes Research Foundation, the PENCIL Foundation, Nashville Public Television, Nashville's Table, the Second Harvest Food Bank, and St. Luke's Community House.

Left: AGLA continues to change the way Americans think about, purchase, and use life insurance. Its "Quality of Life . . . Insurance" offers customers life insurance protection and the flexibility to receive benefits during their lifetime or build cash value for retirement and other needs. Through its insurance products, AGLA offers a way for one generation to care for the next generation.

One of the foremost credit unions in Nashville, this institution provides its 28,000 members—people from all walks of life in the state of Tennessee—with a benefit-rich, cooperative solution to meet their financial needs, offering full-service savings and checking accounts, credit cards, auto loans, mortgages, insurance, and investing.

What began as a venture to make banking affordable for Nashville teachers has become a booming financial institution whose services span the rolling hills of the Volunteer State.

The Tennessee Credit Union was founded in 1950 by an enterprising group of public school educators. Nashville was a bustling city then, full of music, history, and opportunity, and it is even more so today. Modern-day Nashville is one of the country's most active markets for businesses and professionals seeking new opportunities. So many people have flocked to this Tennessee city that Nashville's population has more than doubled since 1960, to more than 1.2 million residents.

And like its beloved city, The Tennessee Credit Union has grown steadily and successfully. The second-largest credit union in Nashville and the fifth-largest in the state, it has nearly 28,000 members and more than $203 million in assets. Its members include active or retired educators, plus people in other fields working for a Select Employee Group or people working or residing in Williamson and Hamblen counties.

From its headquarters in Nashville, The Tennessee Credit Union operates 12 other branches that are located across the state of Tennessee. This credit union also belongs to a network of credit unions with more than 2,100 branches worldwide—as such, its members can access services at convenient locations and more ATMs than any one credit union could offer. Sharing branches helps The Tennessee Credit Union and its partners to better compete with traditional banks.

Right: Shown here is The Tennessee Credit Union's Cool Springs Branch—the most recently added facility. This modern branch provides top-of-the-line financial services to people who live or work in Williamson County.

Helping Its Members Profit

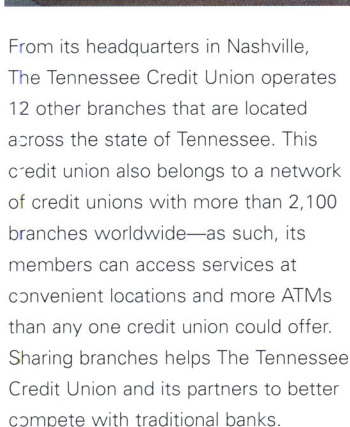

Among the several major differences between banks and credit unions, banks have a paid board of directors, which hires managers and holds them accountable for creating value for shareholders. Credit unions are cooperative, not-for-profit organizations, and the people who do business at a credit union are essentially the shareholders. Any profits are returned to these shareholders, or members, in the form of lower loan rates, better savings rates, and better technology in the branches, mainly through online and on-time services. For all intents and purposes, credit unions are in business to help their members profit since they are the owners of the business. Credit unions are more democratically run than banks, with all credit union members holding one vote regardless of their savings account balance, or "membership share account."

Credit unions appeal to their more than 85 million members because they focus on serving the member and offer an impressive diversity of products and services. The Tennessee Credit Union, specifically, offers members checking and savings accounts, mortgages, auto loans, insurance, investment products, and a full suite of additional financial services.

A Credit Union for Today and Tomorrow

The Tennessee Credit Union is the second-largest credit union in Nashville, and has plans to grow, primarily by reaching out to more potential members already in its field of membership. Additionally, increasing the awareness of the "credit union difference" among young people—who would most benefit from the credit union philosophy of savings and the wise use of credit—will help solidify a future membership base.

The Tennessee Credit Union has a proven track record of success. Every quarter from 2002 to 2006, this credit union has earned a "Five-Star Superior" rating from BauerFinancial, Inc. This rating from BauerFinancial, one of the nation's leading independent financial rating firms, is confirmation of financial strength and performance, and indicates that The Tennessee Credit Union is one of the safest in the United States. Companies that want a credit union for their employees have relied on The Tennessee Credit Union for many years, and today this credit union serves more than 250 Select Employee Group firms.

This type of growth improves The Tennessee Credit Union's performance, which translates into more resources for its members. A broader membership base means that The Tennessee Credit Union can offer better rates and more products to more people in Tennessee. Founded to serve teachers in 1950, today the credit union helps legions of people in numerous walks of life.

Making a Difference in Its Community

In addition to providing superior financial services for its members, The Tennessee Credit Union strongly supports educational charitable causes and community organizations. For more than 20 years, this credit union has partnered with Cheekwood Botanical Garden & Museum of Art to fully sponsor the Scholastic Art Competition, which nurtures art education in Tennessee schools. Additionally, this credit union has supported PENCIL Foundation since its inception. PENCIL Foundation creates and cultivates education partnerships, linking businesses with Nashville public schools to help young people achieve academic success and prepare for life. The Tennessee Credit Union also provides annual funding to the Nashville Alliance for Public Education and other groups that help schools improve education for future generations.

Community service symbolizes the way The Tennessee Credit Union remains close to its roots as it grows and evolves. In its financial and humanitarian capacities and work, The Tennessee Credit Union strives to make a difference in the lives of those it serves, every day.

Above left: In 1967, Betty G. Hobbs became the first full-time employee of The Tennessee Credit Union. She served as its president and CEO for 40 years.

Above right: The Tennessee Credit Union's Main Branch (shown here) is located in Nashville. Serving 28,000 members, The Tennessee Credit Union has 13 branches located across the state and, through its partnership with other credit unions, offers members access to branches and ATMs worldwide.

Franklin American Mortgage Company

Combining personalized service, state-of-the-art technology, and a hands-on sales approach, this full-service Tennessee mortgage banking firm is quickly becoming the lender of choice for mortgage professionals throughout the country.

Above left: Franklin American Mortgage Company (FAMC) is headquartered in Franklin, Tennessee. Above right: Dan Crockett is founder, chairman, president, and CEO of FAMC.

Committed to helping thousands of people achieve the dream of home ownership, Franklin American Mortgage Company (FAMC), based in Franklin, Tennessee, builds long-term relationships by providing outstanding service. Specializing in residential mortgages, FAMC is a full-service licensed lender offering competitive mortgage rates, personalized service, and mortgage packages to suit any customer purchasing or refinancing a home.

FAMC believes that buying a home should be a pleasurable experience, and its associates meet closing deadlines to keep it that way. Although the mortgage industry has its obstacles, FAMC professionals know how to overcome them to keep the mortgage process moving smoothly. Delays are never acceptable at this company, known nationally as an industry trendsetter.

The company operates three loan production channels: correspondent, wholesale, and retail. The correspondent division helps small to large lenders across the nation compete with the growing number of "megabanks." The correspondent lending program was established on the tenet that customer service is critical to success in the secondary market. Clients who want individual attention and quick responses from their investors will always find that level of service at FAMC. The correspondent division prides itself on personalized service, an accessible staff, fast fundings, commitment to using the latest technology, and consistent, aggressive pricing.

The wholesale division funds and underwrites loans for mortgage brokers, again with outstanding efficiency due to its advanced technology. The company's approved mortgage lending partners have online access to locking, status, closing, forms, product descriptions, and other information that helps expedite the process. FAMC is the underwriting institution for these mortgages.

The retail division, the company's oldest, offers mortgages directly to home buyers. FAMC handles the mortgage process from start to finish, giving the company total control over the level of service that its customers experience.

Relationships Built on Service

By delivering unparalleled service in all three divisions and placing a high value on relationships with customers and fellow mortgage professionals, FAMC has become one of the fastest-growing mortgage bankers in the nation. What began as a small brokerage with five employees is now a 370-person, full-service mortgage lender. Company founder, chairman, president, and CEO Dan Crockett, who started FAMC in 1993, attributes the firm's phenomenal growth to a staff that lives the company's values every day and maintains high standards in all business practices.

"We strive to earn our customers' complete satisfaction because their communication of a positive experience with us to friends, family members, and coworkers will provide us with our foundation for the future," says Crockett.

Locally Owned... Nationally Recognized

"We set our goals and expectations along the way and created a mortgage business that was what we thought it should be. We wanted our values, integrity, and behavior to better the industry."

The company's meteoric rise (its revenues increased 660 percent over five years) has not gone unnoticed. FAMC has won *Inc.* magazine's Inc. 500 Award six times, earning a place in the Inc. 500 Hall of Fame, which honors companies that have won the award at least five times since the competition began in 1982.

In 2004, FAMC was named Nashville's Top Company with 101 to 500 employees, an award sponsored by the *Nashville Business Journal* in tandem with the paper's Best in Business Awards. In 2003, the *Journal* named Crockett its Entrepreneur of the Year. *Business Nashville* magazine has recognized FAMC as one of the fastest-growing companies in Middle Tennessee, and the Nashville Chamber of Commerce recognizes FAMC as a Music City Future 50 Hall of Fame member.

Mandatory Delivery Program

Recognizing the value of technology in an information-driven industry, FAMC launched a mandatory delivery program in 2005 that offers lenders another way to sell closed loans to the company. Using a comprehensive Web site, lenders can monitor pricing, credit limits, and trade statuses, and they get additional revenue opportunities supported by real-time data technology. The program is offered through the correspondent lending division, which purchases closed loans from about 600 lenders nationwide.

FAMC is based in Franklin, Tennessee, with a large regional operation center in Dallas, Texas. The company is an approved Fannie Mae and Freddie Mac seller and servicer, is endorsed by the Federal Housing Administration, is Veterans Affairs Automatic approved, and has Lender Appraisal Processing authority.

Franklin American Mortgage Company is always working to make people feel at home in Tennessee and throughout its service area.

Above left: Franklin American Mortgage Company (FAMC) is committed to helping families achieve the dream of home ownership. Above right: FAMC has earned numerous awards for its business practices and customer service.

This successful insurance and casualty company strives to provide clients with the best possible insurance protection at the lowest possible price. It attributes its growth to its continual pursuit of superior customer service.

Above: Consumers Insurance Group, Inc.—established in 1995 in Cookeville, Tennessee—has been proudly headquartered in Murfreesboro, Tennessee, since 1997.

While many insurance companies may claim to provide personal attention, Consumers Insurance Group, Inc. is one company that takes this policy to heart. In fact, one of the company's mottoes is "When You're With Us . . . You're Family." This phrase speaks volumes about the company's philosophy, the way it does business, and its agents.

Bill Wheeler, president, states, "It takes a lot of courage to put that statement on every policy, endorsement, bill, and check that leaves our office. However, Consumers Insurance is dedicated to the belief that we are the friendliest insurance company and the easiest with whom anyone will ever do business."

Jimmy Clift, CEO, explains the company's "personal" approach: "Our agencies represent multiple insurance companies. They have a choice of which policies to promote and sell. At Consumers Insurance, we really focus on building personal relationships with our agencies. We are there to help them and their agents during a crisis, as well as to acknowledge and celebrate their successes. We offer unique training opportunities and significant travel incentives. When it comes to the consumer, we make sure our claims department extends the same personal approach."

The Consumers Insurance mission is to be a substantial regional insurance company that retains the family culture with which it began as a small, one-state company. Says Clift, "We want to be an example to our employees, agents, policyholders, and shareholders of what can be accomplished through hard work, integrity, honesty, dedication, ethics, and prayer."

History of Meeting Needs

Consumers Insurance was established in 1995 in Cookeville, Tennessee, by 40 independent Tennessee insurance agents who specialized in commercial insurance. They wanted their company to provide customer service that was more responsive than the norm and to be more fully attuned to the needs of independent agents. Consumers Insurance has not only met these goals; it has helped raise the standard for service throughout the independent agent network. Today Consumers Insurance has more than 500 agencies across six states, and now offers both personal and commercial auto insurance, which includes coverage for used-car dealers, garage repair shops, tow truck companies, business automobiles, and trucking fleets.

When Wheeler joined the company in 1997, he brought additional services and products to Consumers Insurance's portfolio. Within a year, he also relocated the company closer to Nashville in the fast-growing suburb of Murfreesboro, to take advantage of Nashville's employment base.

Since then, Consumers Insurance has enjoyed steady growth, both within Tennessee and outside of the state.

In 2001 the company expanded into Missouri. Then in 2004, it moved into Illinois and Virginia, as well. During 2005, Consumers Insurance expanded into Arkansas and in 2006, into Alabama.

Finding a Niche

One of the top three insurance companies for used-car dealerships in Tennessee and Missouri, Consumers Insurance is also one of the most technologically advanced insurance companies in the United States. It was among the first to process insurance policies between agents and company via the Internet.

Wheeler says, "We have spent considerable time and effort on our technology. We created software in-house and patented and copyrighted it. The ease of doing business is paramount to us. When an agent has a question, we respond in four to six minutes, whereas many companies have a 24-hour turnaround time. Our fast response time is an asset for the agents, and the policyholder is provided with better service."

Positioned for Growth

While Consumers Insurance may not be a large company by business standards, Clift says, "Consumers Insurance is definitely on the radar screen within the insurance industry as one of the fastest-growing and most profitable companies."

The company hopes to grow at about 15 percent annually and to expand into additional states. The challenge, according to Clift, is keeping pace with changes in technology. "We need to have the right infrastructure and technology in place to handle the growth and geographic expansion."

With Consumers Insurance Group, Inc.'s commitment to personal service and leading-edge technology, the company will achieve and exceed its goals.

Left: Bill Wheeler (kneeling, far left), who serves as president of Consumers Insurance; Jimmy Clift (standing in the first row, second from far right), who serves as CEO; and the many dedicated staff members shown here work hard to ensure the success of their company and the insurance protection of their clients. Above: Every day, these professionals put into practice the company's motto: "When You're With Us . . . You're Family."

This recently merged banking institution provides consumer and commercial banking as well as trust, securities brokerage, mortgage, and insurance products and services to five million customer households and businesses throughout the southern and midwestern United States.

Right: AmSouth Bank is a leader among regional banks in the Southeast because its customer relationships are at the heart of all its operations. Known as "the relationship people," AmSouth employees are committed to exceptional customer service.

The 2006 merger of AmSouth Bancorporation and Regions Financial Corporation has given the combined financial institution a powerful presence in Nashville and throughout much of the nation. The new bank, which will operate under the Regions name and keep AmSouth CEO Dowd Ritter, has $140 billion in assets, a market capitalization of $26 billion, and 2,000 branches, making it one of the top 10 U.S. bank holding companies. In the spirit of collaboration, the boards of directors have combined, and their mutual goal is to make the transition as invisible and seamless as possible for customers. Company headquarters remain in Birmingham, Alabama.

The new Regions Bank is a full-service institution with complete trust, asset management, mortgage banking, securities brokerage, insurance, and traditional banking products and services. The $10 billion merger exchanged AmSouth shares for Regions stock. Regions operates in 16 states: Alabama, Arkansas, Florida, Georgia, Illinois, Indiana, Iowa, Kentucky, Louisiana, Mississippi, Missouri, North Carolina, South Carolina, Tennessee, Texas, and Virginia.

Both organizations have a long history of successful business decisions and customer satisfaction. Alabama's first multibank holding company, Regions formed in 1871 as First Alabama Bancshares Inc., a consolidation of three reputable banks with $543 million in assets and 40 locations in Birmingham, Huntsville, and Montgomery. To reflect its growing presence throughout the South, the company changed its name to Regions in 1994. Ten years later, it merged with Union Planters Corporation, making it one of the top 15 banks in the country.

AmSouth Bank began as the First National Bank of Birmingham in the 1870s. The company has always been committed to understanding and meeting the needs of its customers, investors, employees, and the communities it serves. Over the years, the bank and its staff became known as "the relationship people" because customer satisfaction and unparalleled service were at the heart of the organization and its policies. As Ritter takes the helm of the new Regions Bank, he sums up the benefits of the merger: "With the combination of these two great companies, we have redoubled our commitment to providing great service to our customers and forming strong relationships with our communities."

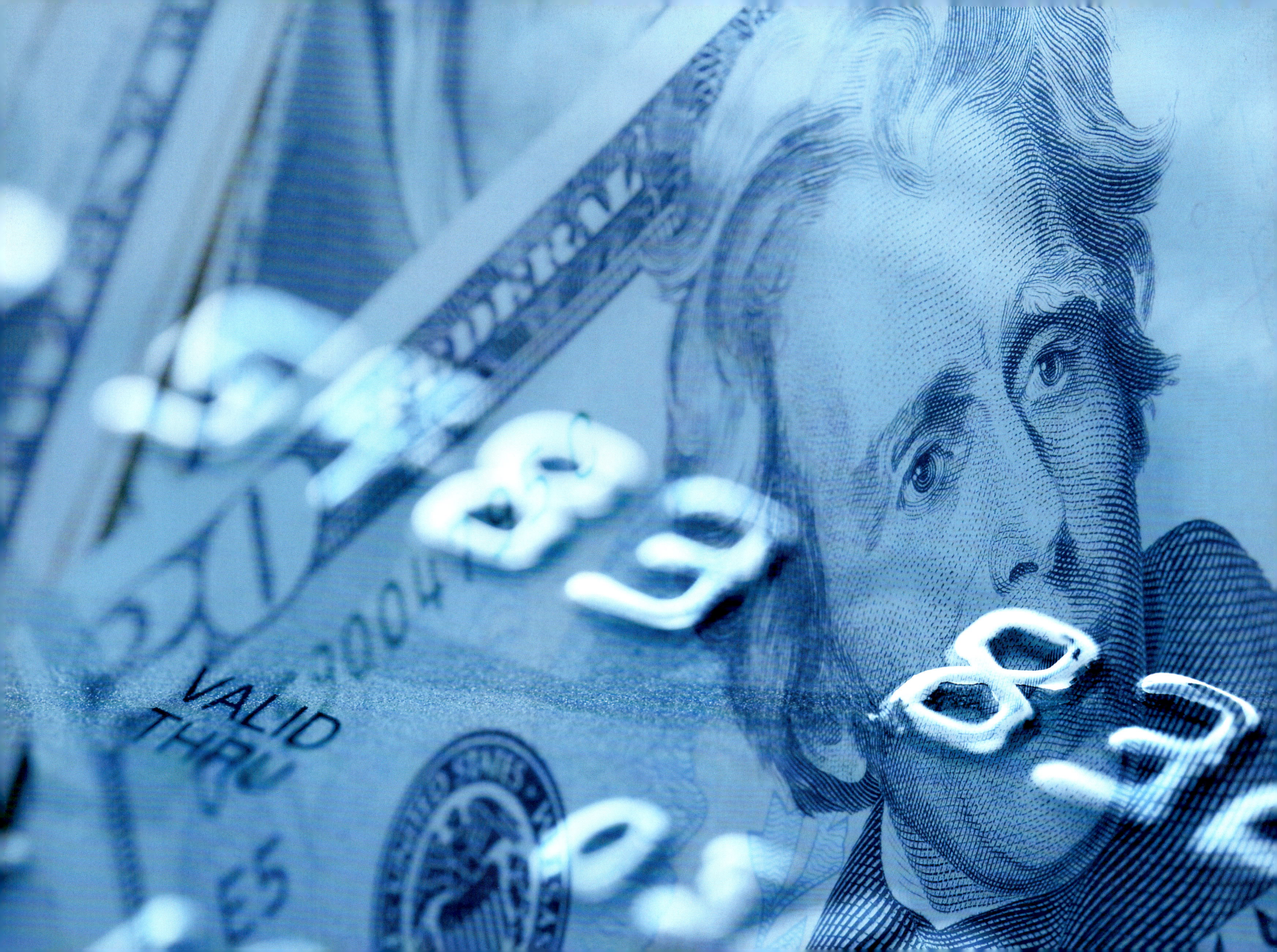
VALID
THRU

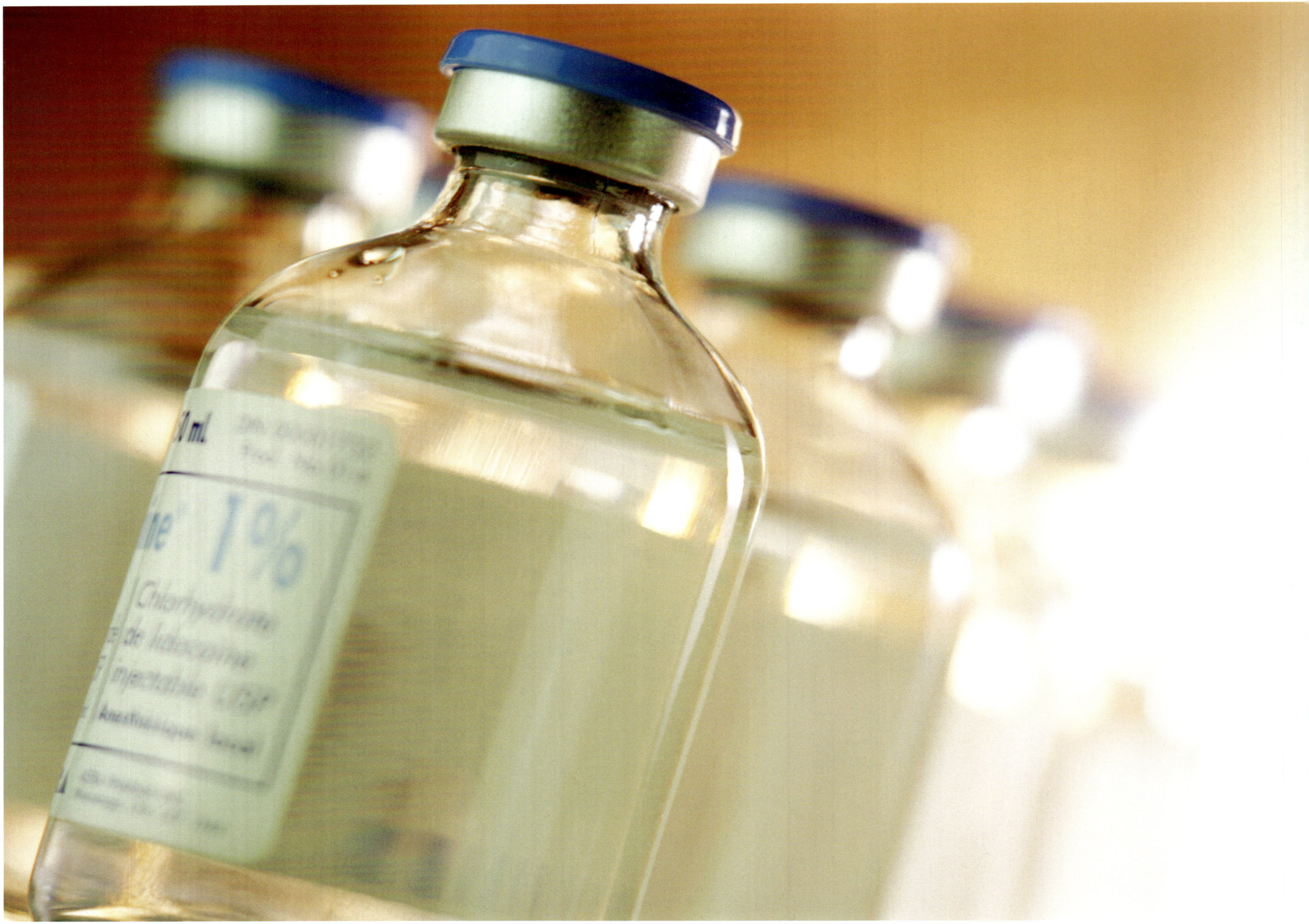
1%

PROFILES OF COMPANIES AND ORGANIZATIONS
Health Care and Biotechnology

From its founding in 1968 to its rescue airlift at New Orleans' Tulane University Hospital & Clinic in 2005 to its proactive work today, this leading Nashville-based health care organization—with 172 hospitals and 107 outpatient centers—has made treating people well its highest priority.

Above: In 1968, Thomas Frist Sr., M.D. (left), his son Thomas F. Frist Jr., M.D. (right), and Jack Massey (center) joined forces to found the Hospital Corporation of America.

Hospital Corporation of America (HCA) stands alone in the Nashville business landscape. It is the only organization in the community that began an industry. It is the only company that created a "family tree" of other firms so large that it fills a poster (which can be found hanging in many Nashville offices). Its success has been vital to the success of so many not-for-profit organizations that the Nashville community-service and cultural landscape would be diminished without it. Today, through its TriStar Health System, HCA operates 10 hospitals in the metropolitan Nashville area—Centennial Medical Center, Centennial Medical Center at Ashland City, Hendersonville Medical Center, Horizon Medical Center, Portland Medical Center, Skyline Medical Center, Southern Hills Medical Center, StoneCrest Medical Center, Summit Medical Center, and Tennessee Christian Medical Center.

The inspiration for, and concept of, a Nashville-based hospital company emerged in the spring of 1968, when a group of Nashville physicians tried to sell a medical facility that was located adjacent to Nashville's Centennial Park. Their original plan was to sell Park View Hospital to the city of Nashville. When that plan failed, some of the physicians—led by cardiologist Thomas Frist Sr., M.D.—began discussing the fate of the hospital with his son, Thomas F. Frist Jr. (also an M.D.), his close friend Jack Massey, and a young lawyer named Henry Hooker.

These men were an interesting group. Frist Sr. seemed to know physicians in every corner of the South. He was also part owner of several doctor-owned hospitals in Tennessee, and more than once had helped doctors who were trying to start hospitals to connect with architects and bankers who could help them realize their vision.

Massey was the former owner of a successful surgical supply business, the founding chair of Nashville's Baptist Hospital, and the chairman of Kentucky Fried Chicken. Perhaps most importantly, however, he was a financial genius who knew his way around Wall Street, and he was the kind of person who could negotiate a good, fair price on anything he bought.

Frist Jr. was a U.S. Air Force flight surgeon, a licensed pilot, and a close follower of the stock market who, when he got out of the service, could not decide whether he wanted to practice medicine or go into business. But no matter what he did, the younger Frist was eager to dive in with both feet.

Somewhere along the way, one of these visionary men suggested the idea of starting a chain of hospitals that would be run like a business, produce profits, and pay taxes like every other successful company—thereby enabling its caregivers to provide superior health care.

At a time when equipment was becoming more expensive and medical care billing more complicated, it made sense for hospitals to combine their operations in order to better meet their patients' needs. Not only could merged hospitals save money by sharing expensive equipment, they could also reduce costs by buying supplies and pharmaceuticals in bulk. When it came time to invest more money in hospitals, the logic went, a for-profit hospital chain would have an easier time raising capital from the public markets than a public hospital would from the local government. All of this would add up to shareholder value, and it also would result in a higher quality of health care than Americans were accustomed to receiving in that era.

Realizing the Vision and Mission

Auspiciously, in May 1968, Park View Hospital's physician-owners voted to exchange their Park View stock for stock in this new company, HCA. (Park View Hospital's name later became Centennial Medical Center.) Soon HCA had bought, or was negotiating to buy, nearly a dozen other hospitals. Less than a year after the company was formed, it began public trading; it was a successful day for its founders and for the original Park View Hospital physician-owners.

Many early HCA acquisitions were not exactly evidence that the company was headed for the big time. Some of the first hospitals were tiny rural facilities in places such as Erin and Lewisburg, Tennessee. Three of them were not hospitals at all, only plans for building new hospitals in Chattanooga, Tennessee, and in Macon and Columbus, Georgia. At the time, even HCA's headquarters was located in an old house near Park View Hospital, and its board of directors met at a Holiday Inn near Nashville International Airport. Wall Street was not impressed, at least not so far. Those who believed in HCA early on did so largely on the basis of Frist Sr.'s reputation among doctors and Massey's success with Kentucky Fried Chicken. It is no wonder that the first-ever story about HCA in a national publication (*BusinessWeek*) was headlined "Southern Fried Hospitals"—a title reflecting the early skepticism many felt about hospital chains.

Nevertheless, HCA had arrived—to stay. Its founders were enthusiastic and hard working, flying across the country to meet with hospital boards and administrators. The fact that one of HCA's founders, Frist Jr., was a private pilot helped immeasurably in this process.

Soon HCA began acquiring larger and more established hospitals, including Johnston-Willis Hospital in Richmond, Virginia, and a chain of four small hospitals in San Francisco—the Ross Medical Corp. HCA brought on board more top-notch executives, including John Hill, who served as CEO from 1970 to 1973; John Neff, who served as CFO in HCA's early years and also from 1973 to 1975; and Sam Brooks, who was named comptroller in 1969 and eventually became the company's CFO. By 1972 HCA was able to raise $25 million through a consortium of insurance companies. This money enabled HCA to continue to acquire more assets. And as HCA purchased additional facilities, as its revenue climbed, and as its stock price rose, reporters could hardly keep up with its acquisitions and successes.

There is perhaps no better indication of what a good idea HCA was than the fact that it began being imitated. By 1970, there were two other for-profit hospital chains established in Nashville: the Hospital Affiliates International and the General Care Corporation, each following a business plan like HCA's. Eventually, in 1980 and 1981, HCA acquired these two companies, creating a firm with nearly 200 facilities.

By that time, HCA had caused reverberations in many sectors of the Nashville business community, not only in the realm of health care. In HCA's early years, practically all of its hospitals were built by Nashville general contractor Joe Rodgers, turning his business from a small-time operation into one of the largest construction companies in Nashville. Meanwhile, nearly all of HCA's architectural work went to a firm co-owned by Batey Gresham, who fortuitously had been a patient of Frist Sr. By 1980, Gresham's company had nearly 100 employees, most of whom worked on HCA projects. Today, Gresham, Smith and Partners is one of the largest architectural and engineering firms in the South.

As HCA's 10th anniversary neared, its founders remembered a goal they had set in 1968, when they convinced the physician-owners of Park View Hospital to exchange stock in their hospital for stock in HCA. Within 10 years, Massey had told them, HCA would have 100 hospitals. As the 10-year mark neared, HCA executives such as Frist Jr. and Clayton McWhorter, who had started

Above: At HCA hospitals, an electronic medication administration record (eMAR) by Meditech uses bar-code technology to help prevent medication errors. An HCA nurse scans the bar code on a medication label, and the system checks a patient's records to help ensure that the patient receives the right dose of the right drug at the right time through the right delivery system.

Hospital Corporation of America

Above: In 1968, the newly formed HCA acquired Park View Hospital from its physician-owners through a stock offering.

with the company as a pharmacist at a hospital in Albany, Georgia, remembered that pledge. Thus in 1978, as the company celebrated its 10th birthday, it did indeed purchase its 100th hospital.

Setting the Bar High

Today, HCA owns and operates 172 hospitals and 107 outpatient centers. It has 194,000 employees working across the country but largely centered in the Southeast. An estimated 37,000 physicians practice at HCA hospitals. Annually, about 225,000 babies are delivered at HCA facilities—more than 5 percent of all those born in the United States.

Under the leadership of chairman and CEO Jack O. Bovender Jr. and president and COO Richard M. Bracken, a primary HCA focus in recent years has been the continual improvement and advancement of health care. One example of these efforts is the full implementation of the eMAR (electronic medication administration record) bar-coding system to improve medication safety. In 1999, a report by the Institute of Medicine of the National Academies concluded that every year nearly 98,000 people in the United States die as a result of preventable medical errors. Largely as a result of this information, HCA was quick to create an eMAR system. Using eMAR, patients at HCA hospitals have a bar code on their wristbands. Before giving medications, nurses scan the bar-coded label on the medication to help ensure that the patient receives the right dose of the right medication at the right time through the right delivery system. As recently as 2005, it was estimated that less than 10 percent of hospitals in the United States had instituted systems like eMAR. However, HCA has installed eMAR in all its U.S. hospitals.

Perinatal safety is another area that has been emphasized at HCA under the leadership of Bovender and Bracken. Historically, nurses have learned on the job how to read fetal heart monitors.

A few years ago, however, HCA saw to it that its more than 5,000 obstetrics-gynecology nurses underwent formal training on how to read fetal heart monitors. HCA has also taken the lead nationally in steps to prevent and treat kernicterus, a disease caused by untreated severe jaundice that can cause brain damage if not properly identified and treated. In 2005, HCA began testing babies born in its hospitals for kernicterus before the babies are discharged to go home.

HCA's emphasis on perinatal safety has paid off—most importantly, in terms of great benefits to patients as well as in operating costs for HCA. Through initiatives like these, HCA has reduced the cost of its obstetrics-related malpractice insurance claims by nearly half—which translates into an annual savings of about $40 million. Such innovations and successes continue to provide evidence that HCA's founding and current philosophy has great merit: "What's good for the patient is good for business."

Caring for Communities

Then there are things that HCA and its people have done for the Nashville community. The company's leaders today, like the company's founders, believe that the HCA family should set an example of volunteerism in the communities it serves. The following are just a few of HCA's most significant examples:

- HCA has contributed $7.5 million to help fund the construction of The Gordon E. Inman Center for health sciences and nursing at Belmont University. The new building, and the programs made possible because of it, will help alleviate the nursing shortage in Nashville.
- HCA started The Sarah Cannon Cancer Center for cancer testing and treatment. In addition, HCA helps underwrite two not-for-profit organizations related to The Sarah Cannon Cancer Center: The Minnie Pearl Cancer Foundation, which provides services to people with cancer and family members of people with cancer; and the Sarah Cannon Research Institute, which HCA formed along with Tennessee Oncology, PLLC. This research institute gives cancer patients access to clinical trials.
- In recent years, HCA has given seven-figure donations to the Frist Center for the Visual Arts; the Nashville Symphony and the Schermerhorn Symphony Center; the Adventure Science Center; the Siloam Family Health Center; and the Nashville Zoo at Grassmere.
- The HCA Foundation also provides about $12 million per year to

countless programs focusing on health and children's well-being in Middle Tennessee. Programs range from local health clinics to the Boys & Girls Clubs of America.

HCA confers two annual Frist Humanitarian Awards—one to an employee who goes beyond day-to-day responsibilities in his or her overall service to the community and the other to a volunteer who gives unselfishly to his or her community and to patients in HCA facilities. The 2005 Frist Humanitarian Award for an employee went to a remarkable, longtime worker at the Redmond Regional Medical Center in Rome, Georgia, who agreed to be a donor when a coworker needed a kidney transplant. The volunteer award went to a dedicated volunteer at the Sunrise Hospital & Medical Center in Las Vegas, Nevada, who had logged 15,500 volunteer hours in 13 years.

The HCA Foundation and HCA also prominently sponsor Habitat for Humanity. By the end of 2005, more than 7,000 HCA employees had helped build 39 Habitat houses across the country, and the foundation's support to build the houses totaled $2.5 million. Also in 2005, after so many hurricanes hit Florida, HCA created a nonprofit employee assistance fund called the HCA Hope Fund to help its employees who are suffering financial hardship as a result of the disaster, extended illness or injury, or other situations. HCA donated $4 million in corporate money to the fund, which then grew by another $2 million dollars with the help of employees, vendors, and physicians.

Leaving No One Behind

HCA perhaps best demonstrated its commitment to its patients, staff, and family members during the days following Hurricane Katrina in 2005. Half a dozen HCA facilities took a direct hit when Katrina came ashore. However, all HCA facilities—including the HCA-owned Tulane University Hospital & Clinic in downtown New Orleans—managed to operate and to provide good health care throughout the storm.

When New Orleans flooded, HCA and the HCA-owned hospitals in the area successfully and safely evacuated by air an estimated 1,400 patients, staff members, and family members of patients and staff from Tulane. "Yes, it is expensive to fly everyone out by helicopter," Bovender later explained to a reporter, "but as we went through this process, there never was a thought about how much this would cost. We were operating under the old military axiom that says, 'Leave no one behind.' We were not going to lose these patients. We weren't going to lose these staff members. We weren't even going to lose a dog or cat."

When government officials and journalists pieced together the story of the Katrina flood, the Tulane airlift, which was planned, executed, and funded by HCA, emerged as one of the most remarkable stories of the ordeal. "HCA's evacuation of critically ill patients in the midst of poor flying conditions, no electricity, weak phone links, and frequent sniper fire stands out among rescue operations in New Orleans in the aftermath of the hurricane," stated the *Wall Street Journal*. "Hospital Corporation of America would act decisively, not waiting for—or even expecting—government help," reported *The Atlanta Journal-Constitution*. "[The company] launched a sweeping plan that would later be regarded as a textbook example of disaster response."

By putting its patients first and by treating its staff, its investors, and the doctors who practice at its hospitals exceedingly well, Hospital Corporation of American believes its facilities will continue to be thought of as textbook examples of how things should be done. As Frist Sr. said many years ago when speaking on his philosophy of how to run an organization: "Good people beget good people."

Above: In 2002, Jack O. Bovender Jr. (right) became chairman and CEO and Richard M. Bracken (left) became president and COO of HCA.

This family of four hospitals, part of the country's largest not-for-profit health care system, is Tennessee's leading faith-based health provider. Top physicians and staff always put the patient first here, and the organization partners with other groups to enrich the communities it serves.

Above: Saint Thomas Hospital in Nashville, renowned for its cardiac care, is one of four Saint Thomas Health Services hospitals.

Saint Thomas Health Services (STHS) is a faith-based ministry serving the people of Middle Tennessee with four hospitals—Saint Thomas Hospital and Baptist Hospital, both in Nashville; Middle Tennessee Medical Center in Murfreesboro; and Hickman Community Hospital in Centerville. This family of hospitals is united by a single purpose: to provide spiritually centered, holistic care that sustains and improves the health of the communities it serves.

Recognized as the leading faith-based health system in Tennessee, STHS is part of St. Louis, Missouri–based Ascension Health, the largest not-for-profit health care system in the United States. STHS is committed to healing and is dedicated to service—especially to persons who are poor or needy, which reflects the spiritual core of its mission, vision, and values.

The Ascension Health and Saint Thomas Health Services mission statement outlines the system's priorities: "Rooted in the loving ministry of Jesus as healer, STHS associates are committed to serving all persons, with special attention to those who are poor and vulnerable. Our Catholic health ministry is dedicated to spiritually centered, holistic care that sustains and improves the health of individuals and communities. We are advocates for a compassionate and just society through our actions and our words."

A Commitment to Quality

In the 2006 HealthGrades hospital quality ratings, Saint Thomas Hospital received the highest marks and ranked in the top five percent in the nation for its heart surgery and cardiac services. Saint Thomas Hospital, with its award-winning physicians and staff, has provided some of the best cardiac care in Tennessee for more than 100 years. Baptist Hospital delivers more babies and performs more joint replacements than any other Tennessee hospital, and it ranks number one in Middle Tennessee for stroke care, according to HealthGrades in 2006. Middle Tennessee Medical Center has the region's busiest emergency department, with more than 55,000 visits each year. And Hickman Community Hospital is an essential access facility that provides acute and long-term care to the residents of Hickman County.

The hospitals of STHS are competitive about providing the best possible care, and many of their patients are just as competitive. Entire teams of professional athletes depend on Baptist Sports Medicine for health care. The official sports medicine provider for the NHL's Nashville Predators and the NFL's Tennessee Titans, Baptist Sports Medicine has earned the trust of athletes throughout the region.

Saint Thomas Health Services Hospitals

- Saint Thomas Hospital, in Nashville
- Baptist Hospital, in Nashville
- Middle Tennessee Medical Center, in Murfreesboro
- Hickman Community Hospital, in Centerville

Vision and Values

STHS traces its healing ministry back more than 350 years to the mission of St. Vincent de Paul and St. Louise de Marillac. The vision of STHS is to be the premier spiritually based health care ministry as seen through the eyes of the patient. Patients are the top priority in everything STHS does and how it does it. Each day the four hospitals give life to the system's values:

- Service of the Poor—generosity of spirit for persons most in need
- Reverence—respect and compassion for the dignity and diversity of life
- Integrity—inspiring trust through personal leadership
- Wisdom—integrating excellence and stewardship
- Creativity—courageous innovation
- Dedication—affirming the hope and joy of the STHS ministry.

Community Care

Consistent efforts to create a healthier community extend beyond providing health care. STHS sponsors three Nashville clinics, the Saint Thomas Family Health Centers, to support its mission of serving the poor and vulnerable. STHS is committed to helping people live healthier lives, and that is why it has teamed with other local organizations to improve the mental, physical, and spiritual health of each community it serves. The American Heart Association, the YMCA of Middle Tennessee, the NFL's Tennessee Titans, and the NHL's Nashville Predators are just some of the community organizations STHS partners with and supports. Together they work to make Middle Tennessee a healthier place to live.

The People of Saint Thomas Health Services

Each leader of the STHS executive management team is dedicated to serving the hospitals and communities where they live. This commitment extends to all STHS associates. To attract the best physicians, nurses, and staff, STHS provides a work environment that is spiritually based and respects the professional lives of associates and their families. By employing the best people and taking care of them, STHS is able to provide the best possible care and to maintain its vision of being "the premier spiritually based health care ministry, as seen through the eyes of the patient."

Far left: Baptist Hospital—also one of four Saint Thomas Health Services hospitals—has received awards for its sports medicine, obstetric, cardiac, and stroke care. Above left: Jim Houser, CEO of Saint Thomas Health Services, was officially commissioned to the position in 2006. His wife, Liz, took part in the commissioning ceremony.

Reaching out to underserved nonurban populations in need of well-managed, leading-edge health care, this trusted multibillion-dollar organization owns, leases, or operates more than 75 hospitals in 22 states from its headquarters in Franklin, Tennessee.

The United States hospital industry is broadly defined to include acute care, rehabilitation, and psychiatric facilities that are either public (government owned and operated), not-for-profit private (religious or secular), or for-profit (investor owned) institutions. According to the American Hospital Association, there are only about 4,900 hospitals in the United States that are not-for-profit privately owned, investor owned, or state or local government owned. Investor-owned hospitals represent approximately 17 percent of that total. Only 2,000 of these facilities, or 40 percent, are located in nonurban communities.

Community Health Systems, Inc. focuses on acute-care hospitals in nonurban America. "We believe the rural market is underserved and represents a very strong market niche for a proven operator like Community Health Systems," states Wayne T. Smith, who serves as Community Health Systems' chairman, president, and CEO. "Rural hospitals often suffer from a lack of capital and have difficulty recruiting physicians and retaining a higher level of management expertise. We focus on overcoming these challenges."

Understanding and Serving Its Communities

Community Health Systems' hospitals are located in growing nonurban health care markets, because of the favorable demographic and economic trends and competitive conditions. There are generally fewer hospitals and other health care service providers in these nonurban areas with smaller populations, which means there is less direct competition for hospital-based services.

In addition, Community Health Systems recognizes that a hospital is viewed as a leader in the local community—as a provider of essential health care services, as one of the largest employers, and as a valuable resource for economic development. Certainly, a well-managed community hospital is vital to keeping quality health care close to home. As a partner with such hospitals, Community Health Systems honors this community view and understands the critical need. The sole focus of Community Health Systems is to provide excellent health care in these communities, while also setting a high standard for success. Community Health Systems works with the community to create a partnership that maintains local involvement and provides the necessary resources to expand essential health care services, to recruit physicians, and to advance the use of existing and new technologies.

Succeeding on a Strong, Steady Performance

Community Health Systems is one of the largest nonurban providers of general hospital health care services in the United States. As of August 31, 2006, Community Health Systems owned, leased, or operated 76 hospitals—with an aggregate of 8,953 licensed beds and 30,000 hospital employees—in geographically diverse

Right: President, Chairman, and CEO Wayne T. Smith, of Community Health Systems, Inc., brings more than 30 years of health care industry experience to the organization.
Far right: An artist's rendering depicts Community Health Systems' headquarters in Franklin, Tennessee, which is just south of Nashville.

areas across 22 states. In more than 85 percent of its markets, Community Health Systems is the sole hospital provider. In the remaining markets, Community Health Systems is one of two providers.

Making Corporate History

In June 1996, an affiliate of Forstmann Little & Co. acquired Community Health Systems in a leveraged buyout for a purchase price of $1.1 billion. Wayne T. Smith was recruited to serve as president and CEO in early 1997. Smith, who came to the company with more than 30 years of health care industry experience, strengthened the senior management team, standardized and centralized operations, and implemented a disciplined acquisition program. In June 2000, Community Health Systems was taken public again on the New York Stock Exchange at a price of $13 per share (NYSE: CYH). Smith was named chairman in February 2001.

Since Wayne Smith's arrival, Community Health Systems has grown from $742 million in net revenue to more than $3.7 billion in 2005. This represents a compound annual growth rate of 22 percent—the strongest revenue growth in the industry. The company has also had outstanding earnings growth. Since 2001, Community Health Systems' earnings per share has grown 26.9 percent on a compound annual growth rate basis.

Currently, Community Health Systems has more than 700 corporate employees and is looking forward to moving into its new corporate headquarters located just south of Nashville in Franklin, Tennessee. The company has a clear, executable strategy with predictable and sustainable growth. Community Health Systems is well positioned to capitalize on the opportunities in the underserved nonurban market segment that has little competition and great potential for strong organic growth. Community Health Systems has earned its reputation as the company that many communities trust to run their local hospital.

In 2006, Community Health Systems was recognized by *Forbes* magazine on its Platinum 400 list of "The Best Big Companies in America" for the third year in a row.

Community Health Systems, Inc. is proud to be a vibrant part of the greater Nashville business community and a contributor to the quality of health care and life in its home state.

Above: Community Health Systems' Laredo Medical Center is at the heart of health care in Laredo, Texas. Left: The company owns, leases, or operates 76 hospitals in geographically diverse nonurban areas across 22 states.

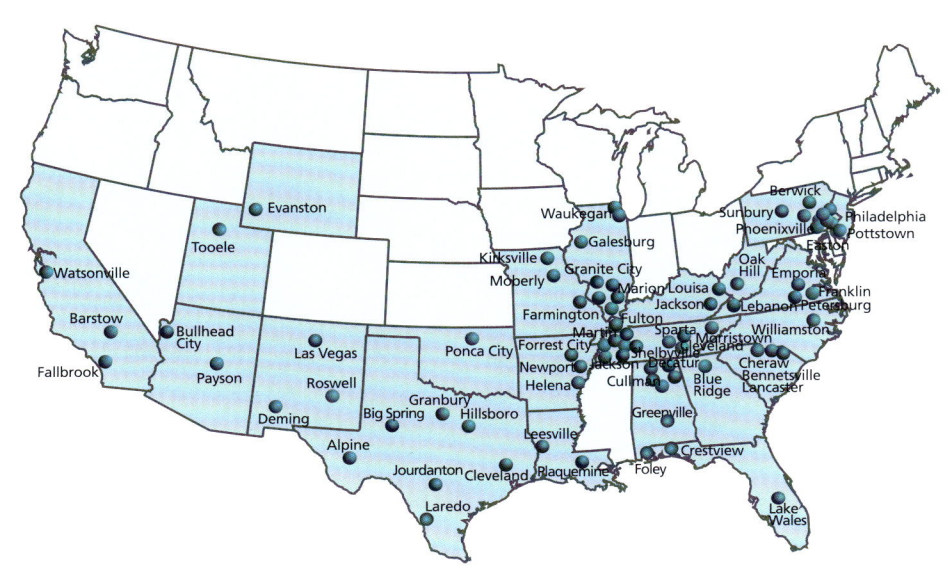

Distinguished by its service delivery, professional expertise, and use of advanced technologies, this company—one of Tennessee's largest private radiology practices—provides outstanding diagnostic and therapeutic imaging for its patients as well as practice stability for its physicians.

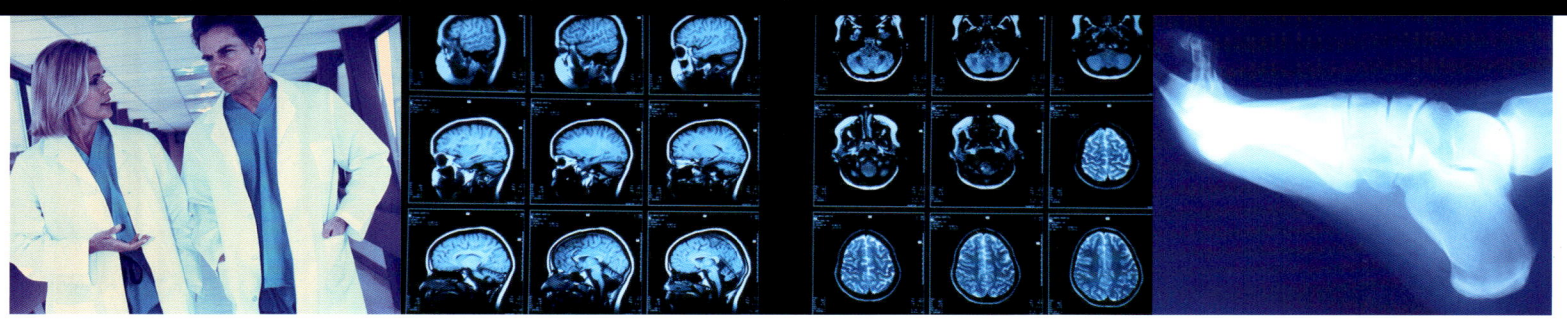

Above: Radiology Alliance, one of Tennessee's largest private radiology practice groups, offers a full range of high-quality imaging and professional radiology services.

In 2001, three successful radiology practices merged to create Nashville's highly regarded Radiology Alliance. Today, with 50 board certified diagnostic and interventional radiologists and radiation oncologists, along with more than 65 additional staff members, Radiology Alliance succeeds as one of the largest private radiology practices in the state of Tennessee. And it is quickly becoming the preferred provider of radiology services in each of the communities it serves.

Then as now, the mission of Radiology Alliance is to provide high quality diagnostic and therapeutic imaging and medical management services to the Nashville community. "Patient care and service is our number one priority," states Keith Radecic, who serves as CEO of the company. "Our goal is to provide the highest level of patient care as well as responsive customer service to our referring physicians. This includes a fast turnaround time of reports and clear, consistent formats." In fact, while most radiologists typically turn around reports within 24 hours, Radiology Alliance averages a remarkable four hours when its voice-recognition system is used.

Radiology Alliance has offices at six hospitals in Nashville and the Middle Tennessee region: Baptist Hospital, Centennial Medical Center, and Saint Thomas Hospital in Nashville; Perry Community Hospital in Linden; University Medical Center in Lebanon; and Cookeville Regional Medical Center in Cookeville. Additionally, the company services seven private offices in Nashville, including the first dedicated breast magnetic resonance imaging (MRI) facility in the mid-state area.

The Full Scope of Services and Specialties

Aside from its geographical reach, Radiology Alliance differentiates itself with its breadth of subspecialties. This company offers interventional radiology, which uses imaging to guide therapeutic procedures; neuroradiology, which focuses on imaging of the central nervous system; musculoskeletal radiology; and radiation oncology. In addition to general radiology, computed tomography (CT), and ultrasound imaging, Radiology Alliance provides positron emission tomography (PET) imaging. In fact, it is a top provider of PET imaging services in the entire state, averaging more than 20 scans per day.

Moreover, Radiology Alliance is ahead of the curve in anticipating changes and advances in imaging technology. This company keeps pace with physicians' needs and desires for faster diagnoses and better medical solutions, as well as patients' all-important needs for immediate information.

Looking toward the future, Radiology Alliance, its principals, and its experts are working to ensure the company's continued growth, particularly into underserved areas in the mid-state region. While this company continues to grow and change, Radiology Alliance's emphasis on outstanding patient care and physician-customer service will endure unaffected.

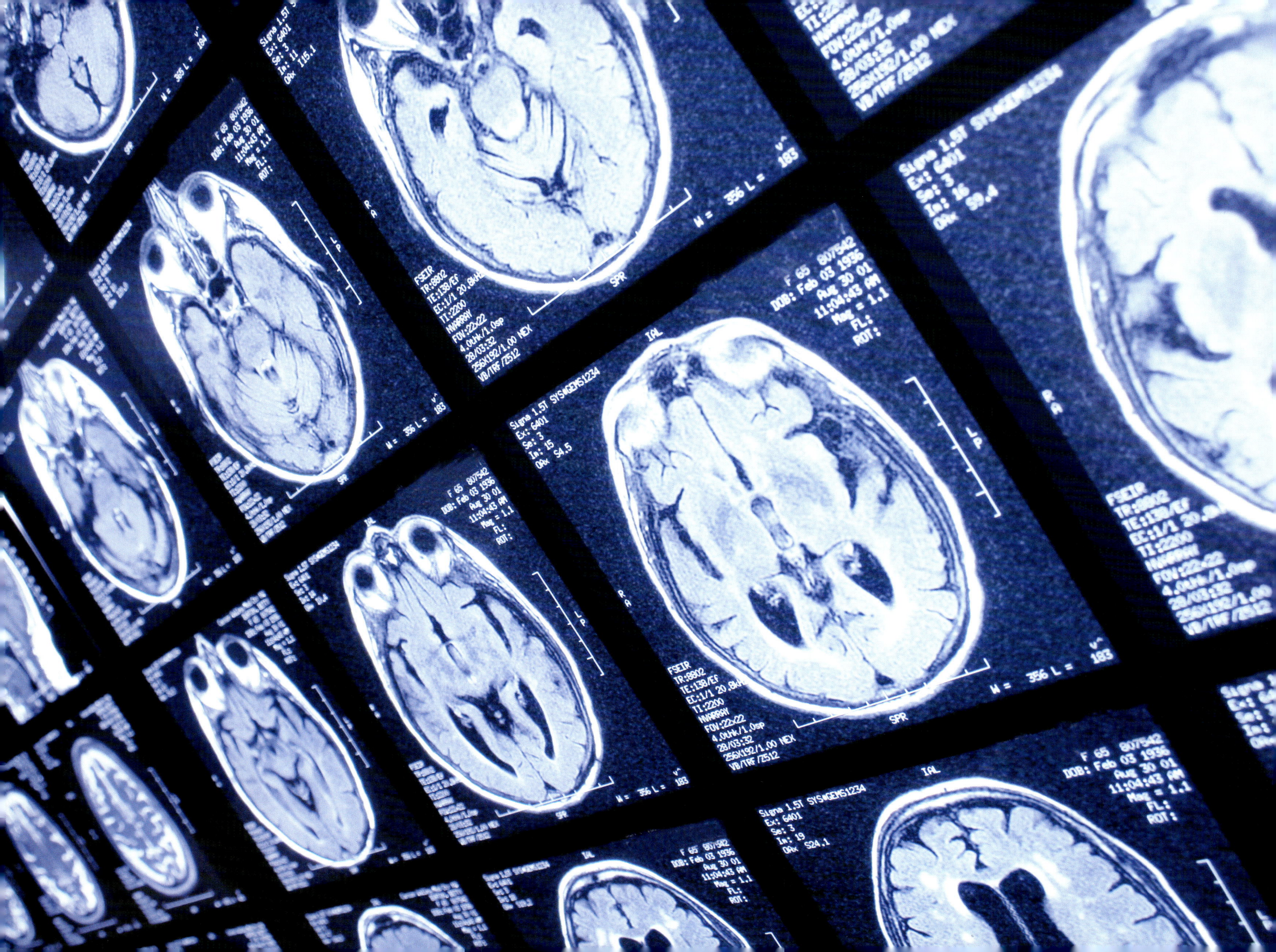
F 65 807542
DOB: Feb 03 1936
Aug 30 01
11:04:43 AM
Mag = 1.1
FL:
ROT:
IAL
Signa 1.5T SYS#GEMS1234
Ex: 6401
Se: 3
Im: 15
FSEIR
TR:8802
TI:2200
W = 356 L = 183
SPR

140 | PORTRAITS OF SUCCESS Profiles of Companies and Organizations

PROFILES OF COMPANIES AND ORGANIZATIONS
Manufacturing and Distribution

Headquartered in Nashville, this company—a leader in advanced tire technology—through its subsidiaries develops, manufactures, and markets Bridgestone, Firestone, and associate brand tires, as well as other rubber products, building materials, and industrial fibers and textiles with 45 production facilities throughout the Americas.

Above: The owners of vehicles from luxury "driving machines" to off-road trucks and mining equipment trust their ride to Bridgestone, Firestone, and the company's associate brand tires. Bridgestone Americas Holding, Inc.—whose parent company, Bridgestone Corporation, is the world's largest tire and rubber company—develops, manufactures, and markets tires for almost every kind of vehicle.

Bridgestone Americas Holding, Inc. (BSAH) may not have invented the wheel, but it definitely has cornered its market. Its tires come as original equipment on more than 200 different cars and light truck models sold in the United States and Canada.

Headquartered in Nashville, the entity now known as "Bridgestone Americas" traces its roots to the 1988 acquisition of the Firestone Tire & Rubber Company by Bridgestone Corporation. It is the largest subsidiary of Tokyo-based Bridgestone Corporation, and it operates manufacturing and sales subsidiaries in the United States, Canada, Mexico, Costa Rica, Venezuela, Argentina, Chile, Brazil, and Colombia, and has sales representation throughout Latin America and the Caribbean.

Through its subsidiaries, Bridgestone Americas sells more than 8,000 different types and sizes of tires for vehicles in a variety of categories—including passenger, light truck, truck, bus, off-road, agricultural, motorcycle, and kart—through more than 7,600 "Family Channel" outlets in North and South America made up of company-owned stores and independent dealers. The company also reaches its customers through warehouse clubs and other outlets such as truck stops. Bridgestone Americas's Firestone Complete Auto Care chain is the world's largest provider of retail automotive service and tire sales.

In addition, other company-owned outlets serving consumers are ExpertTire, Tires Plus, Hibdon Tire, Mark Morris, and Wheel Works. The company's GCR Tire Centers serve the commercial sector with tire sales, service, and retreading for truck tires. The outlets also provide tire sales and service for agricultural, forestry, mining, and construction vehicles.

Bridgestone Americas Business Units

Through its five main business units, Bridgestone Americas operates 45 manufacturing facilities in the Western Hemisphere:

- Bridgestone Firestone North American Tire, LLC in Nashville—a tire manufacturing, wholesale, and original equipment sales group for consumer automotive, commercial truck and bus, agricultural, and off-road tires;
- BFS Retail & Commercial Operations, LLC in Bloomingdale, Illinois—a family of company-owned consumer and commercial stores in the United States and Canada;
- Bridgestone Firestone Diversified Products, LLC in Indianapolis, Indiana—an operation focused on the manufacturing and sale of non-tire products such as roofing and building materials, air springs, synthetic and natural rubber, polymers, and industrial fibers and textiles;
- Bridgestone Firestone Latin American Tire Operations, based in Nashville, Tennessee—the operating unit that oversees Bridgestone Americas' presence in Latin America, consisting of production facilities in Mexico, Brazil, Argentina, Costa Rica, and Venezuela; proving grounds in Acuña, Mexico, and Sao Pedro, Brazil; and sales representation throughout Latin America and the Caribbean; and
- Bridgestone Metalpha U.S.A., Inc. in Clarksville, Tennessee—the company's steel cord manufacturer.

A Blend of the Best

Bridgestone Americas traces its American roots to the formation of the Firestone Tire & Rubber Company in 1900. At that time Harvey S. Firestone, an unemployed buggy salesman, began producing tires in an old foundry in Akron, Ohio, with 12 employees and some secondhand machinery. Previously employed by the Columbus Buggy Company, Firestone dreamed of replacing the steel-rim wheels on buggies with rubber tires for a smoother ride. His idea proved to be successful; it evolved into the business of supplying tires to the automotive industry, and soon Firestone was taking tire orders from Henry Ford.

The company's Japanese heritage comes from Shojiro Ishibashi, a rubber footwear entrepreneur, and his creation of the Bridgestone Tire Company Ltd. (later, Bridgestone Corporation) in 1931. Ishibashi had invented and mass produced rubber-soled footwear that was more durable than the traditional straw sandal. His footwear became popular, and as Ishibashi prospered he decided to apply his knowledge of rubber to another business—tire production—and planned to sell the tires in Europe and America. To give his new company universal appeal, Ishibashi reversed the English translation of his name ("stone bridge"), and "Bridgestone" quickly became a household name.

The company mottoes established by the two company founders serve as the now-blended company's guiding philosophy. Ishibashi's mission statement reflects an ideal to which the company aspires: "Serve Society with Superior Quality." Firestone's motto, "Best Today—Still Better Tomorrow" also is a guiding force that has been incorporated into the company's philosophy. Today more than 50,000 Bridgestone Americas employees carry on the tradition of excellence established by Ishibashi and Firestone, combining both Japanese and American cultures to create the company's high quality products.

Finishing First in Technology

The global Bridgestone Group as well as Bridgestone Americas are innovators in tire technology, using resources from around the world to produce superior tires. The Bridgestone Group operates tri-polar research and development centers, with locations in Tokyo, Japan, and Rome, Italy; Bridgestone Americas's tech center is located in Akron, Ohio. In addition, Bridgestone Americas operates world-class proving grounds in Fort Stockton, Texas; Sao Pedro, Brazil; and Acuña, Mexico.

Motorsports are a key part of Bridgestone Americas's DNA. Through participation in series such as the CHAMP Car World Series and the Indy Racing League, and from the Bridgestone Group's participation in Formula One, the company derives valuable information and testing opportunities that can be applied to the design and manufacture of tires that Americans ride on everyday. An example of this innovation is the recently announced Serenity Technology, now incorporated in the all-new Bridgestone Turanza. Serenity Technology focuses on four key benefits that are paramount to consumers: quiet, comfort, wet performance, and long wear. With its elegant design, Turanza with Serenity Technology incorporates many features from other company innovations and provides the ultimate in ride and comfort for premium touring cars.

Community Support

Since 1952, the Bridgestone Firestone Trust Fund, the philanthropic arm of Bridgestone Americas, has donated millions of dollars in the United States to support education, the welfare of children, and environmental and conservation efforts. It has also provided support to arts programs such as local opera, symphony, and ballet events; public radio and television; and civic improvements ranging from libraries to softball fields.

Above left: The corporate headquarters of Bridgestone Americas Holding, Inc. (known as the "Americas Support Center") is located in Nashville, Tennessee. Above right: In February 2007, Bridgestone Firestone launched the new Bridgestone Turanza with Serenity Technology, an all-season tire with an asymmetrical tread pattern designed to deliver outstanding wet and dry performance for premium touring cars, all year long.

Manufacturing and Distribution | 143

Odom's Tennessee Pride Sausage, Inc.

Proud of its outstanding food-safety record, this breakfast sausage company—one of the largest in the nation—attributes its success to a following of loyal customers, hundreds of dedicated associates, and a commitment to quality and taste in its authentic country sausage products.

Above: Odom's Tennessee Pride Sausage, Inc. is the creator and producer of a great variety of high quality breakfast foods, which are also convenient and delicious for lunch, dinner, and snacks. These fine products are sold across the United States.

For more than 60 years and three generations, Odom's Tennessee Pride Sausage, Inc. has delighted consumers with its products while upholding its commitment to quality, good taste, and food safety. From the first pound of sausage produced in 1943 to all the products it manufactures today, the company has never compromised the quality or flavor of its products—which is just one reason for the company's success.

One of the first companies to market sausage and biscuit sandwiches in the United States, Tennessee Pride is one of the largest breakfast sausage companies in the country and holds the number one retail market share in several cities. The company's products, which include cooked and ready-to-eat links and patties, roll sausage, breakfast sandwiches, sausage balls, and gravy, are sold through major retailers and food-service operators nationwide.

Tennessee Pride's catchy jingle and distinctive Farmboy logo—a character that often appears in person at stores and special events—are favorites with customers, who know the company's advertisements from television, radio, newspapers, and the Grand Ole Opry. Odom's sausage products are easy to find at retailers such as Wal-Mart, Kroger, and Publix, and at major restaurant chains throughout the United States.

Safety and Quality Assurance

Tennessee Pride's commitment to the highest standards of quality, consistency, and flavor has enabled the company to grow and expand. In addition to its headquarters in Madison, Tennessee, it has plants in Dickson, Tennessee, and in Little Rock, Arkansas. Rising demand for handheld foods such as breakfast sandwiches prompted an expansion at the Dickson plant. The company added 33,000 square feet, enough space to double its sandwich production. The renovation of another 25,000 square feet at Dickson added a new cooler and maintenance area, new facilities for employees, and a new cook line for sausage patties as well as for gravy and sausage ball production.

Tennessee Pride has an outstanding record of food safety and humane animal handling. For three consecutive years, from 2003 to 2005, personnel at the Little Rock plant received the American Meat Institute (AMI) Award of Honor for worker health and safety. AMI is a national trade association representing U.S. meat and poultry companies. Employee training in food safety and in other good manufacturing practices ensures safety, quality, and cleanliness. Procedures include steam pasteurization, using fresh seasonings, temperature-control monitoring, and microbiological testing.

At Tennessee Pride, commitment to quality means more than making great sausage; it means improving the whole industry, which is why Larry Odom, chairman and CEO, participates in the AMI. Other company executives serve on committees that address animal handling, human resources, and safety. Tennessee Pride also won the 2002 and 2004 Pollution Prevention awards from the Little Rock Wastewater Utility. Tennessee Pride is a good neighbor wherever it operates.

The 'Secret Recipe'

Odom's Tennessee Pride owes much of its success to the spice formula developed by its founder, Douglas Odom Sr. From working in the meat business all his life, he knew about making sausage. After some experimenting, he found a perfect blend of seasonings, the "secret recipe" that gives Tennessee Pride sausage its great flavor.

Odom was born in 1902 and raised in Nashville, where he attended school and held his first job, which was delivering telegrams for Western Union. With his earnings, he bought a new bicycle to help him make deliveries and start a newspaper route. When he turned 18, he and his brother, William Odom Jr., opened a meat market in Nashville. Their father, William Odom Sr., financed the business.

Having worked in the meat business as deliverer, manager, and owner, Douglas had the knowledge to start another business. He recognized that Nashville lacked a good sausage product and knew he could make one. With equal parts confidence and experience, he moved to Madison in 1941 and began the Odom Sausage Company in 1943. He had the support and enthusiasm of his wife, Louise, and his father. The company's corporate office is still in Madison, on the same property bought during the company's infancy.

Today, the third generation of Odoms leads Odom's Tennessee Pride Sausage, Inc.—keeping it true to its roots and ensuring that every area of production lives up to the Tennessee Pride tradition. Larry Odom, the founder's grandson, gives customers his personal guarantee in writing: "We make every effort each day to not compromise the quality or flavor of our products. Tennessee Pride is an industry leader in thinking and being food safe. That is our commitment to you."

Above left: Chairman and CEO Larry Odom stands with a bronze replica of the company's distinctive and popular Farmboy character. Above right: The Odom's Tennessee Pride Sausage, Inc. board of directors includes, from left, standing, Harold Boone, chief financial officer; Charles "Chuck" Odom, board member; James Stonehocker, executive vice president and chief operating officer; and Larry Odom, chairman and CEO; and, seated, Richard Odom and Douglas Odom Jr., board members and former chairmen.

Manufacturing and Distribution | 145

This leading designer and manufacturer of filtration products and exhaust systems for diesel- and gasoline-powered equipment has an impressive global presence. After nearly half a century in business, today it has more than 5,500 employees, 22 manufacturing plants, and 16 distribution centers across six continents.

Above: A leader and innovator in filtration, Cummins Filtration offers products that are used all over the world.

Headquartered in Nashville, Tennessee, Cummins Filtration is a global specialist in filtration products, chemicals, and exhaust systems for diesel- and gasoline-powered engines. This company's market segments include the on-highway trucking, agriculture, construction, oil and gas, mining, and marine industries.

To meet the needs of these industries, Cummins Filtration employs more than 5,500 people in 22 production plants and 16 distribution centers on six continents.

Industry Innovation

Cummins Filtration began in 1958 as the Seymour Filter Company of Seymour, Indiana, with two employees making cloth-bag oil filters for Cummins diesel engines. Within a year, the company grew to meet market demands for quality filters and filtration products. In 1963, the company introduced its Fleetguard® brand. Five years later, it moved production from Indiana to Cookeville, Tennessee. In 1989, the company established its global headquarters in Nashville, Tennessee.

Cummins Filtration has always developed products to increase vehicle uptime, minimize environmental impact, optimize diesel engine performance, and lower operating costs. Among its significant technological advancements are combination full-flow/bypass filtration and multilayered StrataPore™ media.

The company has more than 200 global patents for its award-winning product technology. For example, its Centriguard™ centrifugal filtration system and ConeStaC™ technology dramatically improve centrifugal filtration efficiency, and its new user-friendly lube and hydraulic filters are made from advanced composite polymers. This line of filters has been recognized by leading industry publications as one of the most innovative products released in 2006.

Continually investing in research and development tools and capabilities, Cummins Filtration uses technology such as a scanning electron microscope and engine test cells. It equips its

146 | PORTRAITS OF SUCCESS Profiles of Companies and Organizations

laboratories with commercial testing machines that provide real-world results.

Products and Market Scope

Cummins Filtration markets dependable products for trucks (heavy, medium, and light), industrial equipment, power generation, and small-engine applications. According to MacKay & Company, an independent market researcher focused on commercial vehicles and construction and farm equipment, Cummins Filtration ranks number one in worldwide market share and brand preference of commercial diesel engine filtration. It also has the top North American market share for commercial diesel exhaust systems and small-engine exhaust and air filtration.

Cummins Filtration offers the broadest product coverage in the industry—more than 12,000 filtration, exhaust, and chemical products. From the intake to the exhaust, Cummins Filtration provides quality component solutions, including air-intake systems, coolant, lube and fuel filters, fuel processors, oil water separators, mufflers, exhaust stacks, crankcase ventilation systems, clamps, tubes, and hoses.

Overall, Cummins Filtration serves hundreds of global original equipment manufacturers (OEMs), more than 15,000 dealer and distributor outlets, and tens of thousands of end users. Whether products are private labeled or bear one of this company's two brand names—Fleetguard and Universal Silencer™—customers depend on Cummins Filtration to protect their equipment and the environment.

Dependability, Service, and Community

Beyond the point of sale, every Cummins Filtration product is supported by a warranty that is among the industry's best. The Cummins Filtration warranty protects each product from the point of purchase throughout its recommended life span.

Cummins Filtration also has a worldwide network of customer assistance centers. The company's service engineering staff helps customers troubleshoot equipment problems, preventing costly downtime. These specialists have the expertise in filtration and exhaust systems to answer any question or help solve any problem.

Beyond service and quality, Cummins Filtration is committed to its employees, customers, and communities. It contributes to many programs focusing on youth and education, equity, economic development, community development, and arts and culture. Each year, at each company location, a committee of employees picks projects to support through monetary contributions and volunteerism.

Says Pamela Carter, president, "As a worldwide leader in filtration, exhaust, coolant, and chemical technology, with customers in over 174 countries on six continents, Cummins Filtration practices our core system of values in every community in which we do business. At the center of these values is to always do what is right—for our customers, suppliers, employees, and anyone with whom we interact. We strive to maintain a great place to work through principles of diversity, respect, training, community involvement, and human dignity."

Above: Pamela Carter is president of Cummins Filtration. Left: The company offers more than 5,000 exhaust products, from mufflers to industrial silencers.

This manufacturer of premium, stylish luggage, business cases, accessories, and personal leather items—proudly based in Lebanon, Tennessee—has been guided by its founder's philosophy 'to build luggage so fine it will stand as a symbol of excellence' since 1877.

Right: From totes and Mobile Travelers™ to Woodbox Pullman suitcases, The Wings® Collection, a refined, graceful collection from Hartmann®, is designed with modern functionality to withstand the harsh realities of today's travel landscape and still maintain its polished appeal. The collection's combination of craftsmanship and artistry makes for one of the most sophisticated and enduring luggage collections in the world. Above, far right: Carried by President George W. Bush, the Hartmann attaché represents the pinnacle of Hartmann's design and craftsmanship. These attachés are built for those who demand the finest in American luxury.

One of America's oldest and most respected manufacturers of high quality luggage, Hartmann, Inc. produces fine leather goods that are as durable as they are stylish. The company's products, which are often handed down from one generation to another, include wheeled, hardsided, and carry-on luggage, garment bags, briefcases, tote bags, wallets, and other leather travel accessories and gifts. Sold in the United States and internationally, Hartmann's products are available through fine department stores and specialty luggage shops as well as at www.hartmann.com.

The company's luggage, built by hand, undergoes rigorous testing to guarantee that products will stand up to the demands of travel. The tumble test, handle test, wheel test, and three-point test are all designed to simulate harsh baggage-handling conditions as well as repeated pressure on parts that receive the most wear and tear. Products that pass these tests are certified as reaching the Hartmann Standard, and are only then made available to customers.

Hartmann was founded in Racine, Wisconsin, by Bavarian immigrant Joseph S. Hartmann, who started out making trunks and Pullmans for steamship and railway travel. As travel changed over the years, the company developed new products to fit each era's needs. Small, fashionable suitcases were developed for the aircraft travel that blossomed in the 1930s. In 1939, the company's innovations included the development of its own industrial-strength Belting Leather, a strong, durable leather made from steer hide tanned in natural extracts instead of harsh chemicals, giving it superior abrasion resistance and a luxurious appearance.

Product development continued to reflect the times and fuel the company's growth. During the 1950s, Hartmann's distribution base quadrupled; company headquarters and plant facilities were moved to their present home in Lebanon, Tennessee. In the 1960s, the company began designing fashionable luggage for female customers, who represented 80 percent of luggage sales. In the 1970s, Hartmann introduced the three-piece luggage wardrobe, called "the 747 Carry-ons." As business and leisure travel increased over the years, the company created luggage and travel gear to accommodate increased and different demands.

In 2007, Hartmann celebrates 130 years of making the world's finest luggage, business cases, and personal leather accessories. Craftsmanship, quality, functionality, and fashionable styling have become hallmarks of each item that bears the Hartmann name. Today, as in the past, design and innovation, product performance, and superior craftsmanship continue to inspire the creation of new products.

For additional information, visit the Hartmann, Inc. Web site at www.hartmann.com.

Quality Industries, Inc.

With an outstanding track record that spans more than 30 years, this full-service precision metal fabrication company—proudly established and headquartered in Tennessee—combines hard-tool and soft-tool capabilities to produce cost-competitive, high quality products.

Quality Industries, Inc. is probably the only metal fabrication company that was hatched from a bucket of Kentucky Fried Chicken. In 1972, company founders Robert and Georgianna Russell worked with Colonel Harland Sanders to create special stainless-steel breading tables and tumbling marinators for Kentucky Fried Chicken outlets. Building upon this early success, Quality Industries—in less than two years—expanded its production to include truck component parts for PACCAR Inc., the worldwide manufacturer of trucks under the Kenworth, Peterbilt, DAF, and Foden nameplates.

Since then, Quality Industries has continued to succeed, evolve, and diversify, while always maintaining its two charter customers. Over its 30-plus-year history, Quality Industries has built its reputation on precision metal fabrication, meticulous finishing capabilities, and quality assembly services.

Today, Quality Industries is a full-service metal fabrication company that provides quality component parts, subassemblies, and complete product assemblies to a growing customer base. Located in LaVergne, Tennessee, just outside Nashville, Quality Industries employs more than 700 people in its 250,000-square-foot manufacturing facility.

Overall, Quality Industries has extensive experience in fabricating aluminum, stainless, carbon, and specialty steels. Yet, unlike many metal fabricators, Quality Industries is unique in its ability to combine hard-tool and soft-tool capabilities with both sheet and extrusion metals. The end products are consistently functional, cosmetically superior, and cost competitive.

In addition to manufacturing and selling food-service equipment, Quality Industries fabricates and assembles parts for a variety of products including heavy trucks, electrical enclosures, engineered aluminum structures, alternative fuel heating equipment, and custom fabrications and assemblies. Many of these products have specific certification requirements and have finishes that must meet high standards for appearance and cleanliness.

Quality Industries maintains an aggressive internal system to monitor its manufacturing process and to ensure that it operates in accordance with ISO technical specifications for the automotive industry. It employs lean manufacturing techniques and Six Sigma methodology to maximize efficiency and utilize core competencies in product design and cost containment as well as effective manufacturing processes.

Beyond its focus on quality and precision fabrication, Quality Industries maintains a proactive position in environmental and safety compliance, often setting the pace for other companies. For example, Quality Industries deliberately avoids hazardous processes that use heavily chlorinated solvents and heavy metal pretreatments.

This company's attention to quality has not gone unnoticed. In 2005, Quality Industries received an Excellence in Manufacturing Award from the Nashville Area Chamber of Commerce. In 2006, Quality Industries was recognized by the *Nashville Business Journal* as one of the top 100 employers in Greater Nashville.

Fred Appel, Quality Industries' president and CEO, affirms, "Our people are the key to our success. As a team, we work together to provide products and services that meet or exceed the expectations of our customers. Our continued success depends upon—and is ensured by—our ability to improve the quality, cost, and timeliness of our process and services."

Above left: Quality Industries, Inc. manufactures a wide variety of intricate metal parts and assemblies at its 250,000-square-foot Tennessee facility.

150 | PORTRAITS OF SUCCESS Profiles of Companies and Organizations

PROFILES OF COMPANIES AND ORGANIZATIONS
Pet Care

A winning, people-centered culture, a commitment to top customer service, and a passion for the good health and well-being of dogs and cats has made Mars Petcare U.S. a leading pet food marketer and manufacturer, a scientific authority on pet nutrition, a research and development innovator, and a trusted partner for customers.

The love for dogs and cats is big business at Mars Petcare U.S. The things that are most important to pets are top priority for Mars Petcare associates. Mars Petcare has a passion for creating and managing the top pet food products in its market segments. Not only does the company have a reputation of being a "trusted partner of choice" among its customers for quality pet foods, it is a staple of influence in innovation, in pet nutrition, and in research that has been acknowledged by the Waltham Center for Pet Nutrition, earning Mars Petcare a reputation as a leading scientific authority in pet nutrition among pet owners, breeders, veterinarians, and academics worldwide.

Headquartered in the Nashville, Tennessee, area, Mars Petcare U.S. is a leading manufacturer of dry pet food and pet snacks and treats in the United States and is owned by parent company Mars, Incorporated. One of the largest privately held companies in the world, Mars, Incorporated operates in more than 65 countries. Mars Petcare U.S. has 28 pet food manufacturing facilities across the United States.

Happy Customers Make Satisfied Consumers

Customers come first at Mars Petcare—they are the company's main focus. By providing unequaled support to its customers, and by establishing and maintaining consistently high standards in its advanced manufacturing facilities, Mars Petcare is able to deliver top-selling brands to customers and also to pass on efficient solutions through its distribution network. The company's expansive logistics network creates a flexible supply chain that allows the business to rapidly respond to changes in demand and emerging customer needs. This results in a timely product-delivery schedule in which products spend less time on shelves and take up minimal floor space. It also reduces the amount of manpower required for general operations, thus increasing productivity and decreasing costs compared to other delivery systems.

Teamwork Is Key to Success

Offering unlimited associate opportunities and a culture that promotes individual growth and team success, Mars Petcare understands that teamwork is a key element of the framework in which it operates. The company values its associates' engagement and insights, and collaborates with them about ideas, systems, processes, and strategies, which in turn strengthens the very core of the business.

Associates adhere to a strong set of values and are committed to the Mars Five Principles of operations. These principles—quality, responsibility, mutuality, efficiency, and freedom—make up the Mars culture. Coupled with an intentional focus on innovation and customers, these principles greatly benefit Mars teams and enable Mars Petcare to capture a large and growing market share.

Long History of Innovation

Since Frank C. Mars started the company in 1911 in the candy market, Mars, Incorporated has set standards for innovative marketing, advertising, and manufacturing. His original idea—to produce a protective candy coating—was the start of a solid company. Eventually, the company expanded into other food industries, which in turn led it into the pet food industry, where Mars, Incorporated continues to deliver marketing innovation by pioneering modern manufacturing techniques.

During the 20th century, Mars, Incorporated became a global provider of high quality foods. The company brought its expertise to the pet food marketplace when it acquired Chappel Brothers, Ltd. in 1935. More than 70 years later, Mars Petcare U.S. is an industry leader in pet foods and a scientific authority on pet nutrition, and has positioned itself to excel in and lead every pet care sector in which it operates.

Mars Petcare U.S. Brands

Mars Petcare provides many industry-leading petcare products, including the number one dog food, Pedigree®; as well as other top-selling national brands in the wet, dry, and treats categories, including Aquarian®, Royal Canin®, Sheba®, Cesar®, The Goodlife Recipe®, and Whiskas®. Mars brings its strong history and innovative marketing skills to each of its products and works to continually develop teams that create marketplace innovations.

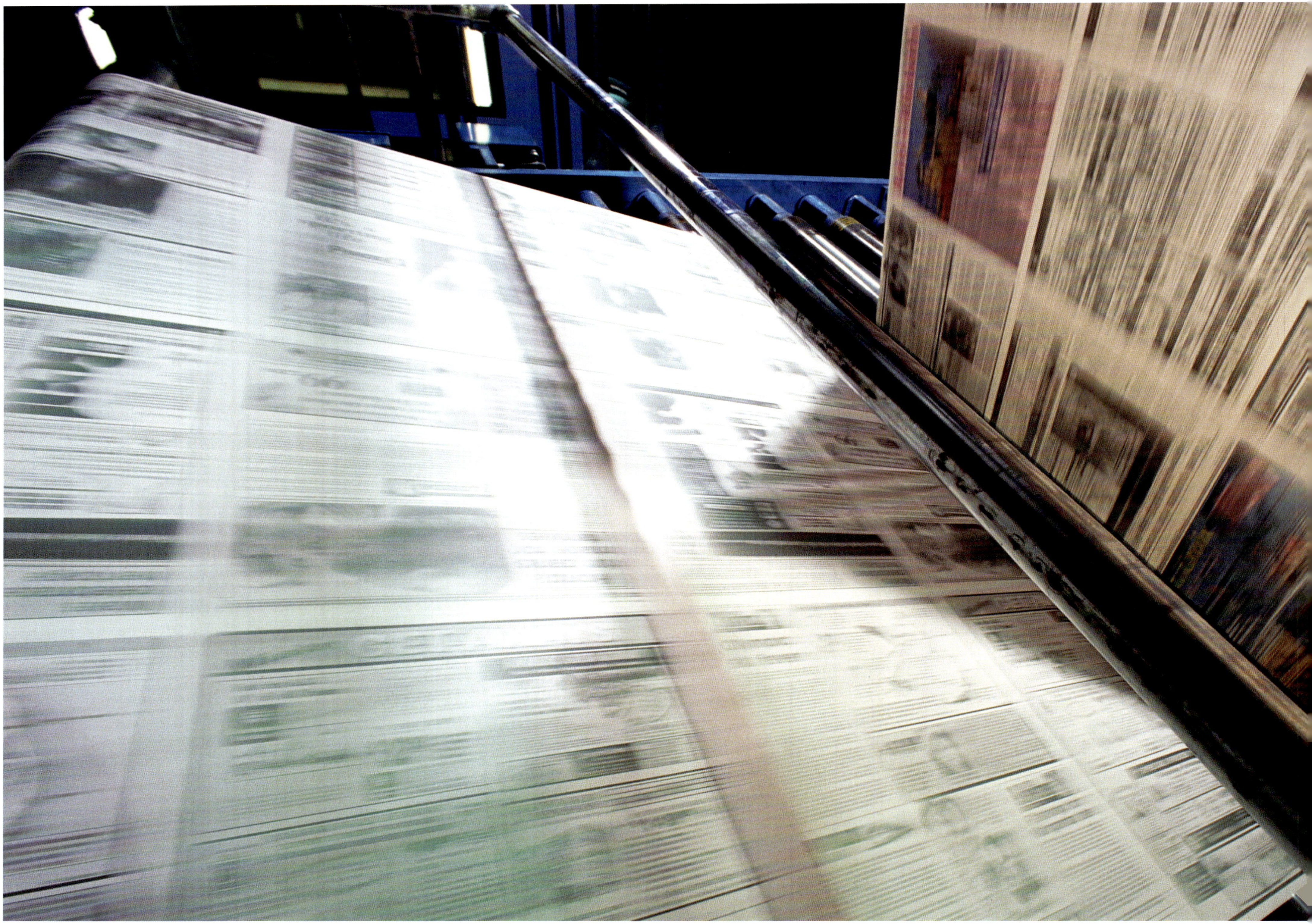

PROFILES OF COMPANIES AND ORGANIZATIONS
Printing and Publishing

This nonprofit Nashville, Tennessee–based institution, started by a driven, visionary Baptist pastor in 1891, has become a mighty force for evangelism, an international ministry, and a revered publisher of Bibles and Christian literature.

Above: One LifeWay Plaza in Nashville is home to 1,400 full-time and part-time employees of LifeWay Christian Resources.

J. M. Frost started small and dreamed big. In 1891, the 43-year-old pastor had a desk in a corner of a newspaper office and a little money that he borrowed from his wife. With the Southern Baptist Convention's approval, he launched what is today one of the world's largest providers of Christian resources—Bibles, church literature, books, music, audio and video recordings, church supplies, and Internet services.

LifeWay Christian Resources, originally the Sunday School Board, began in Nashville publishing Sunday school literature. Today, LifeWay ministries touch lives throughout the United States and the world. An entity of the Southern Baptist Convention, nonprofit LifeWay receives no funding from the denomination and reinvests income above operating expenses in mission work and ministries around the world.

LifeWay people are committed to the company's vision: "As God works through us, we will help people and churches know Jesus Christ and seek His Kingdom by providing biblical solutions that spiritually transform individuals and cultures." LifeWay's presence in Nashville is substantial, with

- more than one million square feet of office, retail, parking, conference, and warehouse space, covering 14.6 acres;
- 1,400 full-time and part-time employees;
- a warehouse on 44 acres in nearby Lebanon and LifeWay Christian Stores in downtown Nashville, Cool Springs, Murfreesboro, and Hendersonville;
- the LifeWay Community Fund, which supports 10 charities in Middle Tennessee; and
- employees involved in the ministry of scores of area churches.

LifeWay directs its ministries through six divisions:

- Church Resources consults with churches and delivers biblical solutions in many ministries and age-group products—Sunday school, Vacation Bible School, leadership development, evangelism, discipleship, music, worship, marriage, and parenting. Solutions include training, enrichment, and resources in print and on CDs, DVDs, and the Internet.

- LifeWay Christian Stores operates more than 130 retail outlets in two dozen states, serving Southern Baptists and the wider evangelical market. The division also serves customers via its Web site (www.lifewaystores.com).

- B&H Publishing Group produces Bibles, books, audio and video products, and church supplies, selling to bookstores and other retailers. The *Holman Christian Standard Bible,* introduced in 2004, quickly became one of the best-selling Bibles in the country for its accuracy and readability.

156 | PORTRAITS OF SUCCESS Profiles of Companies and Organizations

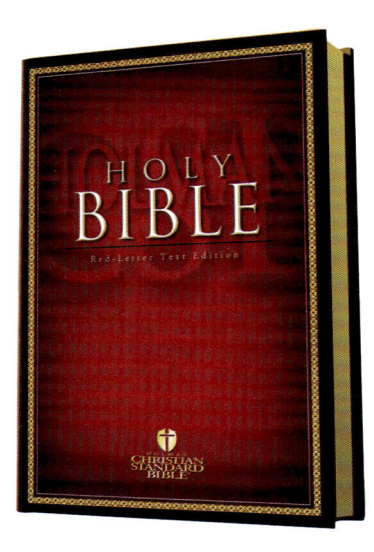

- Corporate Affairs operates conference centers at Ridgecrest, North Carolina, and at Glorieta, New Mexico; handles LifeWay's corporate communications; and raises money through a capital resource development office.

- The Technology division provides five key technology services for LifeWay: strategic; retail; business; enterprise; and Internet technologies, including MyBibleStudy.com, an online resource for Bible teachers and students.

- Finance and Business Services, responsible for LifeWay's financial policies and general accounting, directs many key LifeWay business services—legal, investments, purchasing, real estate, strategic planning, corporate services, and human resources.

The company's international department trains leaders around the world and makes LifeWay products available in many languages. The department also coordinates LifeWay-sponsored, employee-led mission trips. From 1997 through 2005, LifeWay sent more than 800 employees, retirees, and volunteers on 50 mission trips to 30 countries, resulting in 70,000 professions of faith and 200 new church starts.

Finally, LifeWay Research was launched early in 2006 with the goal of becoming the premier Christian research organization in the world. The new organization will help churches become "breakout churches," understanding and impacting the culture for Christ.

Leading LifeWay is President Thom Rainer, the company's ninth chief executive. "From humble beginnings, LifeWay has grown into an international ministry by staying true to our vision of helping people and churches know Jesus Christ," says Rainer. "Nashville is our home—and a wonderful home it is. But the world is our field of labor, and we are passionate about sharing the Gospel and providing biblically sound resources that exalt our Savior and encourage His followers."

Above left: LifeWay employees celebrate the grand opening of a LifeWay Christian Store in Abilene, Texas. LifeWay people are dedicated to making each of the company's more than 130 retail outlets a spiritual oasis for customers. Above right: Beth Moore is one of LifeWay's most popular authors and speakers. Her "Living Proof Live" events, like this one in Indianapolis, attract thousands of women seeking a deeper understanding of Scripture and a more intimate fellowship with Christ. Left: The *Holman Christian Standard Bible* has become one of America's best-selling, most-trusted translations, valued for its accuracy and readability.

Printing and Publishing | 157

Founded as National Baptist Publishing Board more than a century ago, this global publishing concern became a leader in the printing and publishing of Christian literature and religious materials for the African-American market. Four generations of the Boyd family have led the company, each advancing its growth and success.

The R. H. Boyd Publishing Corporation has flourished for more than 110 years, becoming an internationally renowned producer of Christian education materials and a leading producer of religious literature and church supplies for the African-American market. A global name in publishing, it is more than a company; it is a tradition.

R. H. Boyd, a former slave who dared to dream of starting a publishing company, founded the National Baptist Publishing Board (NBPB) in 1896. By 1906, NBPB—today known as the R. H. Boyd Publishing Corporation—had become America's largest black publishing concern.

Success continued under the leadership of R. H. Boyd's son, Dr. Henry Allen Boyd, who took the helm in 1922. By 1934, the company was servicing 20,000 Sunday schools and 8,000 churches. It had published more than 20 different hymnals, as well as music books, Christian education materials, church supplies, and doctrinal resources for ministers and Christian workers. Also under Henry Allen Boyd, the National Baptist Sunday School & Baptist Training Union Congress turned into the major African-American religious event it is today.

Henry's nephew, Dr. T. B. Boyd Jr., assumed leadership of the company in 1959, ushering in a period of innovation and tremendous business growth. Under his leadership, operations modernized and doubled in size, and the company began shipping its literature overseas. One of his greatest accomplishments was completing, in 1974, a million-dollar, ultra-modern facility for publishing and printing. This facility is still located on Centennial Boulevard in Nashville.

In 1979, Dr. T. B. Boyd III was appointed president and CEO, becoming the youngest person in company history to attain those offices. T. B. Boyd III also became chairman of the board of the Citizens Savings and Trust Company, another business that R. H. Boyd helped create. Established in 1904, this savings bank and trust company is the oldest one in America that is owned and operated by African-Americans. During T. B. Boyd III's tenure, the company has developed the new enterprise that honors its founder—the R. H. Boyd Publishing Corporation. Restructured for the new millennium, the corporation provides greater opportunities to publish material that expands the corporate listings of titles in the areas of family, education, and history.

R. H. Boyd Publishing Corporation specializes in developing contemporary Christian education materials that provide positive African-American

Right: The R. H. Boyd Publishing Corporation was founded in 1896. The original bindery is shown in this historic photograph.

imagery and nurturing Christian values for churches and families. The corporation markets a complete range of religious products, including Sunday school literature, Vacation Bible School ministry materials, leadership development and small-group ministry aids, and the renowned *New National Baptist Hymnal* and updated *New National Baptist Hymnal 21st Century*, both worldwide best-selling collections of Christian music.

Publishing and printing these products position the corporation to take advantage of product development and marketing relationships with other major publishers and distributors. It has truly become one of those rare institutions that effectively caters to all the needs of its customers worldwide.

Over the past 100-plus years, the R. H. Boyd legacy has involved four generations of leadership. The Boyd family's innovative, prudent, energetic, and charismatic leadership has driven the success of this publishing company. Unique to the industry, it dually operates as a publisher and printer, and it has excelled and grown phenomenally over 100 years. It remains committed to furnishing the finest literature penned by African-Americans. As a family legacy, the company maintains a spirit of excellence and achievement that will serve many generations to come.

Far left: The R. H. Boyd Publishing Corporation operates a state-of-the-art facility in Nashville.

Left: Four generations of the Boyd family have run the R. H. Boyd Publishing Corporation (from left to right): Richard Henry (R. H.) Boyd, from 1896 until 1922; Dr. T. B. Boyd III, from 1979 until present; Dr. Henry Allen Boyd, from 1922 until 1959; and Dr. T. B. Boyd Jr., from 1959 until 1979.

Printing and Publishing | 159

The United Methodist Publishing House

For more than 215 years, this publishing house has offered programs and resources that help more people in more places come to know God through Jesus Christ, to learn to love God, and to choose to serve God and neighbor. The company is a publisher and retailer to all Christian congregations, their leaders, and their members.

Above left: The United Methodist Publishing House (UMPH) operates 70 Cokesbury Christian Stores across the country, offering resources for the clergy, congregations, and Bible study, including its own and other publishers' titles.

Above right: UMPH publishes books, music, and more, distributing materials in print, on CD and DVD, and online, under the imprints Abingdon Press, Cokesbury, Kingswood Books, and Dimensions for Living.

The United Methodist Publishing House (UMPH) was established in Philadelphia in 1789. Its Nashville operation was opened as the publishing house for the Methodist Episcopal Church South in 1854. At the time, UMPH was located on the Public Square, just north of the City Hotel. In 1906, UMPH was moved from the Public Square to a new building at 810 Broadway Avenue, which also housed this publishing company's retail store. UMPH's current building, located at Eighth Avenue and Demonbreun Street was completed in 1957. Proud of its deep community roots and significant contributions, UMPH is the third-oldest business in Nashville.

Publishing Imprints

UMPH publishes books, music, and other materials, including new works each year, and distributes its titles in print, on CD and DVD, and online, under the imprints Abingdon Press, Cokesbury, Kingswood Books, and Dimensions for Living. UMPH publications include a wide selection of Sunday school curriculum, vacation Bible school programs, professional and academic books for clergy and higher education settings, and resources for every aspect of congregational life and ministry.

Retail Reach

Cokesbury Christian Stores, the retail arm of UMPH, operates 70 stores across the United States, including stores in theological seminaries of various denominations. Cokesbury stocks products published by a wide variety of publishers in order to serve a vast array of churches. Cokesbury's resources and services include Bibles, worship aids, furniture and equipment, church library services, and church and Sunday school supplies.

Financial Contributions

UMPH annual sales top $110 million. The enterprise is fully self-supporting and, as part of its mission, it contributes to United Methodist clergy pensions each year, having given nearly $50 million since 1941. In recent years, a large portion of UMPH's annual $1 million contribution has been designated to provide pensions for clergy in Africa, the Philippines, and Eastern Europe.

"Wherever people gather in Christian fellowship," states President and Publisher Neil M. Alexander, "our aspiration is to provide resources and services so that each congregation will be a more vibrant and faithful center for Christian worship, witness, and service to the world, and for making disciples of Jesus Christ."

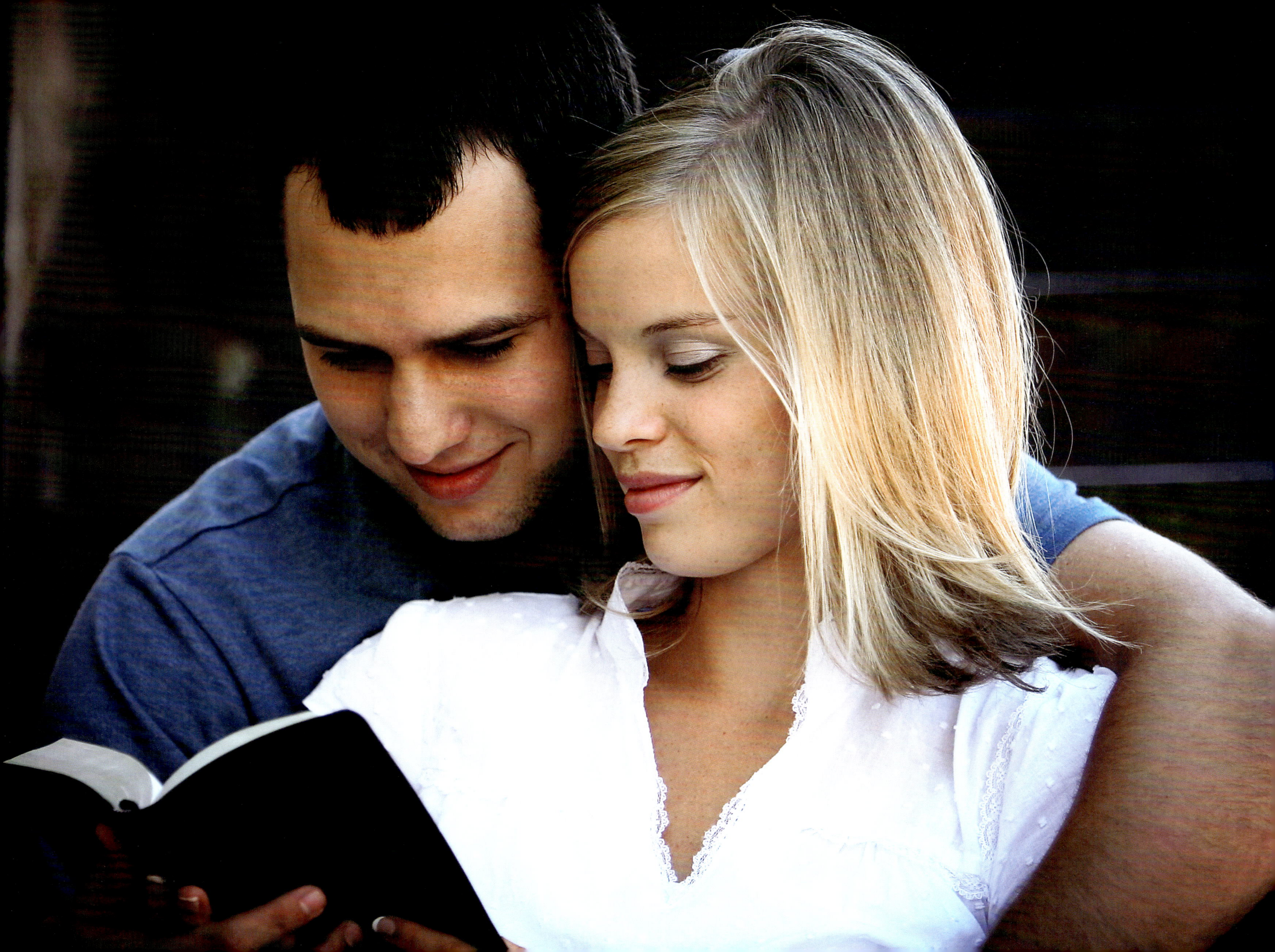

162 | PORTRAITS OF SUCCESS Profiles of Companies and Organizations

PROFILES OF COMPANIES AND ORGANIZATIONS
Professional and Business Services

This growing Tennessee-based company provides businesses with staffing, human resources outsourcing, and manufacturing process outsourcing services that are invaluable for gaining a competitive edge and achieving goals in operational improvements and cost-savings.

When Jim Holland founded The Holland Group in 1991, he intended to make a difference in the staffing services industry. His experience as a human resources (HR) executive who frequently called upon staffing firms to fill position openings had often left him feeling that there must be a better way. From his personal experience, he assessed ways in which staffing firms could improve, and then he started a company in Murfreesboro, Tennessee, that grew to offer full-service HR outsourcing.

By providing custom-tailored solutions that focused on the specific needs of each client, the company gained a competitive edge within its industry, which led to steady growth and development. As more services were offered, such as process management, additional offices were opened throughout the central and southern United States.

Today, The Holland Group still approaches staffing from an HR perspective, providing valuable insights and assistance for a client's business and often improving its procedures. The company operates 57 locations throughout Kentucky, Mississippi, North Carolina, South Carolina, Ohio, Oklahoma, and Tennessee, with headquarters in Murfreesboro. The Holland Group is a leader in the HR and process management industry, specializing in large workforces, process design and management, and workforce training and development.

The company is committed to providing clients with a competitive advantage by enabling them to achieve process improvement and cost-savings goals. It applies Six Sigma methodology—a disciplined, data-driven approach designed to eliminate defects—to define, measure, analyze, improve, and maintain the level of quality in a business's processes.

Hiring, Training, and Managing Workforces

To help clients realize the highest return on their staffing dollar, The Holland Group hires, trains, and manages large workforces, scaling a staff up or down as needed. The advantages of the company's staffing services include solutions custom-designed to address the client's needs; techniques for targeted selections; job candidate screening processes that lead to increased performance and decreased turnover; staffing efficiency that results in reduced cost per hire; a thorough knowledge of compliance issues; an experienced senior management team; and speed of execution in mobilizing the right people with the right skills at the right time.

Maximizing Investment in Human Capital

The Holland Group's human resources outsourcing (HRO) services are in demand by executives who are responsible for developing new human resources (HR) strategies or for transferring existing programs from one location to another. The HR division also specializes in recruitment process outsourcing (RPO), training process outsourcing (TPO), and HR consulting. RPO includes handling all phases of the hiring process from requisition to hire for all employee levels, from hourly to executive. TPO includes training design, delivery, and administration; new-hire orientation; technical and compliance training; and leadership development. HR consulting includes HR auditing; policies, procedures, and handbook creation; legal compliance; organizational development; and day-to-day human resources management.

The company draws from its many qualified professionals to assemble a dedicated team for each project. The Holland Group's formula for success rests on the shoulders of many accomplished staff members, including a

Right: Jim Holland, president and CEO of The Holland Group, founded the company based on his experience in management with large businesses. The company maintains office and on-site locations in Kentucky, Mississippi, North Carolina, South Carolina, Oklahoma, Ohio, and Tennessee.

Recognition of Accomplishments

The American Staffing Association listed The Holland Group as the 88th-largest U.S. staffing firm in 2005.

Business TN magazine named The Holland Group number 94 in its Top 125 Private Companies in 2006.

Music City Future 50 named The Holland Group one of the 50 fastest-growing companies in Nashville in 2003.

Nashville Business Journal named The Holland Group number 55 in its list of Middle Tennessee's Largest Private Companies in 2006.

---

project team dedicated and committed to meeting the client's timeline; on more than 15 years of HR experience in legal compliance; and on seasoned professionals with distinctive HR experience in a variety of fields, including process management, finance, operations, and training in both union and nonunion environments.

Running a Business within a Business

Many clients rely on The Holland Group for manufacturing process outsourcing (MPO) services that reach beyond recruiting, staffing, and relocation management. They trust the company to assume full responsibility for the manufacturing process for some or all of their products. The Holland Group takes charge of all aspects of manufacturing, including needs assessment; plans for production, human capital, and support functions and service agreements; continual process improvement; and delivery of reports to the client.

For example, when a major tire manufacturer began its MPO relationship, The Holland Group took on the task of producing tires at a guaranteed quality level within a guaranteed delivery schedule for a guaranteed price. Highly satisfied with the results, the manufacturer turned to The Holland Group again when it decided to outsource two additional facilities' manufacturing and eventually to staff an entire new facility.

After studying the client's business, The Holland Group's project team began total management of the facilities—from hiring employees as needed, to training some 300 workers, to overseeing the quality, safety, and productivity level of each operation. After just two weeks, all quality and production standards were exceeded ahead of schedule. By outsourcing these tasks, the tire maker's managers and executives gained time to concentrate on other core objectives.

Building for the Future

The Holland Group continues to develop products that offer innovative solutions in the areas of staffing, HR, and manufacturing process outsourcing. Businesses can depend on Holland's valuable insight, planning, communication, and execution to reduce staffing costs and gain higher returns on their investment. Constantly driven by its clients' needs, Holland is entering additional industries in every state of the country and further supporting growth by building an international presence.

The Holland Group
Holland Employment
Holland Outsourcing

237 West Northfield Boulevard, Suite 200
Murfreesboro, Tennessee 37129
Phone: 615-890-9895 or 800-840-8367
Fax: 615-895-4251

www.hollandgroup.com

Above: The Holland Group's corporate office is located in Murfreesboro, Tennessee.

For more than 45 years, Randstad has worked diligently to help employers make better hiring decisions. The company has 23 locations in the Nashville area and is dedicated to delivering staffing solutions that keep businesses humming.

This page: Randstad USA provides 1,900 staffing professionals at 419 branch offices and client-dedicated locations to assist employers. Opposite page, left: The company puts some 48,500 people to work each week nationwide. Opposite page, right: Randstad's goal is to locate the best people to suit its clients' needs.

Matching the right person to the right job is an ongoing challenge for employers. Randstad USA, with 23 locations in the Nashville, Tennessee area, creates smart staffing solutions for its clients each and every day. Its approach is simple: "Deliver the right talent for the right job at the right time."

"Our business is all about the people," says Laquita Stribling, district manager for Randstad in Nashville. "People make work happen, and we simply provide the right people to fill jobs of all types, from clerical to technical, from industrial to professional."

What Makes Randstad Different

Randstad continues to meet the growing demand for greater workforce productivity and flexibility by focusing on its strategy for success: Provide strategic staffing solutions to businesses, while offering a wide variety of opportunities to talented job candidates. When client companies and job candidates work with Randstad, they benefit from Randstad's more than 45 years of building and perfecting its services and staying ahead of workforce trends through continual innovation.

Randstad attracts top business, industrial, and creative talent by offering the best benefits packages in the staffing industry. Job candidates are then assessed by professional agents who know the local Nashville business environment, including its employers and workforce demographics. Randstad candidates have their choice of work opportunities, from short-term and long-term assignments to contract engagements to permanent-placement opportunities.

Just attracting the best talent is not enough for Randstad, which also strives to retain the best talent by nurturing and supporting eligible talent through skills assessments, career counseling, skills-enhancement training, health and dental insurance coverage, paid vacation time, and generous employer contributions to a 401(k) plan.

"Randstad is committed to serving the needs of Nashville's workforce. Our company's mission is to provide rewarding employment opportunities, career guidance, and enough flexibility to allow time to enjoy what life has to offer," Stribling says.

good to know you™

Randstad professional agents make the best matches by merging a thorough understanding of client needs with a detailed assessment of talents' skills. Methodical fact-finding with clients results in a deep understanding of their company's business environment; and rigorous testing of talent evaluates skill sets, experience, and expertise. The combination is designed to lead to a perfect match.

'Good to Know You'

"Randstad's values are summarized through our 'good to know you' philosophy," says Stribling. "At Randstad, 'good to know you' is both our greeting and our guarantee based on our core values—our way of working, our unique agent system, and our in-depth knowledge of employment issues and trends."

The professional agents at each Randstad Nashville–area location devise staffing solutions for their clients and also provide service for them, working with a 360-degree view of both the clients who need talent and with the talent that meets those needs. Its agents also are empowered to make the best decisions in their market specialty based on their knowledge of the local business environment. They work closely with Nashville-area contacts, employers, and recruiters. Many agents are members of local business organizations, furthering their professionalism and their area business contacts.

"Randstad is known among our clients for its commitment to its values—to know, serve, and trust," Stribling concludes. "Our business is the world of work, and our goal is to match our clients' workplace needs with the best people."

The strategy is successful. The employment experts in the Nashville area's Randstad offices put 2,230 people to work each week for a total annual payroll of $63 million in metropolitan Nashville and $231 million in Tennessee. Each Randstad office offers a pleasant, welcoming, professional environment. Clients as well as talent are invited to visit and to meet with the company's professional agents.

About Randstad

Headquartered in Atlanta, Georgia, Randstad USA is a wholly owned subsidiary of Randstad Holding nv, which is an $8.25 billion global provider of professional employment services based in Diemen, the Netherlands, and is one of the largest staffing organizations in the world.

In 2005, Randstad USA's 1,900 staffing professionals put 48,500 people to work in the United States each week through its 419 branches and client-dedicated locations. Randstad USA provides additional information on its Web site (www.randstad.com) about the company and its employment services.

Local Contacts

Randstad offers many convenient locations throughout the Nashville area, including

- West End—615-292-3816
- Donelson—615-316-0755
- Rivergate—615-868-9675
- Williamson County—615-771-2800
- Murfreesboro—615-893-3333
- Smyrna—615-355-3055
- Lebanon—615-449-7077
- Springfield—615-384-8048

A global leader in parking and parking-related services, this Nashville-headquartered company attributes its success to placing integrity and professionalism above all else. With these guiding principles, it is able to pursue aggressive expansion, excel at customer service, and value its employees.

Commitment to Integrity

Central Parking Corporation

Above: Central Parking Corporation's dedication to integrity is demonstrated by its corporate compliance program—"Commitment to Integrity." This comprehensive program includes a code of conduct, key compliance policies, training, and certification requirements.

The world's largest parking services company, Central Parking Corporation (CPC) owns, operates, or manages 1.4 million parking spaces at over 3,000 parking facilities. CPC also offers parking-related services including valet, parking meter collection and enforcement, shuttle bus operation, billing services, and parking consulting. The company's clients include some of the nation's largest owners and developers of mixed-use real estate projects, sports stadiums and arenas, retail centers, and major office buildings, hotels, and hospitals, as well as airports and government agencies. The mission of CPC is to operate a premier parking services company dedicated to integrity, professionalism, growth, value, leadership, and quality service.

Six core values form the foundation of success at CPC:

- unquestioned integrity in every aspect of business,
- a strong work ethic and a commitment to achieving results,
- a commitment to exceeding customer expectations,
- aggressive, persistent, and creative pursuit of opportunities,
- fiscally sound operations, and
- recognition of the importance of its people.

"When I founded the company in 1968, my vision was to create a different kind of parking company—a company based on the highest levels of customer service and professionalism with integrity as our number one value," says CPC chairman and founder Monroe J. Carell Jr.

Beginning with a single parking lot in Nashville, the company grew rapidly under Carell's leadership. CPC became a public company in 1995, and by 1997 annual revenues totaled $223 million and the company operated about 700,000 parking spaces. *Forbes* magazine ranked CPC as one of America's 200 Best Small Companies. CPC continued its expansion in the late 1990s through a series of acquisitions, culminating in the acquisition of the second-largest parking company in the United States, Allright Corporation. For the next several years, CPC focused on integrating these acquisitions.

In 2005, Emanuel J. Eads was named company CEO. A 32-year veteran of CPC, Eads has implemented a number of financial and strategic initiatives to focus the company on its core strengths and to build a platform for robust future growth. Since Eads' appointment, the company has repositioned its geographic footprint to focus on major markets with high growth potential. Additionally, the company has introduced its Operational

Excellence initiative, which is aimed at increasing revenues and reducing costs. Eads' strong leadership and strategic focus have positioned the company for growth and continued profitability.

Today, CPC provides parking and related services in 37 states, the District of Columbia, Canada, Puerto Rico, the United Kingdom, the Republic of Ireland, Chile, Colombia, Peru, Spain, Switzerland, Italy, and Greece.

CPC's dedication to integrity is demonstrated by the company's corporate compliance program, "Commitment to Integrity." This comprehensive program includes a code of conduct, key compliance policies, training, and certification requirements. CPC has also developed a Diversity Mission Statement to create an environment where people understand, value, and respect differences. Treating all employees with dignity and respect is at the heart of CPC culture. The company offers education and training programs to help employees learn and achieve. Executive education and leadership development programs are offered through major universities.

CPC and its employees participate in community outreach as well. Company and employee donations to United Way of Metropolitan Nashville made CPC one of only 32 companies to win that organization's Circle of Honor Award in 2003. Employees also raise funds by participating in walks sponsored by the American Diabetes Association and the American Heart Association. In addition, the company supports the Monroe Carell Jr. Children's Hospital at Vanderbilt in Nashville.

Central Parking Corporation continually seeks new ways to enhance its image and improve its ability to respond to customer needs. It is committed to never taking its customers for granted and considers that this dedication to service has enabled it to flourish in its industry. It has entered the 21st century with confidence and strength.

Above left: Central Parking Corporation (CPC)—"The worldwide parking professionals"—provides parking and related services in 37 U.S. states, the District of Columbia, and Puerto Rico, as well as in Canada, Chile, Colombia, Peru, the United Kingdom, the Republic of Ireland, Spain, Switzerland, Italy, and Greece.
Above right: The world's largest parking services company, CPC owns, operates, or manages 1.4 million parking spaces at more than 3,000 parking facilities, including, shown here, the Commerce Street Garage.

Professional and Business Services | 169

170 | PORTRAITS OF SUCCESS Profiles of Companies and Organizations

PROFILES OF COMPANIES AND ORGANIZATIONS
Real Estate Development and Construction Services

With numerous large projects completed in Nashville and other areas, this general contractor is a recognized leader in the construction industry, providing expertise in specific, specialized sectors and a dedication to exceptional service, 'Exceeding Expectations, Every Day!'

Above: One of Brasfield & Gorrie's notable projects is Roundabout Plaza, located at 1600 Division Street. This nine-story, 220,000-square-foot office building, with a seven-story parking deck, graces the top of Music Row in downtown Nashville.

Brasfield & Gorrie is one of the largest privately held contracting firms in the Southeast, and *Forbes* magazine ranks the company 276th among the nation's 500 Largest Private Companies. Established in 1921 as the Thomas C. Brasfield Company, the Brasfield & Gorrie of today was formed in 1964, when Miller Gorrie purchased Brasfield's construction assets and changed the company name in 1967 to Brasfield & Gorrie.

The year 1968 marked the completion of Brasfield & Gorrie's first multistory concrete project, which was to be the forerunner of hundreds of high-rise and other specialty concrete structures. Since then, Brasfield & Gorrie has grown steadily, opening full-service offices in Atlanta, Georgia, and Orlando, Florida, in 1985 and then adding offices in Raleigh, North Carolina, and Nashville in 1998.

Brasfield & Gorrie is a full-service general contracting, construction management, and design-build service provider. The company's experience is diverse, covering many sectors including health care, industrial, office, educational, institutional, retail, and water treatment facilities. In 2007 Brasfield & Gorrie is still led by founder Miller Gorrie and is a nationally ranked regional general contractor that employs over 3,000 people, with an annual construction volume of nearly $2 billion.

There are 21 operating divisions within Brasfield & Gorrie, which are organized to focus on specific, specialized construction markets. This structure enables the company to better serve the unique needs of clients in each sector; to build expertise among its project managers, estimators, and superintendents dedicated to those sectors; and to respond readily to shifts in the construction market. This strategy has made Brasfield & Gorrie a leader in many types of construction; the company is consistently listed among the nation's top contractors, and approximately 85 percent of its work is from repeat customers.

Brasfield & Gorrie made its mark in the Nashville area in 1991 with the construction of the BellSouth headquarters building downtown—Brasfield & Gorrie's first high-rise in Nashville—which became its signature building in the city. Completed in 1994, the building is referred to by some as the "Batman" building because it reminds them of the mask worn by Batman.

At the same time it was constructing the BellSouth building, Brasfield & Gorrie was building the Vanderbilt Stallworth Rehabilitation Hospital in Nashville. These projects, along with the opportunity for Brasfield & Gorrie to build the Caterpillar Financial Center in Nashville, led to the opening of Brasfield & Gorrie's Nashville office. The next big project for the Nashville office was the 2525 West End office

172 | PORTRAITS OF SUCCESS Profiles of Companies and Organizations

building, a fourteen-story structure with retail stores on the first two floors, and two parking garages. This was the third highly visible structure (along with the BellSouth and Caterpillar buildings) to be completed by Brasfield & Gorrie on Nashville's West End Avenue.

Soon, Brasfield & Gorrie received its first Hospital Corporation of America (HCA) project, a parking deck on HCA's main campus in Nashville. The success of the job led to a second HCA project—an expansion of the Colleton Medical Center near Charleston, South Carolina.

With Nashville's growth and the large number of major health care organizations that are headquartered in the city, the Brasfield & Gorrie Nashville office became home to two new company divisions—the Tennessee Commercial division and the Healthcare division—which have experienced considerable growth.

Completed Nashville projects in Brasfield & Gorrie's impressive portfolio include Roundabout Plaza, the Cool Springs III office building, Nashville Public Square, The Ensworth School, and the corporate headquarters for Country Music Television, Inc. (CMT). Notable projects under construction include, in Nashville, Adelicia, a condominium complex; the Encore residential tower; and the SunTrust Plaza office building; and in Cool Springs, Tennessee, the headquarters for Healthways.

Brasfield & Gorrie has a strong financial position. The company has completed an average of more than $1.18 billion in volume annually from 2001 through 2005, and it has $4.2 billion of work in progress or under contract, with an uncompleted backlog of $1.7 billion.

Brasfield & Gorrie has received impressive industry recognition. The company has been ranked by *Engineering News-Record* as the 28th among the nation's Top 400 Contractors, the 15th among the Top 50 in General Building, and the 7th among the Top 25 in Commercial Offices. It also was ranked number one among the nation's Healthcare General Contractors by *Modern Healthcare*.

The future for Brasfield & Gorrie looks exciting. Each of its offices has built a strong foundation throughout the Southeast, and the company is expanding its business every year. The diversity and scope of its projects continue to broaden the company's industry base. A high level of energy within Brasfield & Gorrie is felt throughout the company, which is well prepared to meet the challenges of the future. Its diversification along with its unique business structure enables Brasfield & Gorrie to respond well to cyclical geographic and market shifts in the construction business.

Brasfield & Gorrie continually seeks better ways to serve its clients. The company is dedicated to better serving not only its clients but also its communities, as well as, significantly, the people who make Brasfield & Gorrie more than simply a place to work—but indeed a rare team- and family-oriented experience.

Above left: Thanks to the work of Brasfield & Gorrie, Caterpillar Financial Center was able to consolidate its operations from four different sites to one site in Nashville—at its new 11-story, 330,000-square-foot office tower located on West End Avenue. This new structure also features a seven-story, 380,000-square-foot parking garage.

Above right: When MTV Networks relocated the headquarters of its Country Music Television, Inc. (CMT) division to downtown Nashville, Brasfield & Gorrie renovated 62,000 square feet of space for the new facility. CMT's new Nashville headquarters also features 18,000 square feet of production and technical areas.

Gould Turner Group, P.C.

In Nashville and nationwide, Gould Turner Group, P.C. is known for its architects' no-nonsense approach—their ability to strike a balance between creativity and practicality—in designing a variety of structures. Local projects include Palmer Plaza, One Belle Meade Place, The Bank of Nashville, and Croft Middle School.

Gould Turner Group, P.C. (GTG) specializes in health care architecture that is both functional and aesthetically compelling and has created beautiful, state-of-the-art facilities nationwide. Above left and center: Among GTG's notable projects is the Northwest Medical Center of Oro Valley—a 2006 ASHE Vista Partnering honorable mention winner—located in Oro Valley, Arizona. Above right: Another GTG stand-out is The Agility Center, which provides advanced neurological and musculoskeletal care, located in Bentonville, Arkansas.

Founded in 1980, Gould Turner Group, P.C. (GTG) is a Nashville-based, full-service architectural, planning, and interior design firm. Since its founding, this firm has acquired a national reputation for excellence in health care design and enjoys local recognition for a multitude of building types, including educational, public, and commercial facilities. Committed to designing buildings that are attractive and operationally efficient, GTG's architects work in collaboration with clients across the country and deliver to all their projects a variety of specialized talents and a depth of knowledge and experience.

Linda S. Marzialo, AIA, ACHA, a principal and the president of GTG, brings more than 30 years of experience to the company. Marzialo describes the firm's underlying philosophy: "Our role is to assist our clients in achieving their vision. We carefully listen to our clients in order to understand the challenges and opportunities they face, and work with them in partnership to provide unique solutions." Marzialo, who holds an American College of Healthcare Architects (ACHA) board certification, states that for health care design, this means helping GTG's clients to create facilities that provide a comforting, calming, healing environment for patients and families as well as a supportive workplace for staff.

Perfecting Evidence-Based Health Care Design

A successful example of GTG's medical facility design approach may be found in its design for the Northwest Medical Center of Oro Valley in Oro Valley, Arizona. This project was featured in the "Architectural Showcase" issue of *Healthcare Design* magazine in September 2005 and is an honorable mention winner of the 2006 prestigious ASHE (American Society for Healthcare Engineering) Vista Partnering award. This project embraces the evidence-based design ideology, which maintains that thoughtful design can produce positive measurable results to a facility's bottom line. Working closely with hospital staff, GTG incorporated such details as decentralized nursing stations to bring nurses closer to patients, wireless communication devices to lessen noise distractions, and views of nature and abundant day lighting to enhance patients' hospital experience. The result is a striking facility that boosts caregiver productivity, is operationally efficient, and champions patient healing and wellness.

Advancing Education

GTG brings to its educational clients innovative translations of their educational programs into architectural solutions that offer not only efficient and cost-effective school buildings but also facilities that are exciting and highly conducive to the learning process. Ted Stanton, a senior architect with GTG, notes, "We want our school buildings to play a key role in advancing the school's educational programs."

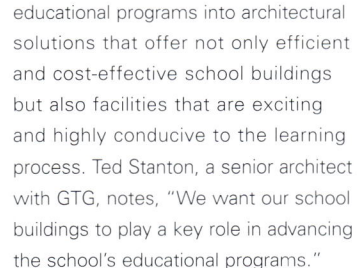

Croft Middle School in Nashville, Tennessee, exemplifies this concept. Sited adjacent to the Nashville Zoo at Grassmere, the school takes advantage of its exceptional location to highlight programs in natural history, biology, zoology, and conservation by featuring centers for "up close" animal encounters and exhibits under the supervision of zoo personnel. Demonstration centers in the facility are also available for use by other schools and by community groups.

Leading in Sustainability

GTG architects remain at the forefront of environmentally responsible and sustainable design. Members of the firm are LEED (Leadership in Energy and Environmental Design) accredited and are active in the U.S. Green Building Council. GTG's design for McKenzie-Willamette Medical Center, a new health care facility in Eugene, Oregon, is one of a limited number of new hospital designs in the nation to pursue LEED certification.

Ed Wansing, Director of Sustainability for GTG, explains the benefits of environmentally responsible design: "By focusing on water and energy efficiency, owners can expect to see long-lasting operational cost savings. Through the use of materials that contribute to good indoor air quality, we are able to create healthier interior environments for the building's occupants; and due to reduced environmental impact and increased open space, the entire community benefits when thoughtful consideration is given to the positioning of a building on its site."

Succeeding through Commitment

Throughout the design process, GTG principals and project architects maintain a hands-on design and delivery approach and remain active during each phase of the project. GTG architects and interior designers use their experience and knowledge to blend creativity with practicality. GTG manages every opportunity with the attitude of providing value and service to its clients. By developing long-term relationships with clients, Gould Turner Group, P.C. enjoys a high level of repeat business from a long list of satisfied customers.

Top left: GTG was honored with the 2006 IIDA (International Interior Design Association) award for health care interior design for its creation of the Swedish Southwest Urgent Care facility in Englewood, Colorado. Top center: GTG designed the illuminated canopy of Wesley Medical Center's Critical Care Tower in Wichita, Kansas, to act as a beacon to welcome visitors. Top right and above right: GTG's award-winning HealthCenter Northwest in Kalispell, Montana, successfully blends the high-tech of surgery and imaging services with the high-touch of soothing colors, natural materials, and day lighting. Below, both photos: GTG also designs innovative school facilities, including Croft Middle School (shown here) in Nashville, Tennessee. This school was the 2003 Tennessee School Board Association's first place winner in the middle school design category.

This awarding-winning, full-service firm—proudly headquartered in Nashville and with a national presence—offers a range of professional services. MJM Architects approaches all projects with its renowned professionalism, competence, and agility and is versatile enough to take on any project.

Above: This artist's rendering of a proposed mixed-use development to be located in downtown Nashville is among MJM Architects' most recent projects.

For more than 20 years, MJM Architects has been recognized as a top architectural firm that provides clients with award-winning design excellence and superior service. MJM is a full-service firm, offering architecture, engineering, site planning, and graphic design. In 2002, this firm relocated to a renovated grain warehouse located on Broadway in Nashville's vibrant Central Business District.

MJM calls upon its experience, skills, and talents to shepherd a project from concept to completion. With a staff of more than 45 professionals, including many licensed architects and engineers, this firm offers comprehensive, customized professional services with a focus on the retail industry, including specialty retailers, big box stores, regional open-air retail centers, and restaurants.

Growth, Innovation, and Honors

MJM is led by partners Robert S. Maxwell, Curtis R. Johanson, Stephen P. Maher, and Mathew B. Root, who have successfully and continually grown the firm by 25 percent annually. In 2005, the firm logged in excess of 300 projects. To remain competitive and provide additional value to its clients, MJM developed a digitally based project-management solution to manage internal documents and processes as well as an external module that enables clients to securely access project information and drawings.

For such success and innovation, MJM has been honored with awards from The American Institute of Architects and from *Chain Store Age* magazine. The firm has also been recognized by *Retail Construction Magazine* as one of the top 20 U.S. retail firms by volume. Most recently, ZweigWhite, management consultants for the architecture, engineering, and construction industries, identified MJM in 2006 as a top 20 architectural firm for which to work.

Notable Client and Community Partnerships

MJM's recognition by its clients is as strong as the firm's recognition by the industry. In fact, more than 80 percent of MJM's work comes from repeat clients and from relationships that have developed since the firm's founding. MJM considers itself fortunate to have worked with numerous clients for more than 15 years. Notably, for the Minneapolis, Minnesota–based Best Buy Co., Inc.—one of MJM's oldest clients—MJM has completed more than 200 projects, totaling 7 million square feet, in 26 U.S. states.

Also nationally, MJM has worked with the Seattle, Washington–based Starbucks Coffee Company on more than 400 projects, including the design and implementation of retail kiosks, store remodels, and ground-up stores. One of MJM's newest and most dynamic clients is the Pittsburgh, Pennsylvania–based Dick's Sporting Goods, Inc. Over the past four years, MJM has worked with this retailer in creating 27 stores in 16 states and in managing its two-story prototype. Additional MJM clients with a national presence include Bed Bath & Beyond Inc.; Lowe's; Panera Bread; PetSmart; Ross Stores, Inc.; Staples, Inc.; T.J.Maxx; and Tire Kingdom.

MJM has worked with many Nashville-based developers, including GBT Realty and Newton Oldacre McDonald. GBT Realty developed the Shoppes of Brentwood Hills, which is anchored by a Target and is located in Brentwood. The amenities of this shopping center include a two-story office building, specialty shops, and numerous restaurants, situated on 14 acres. Newton Oldacre McDonald developed the Nashville West Shopping Center, which is located on Charlotte Pike. This center features a Best Buy and Dick's Sporting Goods as well as many national big box retailers. In addition to its retail projects, MJM provides professional services in the community, corporate office, institutional, recreational, and residential sectors. Recent projects include a car dealership, a medical office building, renovations and additions for secondary schools, higher education facilities, and several upscale homes in Tennessee.

As a community partner, MJM believes in sharing its success by supporting local and regional charities in Middle Tennessee. The firm supports the Boy Scouts of America, the Special Olympics, and Big Brothers Big Sisters. MJM recently partnered with Ronald McDonald House Charities by providing materials and volunteer hours to support this organization's mission and good work.

Overall, the award-winning MJM Architects, with a local and national presence, approaches every project with unsurpassed competence and agility.

Above left: MJM clients with a national presence include Dick's Sporting Goods, Inc. Above right: MJM teamed with GBT Realty to develop the Shoppes of Brentwood Hills, which is located in Brentwood, Tennessee.

Real Estate, Development, and Construction Services | 177

Founded in 1954 in Nashville, this award-winning architectural firm bases its modern design philosophies on methods drawn from its own rich heritage and from architecture throughout time. Street Dixon Rick Architecture, PLC leads in the design of educational, religious, performing arts, and historic institutions.

Right: Daugh W. Smith Middle School at Harpeth Hall in Nashville is part of an entirely new campus master plan designed by Street Dixon Rick Architecture, PLC.
Far right: This artist's rendering shows one of five new freshman residence halls on the Peabody Campus at Vanderbilt University in Nashville. These residence halls will become the second project in Nashville—and the first at Vanderbilt University—to be LEED-certified (Leadership in Energy and Environmental Design) by the U.S. Green Building Council. The first two halls were opened in the fall of 2006, and the final three are scheduled to open for the 2007 school year.

Street Dixon Rick Architecture, PLC is known for its timeless design of landmark institutions located throughout Nashville, for its focus on campus planning, and for its religious architecture. The firm was recognized as a leader in these specialties long before others entered these areas of architecture. Founded in 1954 by the notable Street and Street Architects, Street Dixon Rick is the successor to a rich heritage in architectural practice. Today, E. Baird Dixon, a Nashville native who studied architecture at the University of Virginia, and Stephen P. Rick, a Michigan native who earned his architecture degree at Tulane University, lead the firm. Dixon's and Rick's fine-honed skills and talents have developed Street Dixon Rick's leadership position in campus master planning and in educational, religious, performing arts, and historic design.

A Client-Centered Approach

At Street Dixon Rick, the design process involves more than creativity; it involves communication. Final designs are reached only after numerous discussions with the people who will actually use each building. This disciplined dialogue is used effectively to elicit and nurture great ideas from the minds of the clients, and to convey those ideas into the minds of the architects—thus ensuring that the end product reflects the heart and soul of both the user and the designer.

Integral to the firm's success is the participation of the partners with all clients. "We're a boutique firm, and keeping our practice small to medium in size allows us to be instrumentally involved with all projects," explains Dixon. Although the firm is honored every year with awards of excellence, Dixon emphasizes that client satisfaction is the firm's most important measure of success.

A notable example of Street Dixon Rick's repeat-client satisfaction is the firm's longstanding professional relationship with Harpeth Hall, a leading college preparatory middle and high school for girls, located in Nashville. After completing the designs for the campus master plan, Street Dixon Rick was invited back for every project to complete the plan, resulting in an entirely new and renovated campus. Merrie Clark, department chair at the Daugh W. Smith Middle School at Harpeth Hall, praises the work of Street Dixon Rick: "This school provides an ideal environment for learning and is a splendid place where students can grow and thrive. I am so happy for our girls and so grateful to Street Dixon Rick for making our dreams a reality."

Street Dixon Rick is honored to share this same type of relationship with Nashville's First Presbyterian Church and

The Oak Hill School, for which the firm created a master plan that will lead to the expansion of both the church and its affiliated school.

Integrating Form and Function

In Hendersonville, Our Lady of the Lake Parish called upon Street Dixon Rick when the parish outgrew its church. Working closely with church principals and members, Street Dixon Rick chose a new site, developed a master plan, and designed and constructed a new sanctuary, education spaces, offices, and a social hall. "We translate personal needs and feelings of parishes into spaces that allow and encourage worship," states Rick. "These churches, whether large or small, always become intimate spaces for worship."

While the design of a church focuses a parish toward an altar, orienting an audience toward a stage becomes one of the many complex factors in the design of performance halls. Some projects require a multiform theater space for productions in the round. This was the case for Street Dixon Rick's design for the Halbritter Performing Arts Center at Juniata College, located in Huntingdon, Pennsylvania.

In Nashville, Ingram Hall at Vanderbilt University's Blair School of Music was part of Street Dixon Rick's overall design for the Martha Rivers Ingram Center for the Performing Arts. The 625-seat Ingram Hall accommodates full orchestral and opera productions. And because of Street Dixon Rick's work, the acoustics in Ingram Hall are so excellent that the Nashville Symphony has used it as a practice space and for musical recordings. Ingram Hall also includes instrumental and rehearsal halls, conductors' studios, administrative offices, and a professional recording studio. "The new building is an aesthetic delight," states Mark Wait, dean and professor of music at the Blair School of Music. "Its openness, ample green space, and superb functionality are ideally blended, making it a joy to show up for work each morning."

In its renovation and restoration work, Street Dixon Rick specializes in harmonizing the design of new buildings, additions, and interior spaces with those of older, existing buildings. While similar to the dialogue between client and architect, this process requires vast knowledge, keen observation skills, and an eye for historic design in order to find the forms, materials, and details that will link the new with the old. "We have found many ways to create new structures that meet the needs and ideas of today, while maintaining the integrity of the original and surrounding buildings," states Dixon. Such design sensibility and skill is evident in the two-story glass atrium that Street Dixon Rick designed to function as a "living room" as part of the renovation of the 1875 sandstone hall at The University of the South, located in Sewanee, Tennessee.

Building Nashville's Future

More than 90 percent of Street Dixon Rick's new design projects are for repeat or referred clients. In addition to its longstanding relationships with The University of the South, Vanderbilt University, Juniata College, and Harpeth Hall, the firm has established enduring relationships with Harding Academy, Saint Edward's School, Westminster Presbyterian Church, Middle Tennessee State University, and many other clients located throughout Middle Tennessee.

An educational project under construction is the new Freshman Commons, to be used by 1,600 students, on the Peabody Campus at Vanderbilt University. Street Dixon Rick developed the master plan for five new residence halls that are designed to blend seamlessly with the historic campus. This project is designed to have the lowest possible impact on the environment and is expected to become the second project in Nashville—and the first at Vanderbilt University—to be LEED-certified (Leadership in Energy and Environmental Design) by the U.S. Green Building Council.

Just as Street Dixon Rick is part of Nashville's design landscape, the firm is also part of the community. Active in a number of nonprofit organizations, Street Dixon Rick supports Vanderbilt University's Blair School of Music, the Academic Cultural Enrichment (ACE) Mentorship Program, the Cheekwood Botanical Garden & Museum of Art, the Nashville Shakespeare Festival, and WPLN Nashville Public Radio.

For additional information, visit the Street Dixon Rick Architecture, PLC Web site at www.sdrarch.com.

Above left: Street Dixon Rick developed the master plan for Our Lady of the Lake Parish, which now includes a new sanctuary, offices, a social hall, and education spaces. This parish is located in Hendersonville, Tennessee. Above right: Another notable Street Dixon Rick project, the Martha Rivers Ingram Center for the Performing Arts at Vanderbilt University is renowned for its overall design as well as for the design of its acoustics.

Ross Bryan Associates, Inc.
Consulting Engineers

This award-winning structural engineering firm plays a key role in the precast concrete and construction industries throughout Tennessee and across the country. The firm's seasoned staff brings decades of experience and innovative solutions to each project, enabling the company to handle even the most complex building structures.

Above: Ross Bryan Associates, Inc. was honored with the Atlanta Urban Design Commission's Award of Excellence for its work on the AT&T Promenade II. Above right: Ross Bryan Associates is a diversified firm of more than 30 dedicated professionals.

Ross Bryan Associates, Inc. is an accomplished structural engineering firm based in Nashville, with a practice that extends across the United States and into Canada and Mexico.

Setting a Solid Foundation

Ross H. Bryan, originally from Kansas, made his home in Nashville at the conclusion of his naval service, which included time at the Panama Canal. Bryan, who designed the first U.S. building and bridge structures constructed of prestressed or post-tensioned concrete, founded Ross Bryan Associates in Nashville in 1949.

The firm's initial consulting work included developing rebar drawings for the Nashville federal building on Broadway Avenue. In the mid 1950s, Ross Bryan Associates was chosen to design the monumental Life and Casualty Insurance Company of Tennessee office tower (the L&C tower). At the time of its completion in 1957, the 31-story steel structure was the tallest building in the South.

In the 1960s, T. Henry Clark, James L. Smithey, and Edwin A. McDougle joined Ross Bryan Associates. They are now the firm's principals: Clark is the president, Smithey is the executive vice president, and McDougle is the secretary/treasurer.

In the mid 1960s the firm took on the project of the Revere Copper & Brass Rolling Mill in Scottsboro, Alabama—the largest precast/prestressed structure in the world at the time. The mill was completed in 1968.

Expanding into Precast Audit, Quality Control, and Corporate Identity Solutions

In the late 1960s, Ross Bryan Associates expanded into three areas that continue to be lucrative for the firm even today. In 1967, the Precast/Prestressed Concrete Institute (PCI) hired Ross Bryan Associates to perform audits of 27 precast concrete producer plants across the United States. These plants had voluntarily joined PCI's Plant Certification Program, which ensures that each plant has a reliable, ongoing quality assurance system. The program has grown to include almost 300 plants across the United States, Canada, and Mexico that are audited twice a year by engineers from Ross Bryan Associates.

The firm's engineers also conduct quality control seminars throughout Nashville and across the country to train and certify personnel from participating plants. Over the past quarter century, some 3,000 individuals have taken these courses.

During the 1960s, the concept of corporate identity became integral to the success of Ford Motor Company and General Motors Corporation. Ross Bryan Associates was hired first by Ford and then by General Motors to design sign structures for car dealerships. Since then, the firm has provided corporate identity design services for more than 15,000 dealerships throughout the United States.

Enhancing Cityscapes

Through design, renovation, and expansion projects, Ross Bryan Associates has changed the face of structures across the country.

Medical Centers

The 1970s and 1980s were busy decades for Ross Bryan Associates. Donald E. Yarbrough, R. Mark Dunning, and Elizabeth Surface joined the firm during this time. All three currently serve as the company's project managers. During this period, the firm designed 14 hospitals for Humana, Inc. and headed the patient tower expansion at The University of Tennessee–Knoxville's Memorial Hospital (now The University of Tennessee Medical

180 | PORTRAITS OF SUCCESS Profiles of Companies and Organizations

Center). Other projects during the 1970s and 1980s included expansion projects at Baptist Hospital of East Tennessee in Knoxville, the College of Veterinary Medicine at The University of Tennessee–Knoxville, and James H. Quillen College of Medicine at East Tennessee University in Mountain Home, Tennessee.

Power Plants

During the early 1970s, Ross Bryan Associates worked with Westinghouse Electric Corporation to develop a precast concrete cooling tower to be used at coal-fired and nuclear power plants. An installation of this tower was built for the Florida Power & Light Company and still functions at their power plant in Palatka, Florida.

Convention Centers

The Gaylord Opryland Resort & Convention Center Nashville is a Ross Bryan Associates project that has expanded over the years and helped draw the firm into the convention center business. The firm has designed more than $1 billion worth of centers, including the Pennsylvania Convention Center in Philadelphia; the Washington Convention Center in Washington, D.C.; the Knoxville Convention Center in Tennessee; and the Raleigh Convention Center in North Carolina.

Educational Facilities

Ross Bryan Associates projects have included the design, renovation, and expansion of university facilities in Nashville and beyond, including the following:

**Vanderbilt University—
Nashville, Tennessee**
- Carmichael Towers I, II, III, and IV residence halls
- Olin Hall, which houses the university's Chemical and Mechanical Engineering programs
- Kirkland Hall renovations I, II, and III
- Memorial Gymnasium's east and west balconies
- Married-student apartments (now The Commons)
- University Club
- Old Science Hall (now Benson Science Hall) renovation
- Neely Auditorium, Vanderbilt University Theatre renovation

**Vanderbilt University Medical Center—
Nashville, Tennessee**
- Rudolph A. Light Hall transfer girders
- Nuclear medicine facilities
- Annette and Irwin Eskind Biomedical Library
- Medical Center Garage, phases I and II

**University of Tennessee—
Knoxville, Tennessee**
- Walters Life Sciences building
- Presidential Complex dormitories
- Thompson-Boling Assembly Center and Arena skybox retrofit and concession additions
- Glocker Business Administration complex expansion
- Neyland Stadium, phases I, II, and III
- McClung Tower
- John Hodges Library expansion
- The Howard H. Baker Jr. Center for Public Policy
- Pratt Basketball Practice Pavilion

**Tennessee Technological University—
Cookeville, Tennessee**
- Centers of Excellence
- Angelo and Jennette Volpe Library and Media Center

High-Rise Structures

High-rise structures in structural steel and cast-in-place (CIP) concrete have been part of Ross Bryan Associates for more than 40 years. The L&C tower in Nashville was a "first" in structural steel, utilizing a stiffened truss to support lateral loads. Nashville's Commerce Place (now Bank of America Plaza) utilized architecturally finished CIP concrete walls to support lateral loads, while the 38-story AT&T Promenade II building in Atlanta used a shear core combined with exterior columns to resist such loadings.

Rising to the Challenge

In 2006 Ross Bryan Associates was awarded the annual Engineering Excellence Award by the American Council of Engineering Companies for its work on the restoration of the historic Tennessee Theatre. This is just one of many awards earned by the firm attesting to its quality work and innovative solutions. Ross Bryan Associates continues to support and expand its client base, pursuing challenging projects wherever opportunities are presented.

Above left: Ross Bryan Associates has helped designed more than $1 billion worth of convention centers, including the Washington Convention Center (shown here) in Washington, D.C. This center features 2.4 million square feet of state-of-the-art space.

Above right: Ross Bryan Associates has also designed, renovated, and expanded numerous university facilities, including the Annette and Irwin Eskind Biomedical Library (shown here) at the Vanderbilt University Medical Center in Nashville, Tennessee. This library is the intellectual and geographical heart of the medical center.

Earl Swensson Associates, Inc.

Collaborating with clients on each stage of a project, this influential architectural and design firm creates 'human-centered' environments that balance form and function. Regarded as one of the nation's top 10 designers for the health care field, the firm designs office buildings, resorts, academic buildings, and more.

Founded in 1961, Earl Swensson Associates, Inc. (ESa) provides design services in architecture, interior architecture, master planning, and space planning for clients in the health care, hospitality, education, senior living, and corporate office sectors around the country.

In its headquarters city of Nashville, many of the firm's projects are woven into the fabric of the city's landscape and skyline. Notable projects include the iconic BellSouth Tennessee headquarters skyscraper; Monroe Carell Jr. Children's Hospital at Vanderbilt; the Schermerhorn Symphony Center; Centennial Medical Center; Caterpillar Financial Center; Belmont University's Beaman Student Life Center/Curb Event Center; and Gaylord Opryland Resort & Convention Center.

ESa believes that design is about creating environments. Dedicated to the principle of "human-centered" design, the firm strives in each of its projects to combine style, innovation, technological sophistication, and convenience of use to create aesthetic, functional environments that respond to the needs and imagery of the individual client.

To address the details of each project, the ESa team listens to the client from the conception of the work through its completion. Clients are thus assured of being delivered the best possible solutions for their needs and budgets. This underlying belief in service is validated by the overwhelming number of repeat ESa clients, who total more than 80 percent of the firm's business.

A significant percentage of ESa's work is in the design of medically related facilities. For this work, the firm has been consistently ranked by *Modern Healthcare* magazine as one of the top 10 health care design firms in the nation. In fact, many of ESa's projects have received recognition through design awards and national publicity.

ESa, with more than 190 employees, has architects who are licensed to practice in all 50 states and the District of Columbia. The firm is owned by Earl S. Swensson, FAIA, chairman; Richard L. Miller, FAIA, president; Joe D. Crumpacker, vice president; and Raymond M. Pratt, vice president. These four principals play an active role in the day-to-day operations of the firm, thereby maintaining the high level of personal service that is the firm's primary management objective.

As a member of the U.S. Green Building Council, ESa supports the concept of designing sustainable buildings that are environmentally responsible, high performance, prosperous, and healthy. This forward-looking design firm succeeds in the present, while preserving the future.

Above: Earl Swensson Associates, Inc. (ESa) designed BellSouth's Tennessee headquarters in Nashville. Top right: ESa also designed the Beaman Student Life Center/Curb Event Center at Belmont University. Right: Another notable ESa project is Monroe Carell Jr. Children's Hospital at Vanderbilt.

182 | PORTRAITS OF SUCCESS Profiles of Companies and Organizations

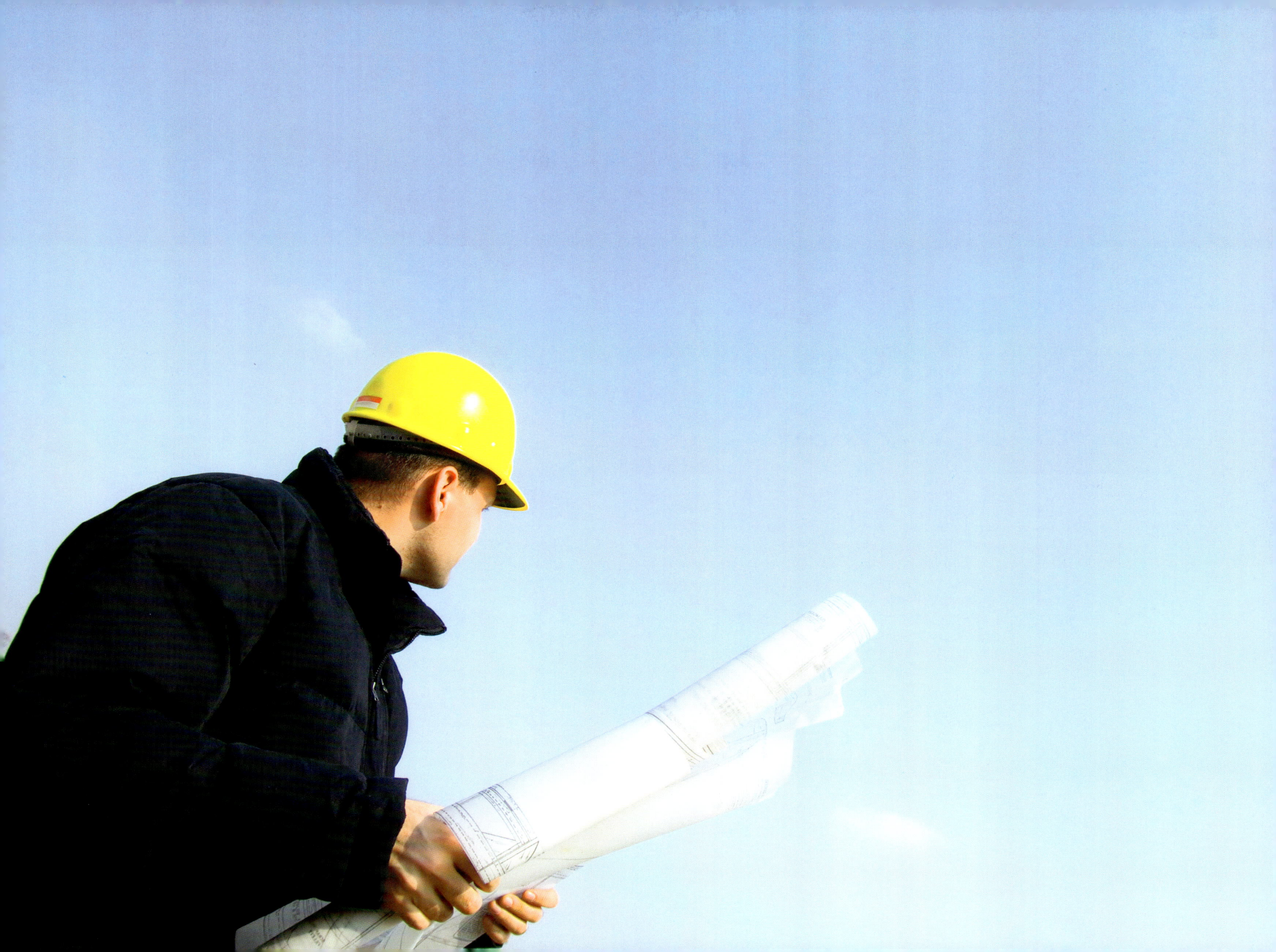

Shirley Zeitlin and Company, Realtors®

Founded in 1979 by notable Nashville Realtor, Shirley Zeitlin, this outstanding real estate firm's more than 100 full-time professionals deliver comprehensive buying, selling, and relocation services throughout the greater Nashville area, including Brentwood, Franklin, Green Hills, Belle Meade, and the urban market.

Above: More than 100 seasoned professionals in three offices—in Nashville, Brentwood, and Franklin—serve the community's real estate needs through Shirley Zeitlin and Company, Realtors®. The management team includes (from left to right): Managing Broker Matt Ligon (Franklin), Co-Broker Mary Frances Ligon (Franklin), Founder and CEO Shirley Zeitlin, President and Managing Broker Patty Carter (Brentwood), and Managing Broker Price Lechleiter (Nashville).

Clients look to Shirley Zeitlin and Company, Realtors® for one-stop real estate services, delivered at the five-star level. This organization is distinguished in the industry by its select group of professionals who are experienced, knowledgeable, and dedicated. Their focus is always on the best interests of their clients, thus ensuring the most complete and satisfying real estate experience before, during, and after sales transactions. The high level of service is based on the goal of forming lifelong relationships that address clients' needs, whenever they might occur. "We want our clients to have the ability and comfort level of calling on their agent for any assistance they may need throughout the years, just as they would with other specialized professionals in their lives," states Shirley Zeitlin, founder and CEO. The service level is of paramount importance, with the targeted standard being to always exceed clients' expectations.

Overall, this independently owned company has stood the test of time, earning the brand of real estate leadership and excellence in the area since 1979. Its Relocation Department was developed at the onset, with an emphasis on providing first-class concierge service to both corporate and individual clients. The department has been highly effective in securing numerous corporate relationships and in being the designated Realtor for the Titans and Predators, the Nashville NFL and NHL teams respectively. Shirley Zeitlin and Company's affiliations with Leading Real Estate Companies of the World, Luxury Portfolio, Residence International, and Who's Who in Luxury Real Estate enhance its marketing and networking abilities and services to clients. The company's Relocation Department is recognized as one of the country's finest.

Whether clients are looking for a downtown loft or a residence in the city, the suburbs, or the country, the company's associates can help them find their dream home at the best value for their investment. Both the relocation team and the associates are eager to introduce newcomers to schools, shopping districts, sports and recreation venues, and the many cultural offerings of each area.

A Partner in Progress

Shirley Zeitlin and Company has grown and changed in tandem with the city it serves. In 2006 The Zeitlin InTown division was created to serve Nashville's downtown and midtown urban developers as well as buyers who want to live in one of the city's most exciting and fastest-growing residential markets. The following developments are currently represented by the Zeitlin InTown team: Terrazzo in the Gulch, Summer Street Lofts, The Ambrose Lofts, Fourth & Monroe, Little Sixteen, and Salem Gardens. Additionally, the Williamson County market has selected Shirley Zeitlin and Company to represent the following communities: The Governors Club, an exclusive golf club and residential community in Brentwood, featuring an Arnold Palmer signature golf course and some of the area's most spectacular homes; and Saddle Springs Estates, a state-of-the-art equestrian community that features some of the finest facilities and home sites in the region.

In addition, the Shirley Zeitlin team takes special pride in giving back to the community through the Shirley Zeitlin Charitable Fund. Contributions are directed to many of Nashville's numerous worthy causes and are supported by both the Realtors and the company. With an eye always on the future, Shirley Zeitlin and Company strives for continual growth and improvement, securing its position of leadership and strength in the Middle Tennessee area.

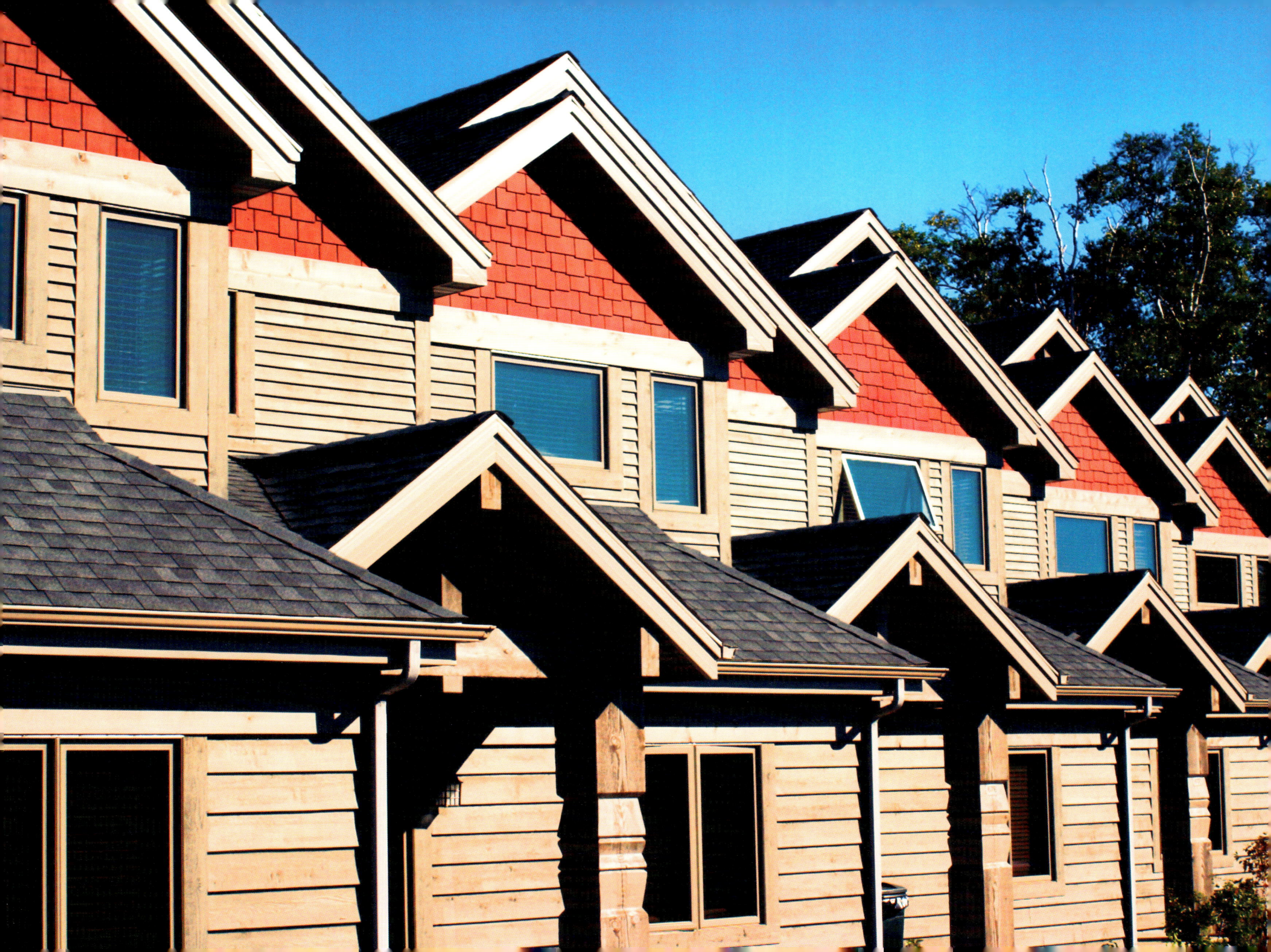

186 | PORTRAITS OF SUCCESS Profiles of Companies and Organizations

PROFILES OF COMPANIES AND ORGANIZATIONS
Recreation and Youth Services

With 29 centers and 332 program locations, this not-for-profit charitable fellowship—with the motto 'We build strong kids, strong families, strong communities'—invites people of all ages, backgrounds, income levels, and abilities to have fun and grow healthier by participating in its diverse range of life-changing programs and services.

The YMCA of Middle Tennessee (the Y) includes 29 centers and 332 program locations in its service area, which covers a 12-county region. Right: The Y's programs for children include preschool, Fun Company before-school and after-school care, kids' gymnastics, and many other programs—even nursery services for children as young as six weeks old. Far right: Among the Y's many programs is Y-Build, a career-development program that offers construction-skills training for young men ages 18 to 24.

The YMCA of Middle Tennessee reaches many lives in its 12-county service area—people of all ages and backgrounds, from all walks of life.

As part of "a worldwide charitable fellowship united by a common loyalty to Jesus Christ for the purpose of helping people grow in spirit, mind, and body," the YMCA of Middle Tennessee (the Y) is built on the values of caring, honesty, respect, and responsibility. The Y's vision is to be a source of strength to its community by providing an environment where people of all ages, faiths, races, backgrounds, and abilities work toward achieving their God-given fullest potential, build friendships, and experience the joy of helping others. To fulfill this vision and mission, the Y has always been blessed with outstanding staff and volunteer leadership, including, in the past, Captain Tom Ryman, Percy Warner, H. G. Hill Sr., and H. G. Hill Jr. Today the Y's board chair is Cal Turner Jr.

Organized in 1855, the Nashville YMCA—which later became the YMCA of Middle Tennessee—disbanded during the Civil War but reemerged in 1875. Originally it offered Bible study and prayer for young men away from home for the first time. Members met in the rooms of the Nashville Library Association until 1888, when the Nashville YMCA moved into a new four-story building on Church Street. With the Nashville YMCA concentrating on physical as well as spiritual conditioning by the early 1900s, a new location was built in 1912 at Seventh Avenue North, featuring four gymnasiums and a swimming pool, plus a dormitory and classrooms. In World War I and World War II, millions of enlisted men used the Nashville YMCA for housing and recreation.

In 1960, a fund drive raised enough money to build the East Nashville YMCA, which was opened in 1962. That decade, the Nashville YMCA introduced popular programs such as camping, basketball, softball, and Indian Guides. In 1972 the Southwest YMCA (now the Green Hills Family YMCA) was opened, and construction was under way on new facilities for the Downtown YMCA and Northwest Family YMCA.

In 1984 the association broadened its outreach internationally when Nashville mayor Richard Fulton led local business and civic leaders on a YMCA-sponsored trip to Venezuela to share ideas and strengthen bonds with the YMCAs of that country. The Uptown YMCA was opened in 1991, followed by the Rutherford County and Franklin YMCAs in 1995. Other centers that were opened in the 1990s included the Maury County Family YMCA, located in Columbia, Tennessee, as well as the Joe C. Davis YMCA Outdoor Center, which is home to Camp Widjiwagan. With these new facilities came many new programs.

In 2002, John Mark "Journey" Johnson succeeded Clark Baker to become the Y's president and CEO, bringing 25 years of experience in working with

188 | PORTRAITS OF SUCCESS Profiles of Companies and Organizations

the YMCA. The successful Preston Taylor Boys & Girls Club/YMCA Youth Development Center also was opened that year, in partnership with the Metropolitan Nashville Public Schools and United Way, providing kids and teens with after-school and summertime academics, life skills, and physical fitness programs.

In 2005 the Y celebrated its 130th anniversary—and added the Putnam County Family YMCA in Cookeville, opened the new North Rutherford YMCA–Ronald Reagan Family Center in Smyrna, and broke ground on a new Bellevue YMCA in partnership with Senior Citizens, Inc.

In 2006, 10,312 "joyful givers" and 1,283 volunteers helped the Y raise more than $4.6 million through its "We Build People" annual giving campaign, which enables the Y to remain available to all, regardless of ability to pay. Partnering with Nashville schools, the Y provided Fun Company—its before-school and after-school program —to 7,500 children at 149 sites. More than 11,500 people, mostly children, were taught to swim, and 20,849 children were shown the importance of character, confidence, and good health by playing sports at the Y. Nearly 3,000 children attended Camp Widjiwagan, which has been named "Middle Tennessee's #1 Day Camp" for nine consecutive years by *Nashville Parent* magazine.

Also in 2006, the Y continued to broaden its reach, enriching more children and adults than ever. It also took important steps toward ensuring a future legacy of service to Nashville and Middle Tennessee, with dreams and plans taking shape for exciting additions to youth and teen programs, camp options, and aquatics opportunities.

Thanks to its tremendous team of donors, volunteers, and staff, the Y opened the beautiful new Bellevue Family YMCA and J. L. Turner Lifelong Learning Center of Senior Citizens, Inc., a hub for people of all ages in a vibrant, fast-growing community.

Each year, the Y reaches more than 260,000 lives, providing people of all ages with a safe place in which to grow and achieve. It provides information about its programs and services on its Web sites (www.ymcamidtn.org and www.ymcafoundation.org). With a solid mission, strong commitment, honorable values, clear vision, and passionate volunteer and staff leadership, the YMCA of Middle Tennessee, a not-for-profit association, is dedicated to helping people fulfill their hopes, dreams, and aspirations in every community it serves.

Counterclockwise from far left: The Y offers 42 indoor and outdoor pools within its service area. In 2006 the Y taught swim lessons to more than 11,500 children and adults; certified some 388 lifeguards; and provided skill clinics, swim teams, scuba certification, and more. Children from ages 3 to 17 participate in athletics such as soccer, hockey, basketball, flag football, and gymnastics, all the while "catching" the values of teamwork and sportsmanship as they enjoy these volunteer-coached programs.

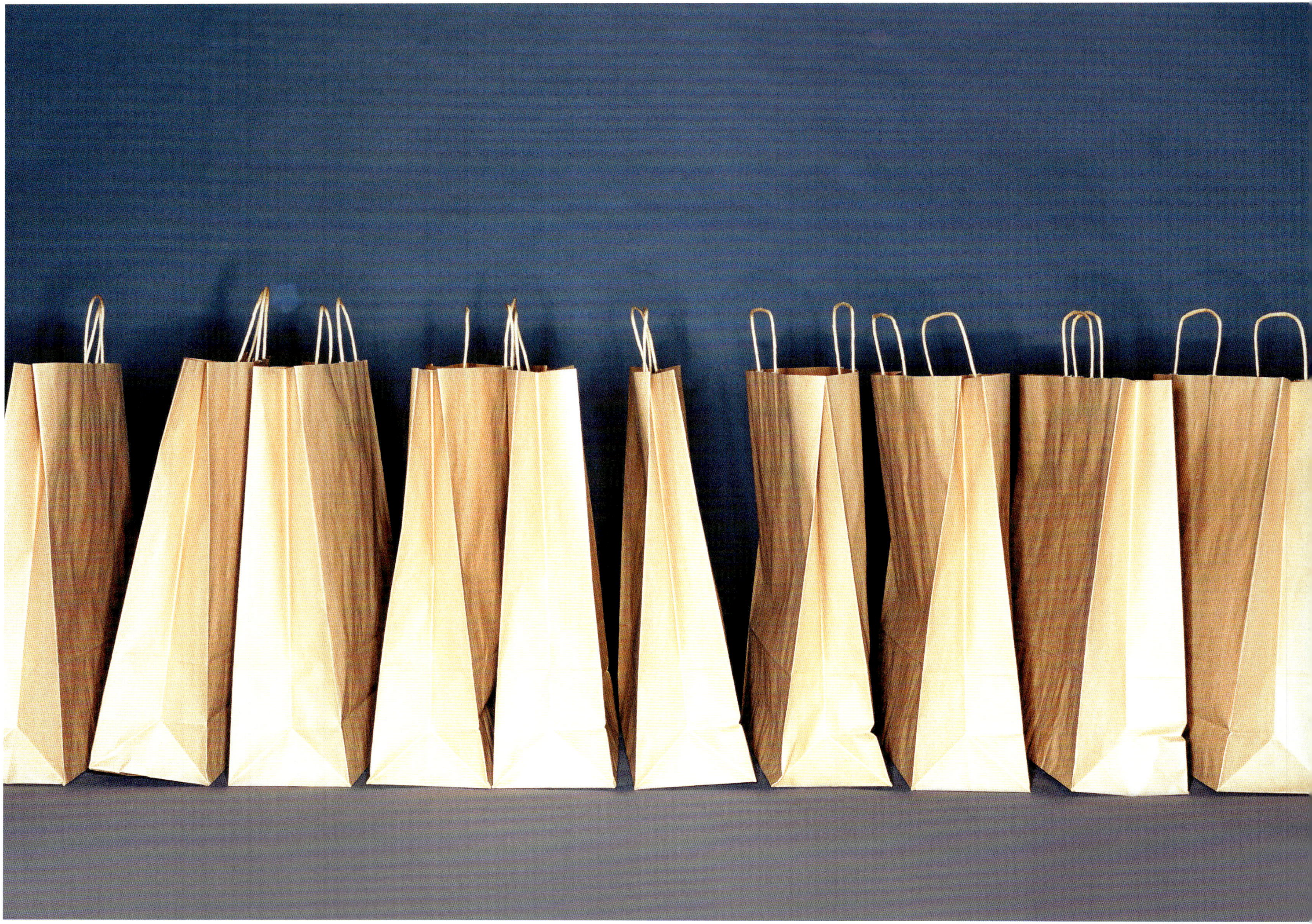

PROFILES OF COMPANIES AND ORGANIZATIONS
Retail and Sales

Tennessee–based company is one of the largest retail farm and ranch store chains in the United States according to industry sources and is the 'store you can trust' according to its customers.

Right: Tractor Supply Company currently encompasses more than 600 stores in 35 states. The typical store features 16,000 to 24,000 square feet of inside selling space with a similar square footage of outside space, which is used to display items such as stock tanks, agricultural fencing, and livestock equipment.

What do you see when you look at a piece of land that extends out toward the horizon? Tractor Supply Company's customers see opportunity. They see something that needs to be tended to and tinkered with; they see the opportunity for growth and success. And whether they have a few acres or a few hundred, they trust Tractor Supply to help them with all their needs, from hauling to fixing.

Tractor Supply Company, proudly based in Brentwood, Tennessee, is one of the largest retail farm and ranch store chains in the United States. This company is focused on serving the needs of people who choose to live a rural lifestyle, helping them take care of their land, property, and animals.

"The return to rural America is not a fad or a trend, it's a commitment to a lifestyle," states Jim Wright, president and CEO of the Tractor Supply Company. "And that commitment presents an incredible opportunity for the future for our customers and our company. We give people the tools and seasoned advice they need for life 'out here,' be it the great heartland or a few acres in the city."

'A Store You Can Trust'

Tractor Supply customers are sometimes described as hobby or part-time farmers or ranchers. It is estimated that this consumer segment spends more than $5.5 billion annually on supplies. Less than 10 percent of Tractor Supply customers classify themselves as full-time farmers or ranchers. In fact, Tractor Supply's largest customer segment does not farm at all. They are more aptly described as rural or suburban home-owners, or "self-reliants." When asked, these customers often describe Tractor Supply as "a store you can trust."

This store that they trust was founded in 1938 as a mail-order catalog business that offered tractor parts to America's family farmers. The first store was opened in Minot, North Dakota, and proved to be such a hit that more stores soon followed. Always mindful of its customers and their needs, Tractor Supply continually modified its product offerings based on what its customers required . . . and this practice continues today.

A Leading-Edge Retailer

Since its founding, Tractor Supply has grown to become a leading-edge retailer. By 2006 Tractor Supply had more than 600 stores in 35 states, surpassed $2 billion in annual sales, and saw its stock traded on the NASDAQ under the symbol TSCO. Tractor Supply also had added a second retail brand with the acquisition of Del's Farm Supply.

Tractor Supply stores are primarily located in rural areas and the outlying suburbs of major cities. The typical store has 16,000 to 24,000 square feet of inside selling space with a similar square footage of outside space, which is used to display items such as stock tanks, agricultural fencing, livestock equipment and horse stalls.

Overall, Tractor Supply features the unique products that support its customers' rural lifestyles. Those products range from welders, generators, and air compressors to animal care products, men's and women's work clothing, and truck hauling equipment and accessories. Tractor Supply stores also carry tools and hardware, home repair products, equine and pet supplies, animal feed, power tools, riding mowers, lawn and garden products, and much more. In addition, each store features teams that include a welder, a farmer or rancher, and a horse owner, who collectively provide an exceptional depth of knowledge and resources.

Moreover, Tractor Supply stores carry specific seasonal and regional products that are designed to meet customers' particular needs at every time of year and in all parts of the country. And the company is a leading retailer for nationally respected brands, including Cub Cadet lawn tractors and Carhartt work clothing. Tractor Supply has also developed its popular private-label brands, including Retriever dog food, Royal Wing bird seed, Huskee lawn tractors, and CE Schmidt work clothing.

As it looks to the future, Tractor Supply Company remains focused on understanding and serving its customers. This company has succeeded and will continue to succeed on its motto, which is posted in every store: "Customer satisfaction guaranteed. Every team member has the authority to do whatever it takes."

Left: Tractor Supply offers the complete range of products that support its customers' rural lifestyles, including riding mowers; lawn and garden products; generators; air compressors; pet, livestock, and equine care products and feed; and agricultural and livestock fencing.

194 | PORTRAITS OF SUCCESS Profiles of Companies and Organizations

PROFILES OF COMPANIES AND ORGANIZATIONS
Tourism and Hospitality

Doubletree Guest Suites Nashville Airport

Located in the heart of friendly Nashville, this full-service, all-suite hotel is a perfect combination of location and luxury. Impeccable accommodations and amenities make guests feel at home while they visit the city's cultural landmarks or conduct business in the hotel's spacious boardrooms and meeting spaces.

This page, all photos: The Doubletree Guest Suites Nashville Airport welcomes visitors with beautiful, well-kept grounds and tastefully appointed, spacious suites with all the comforts of home.

Warm chocolate-chip cookies and comfortable beds piled with mounds of pillows welcome visitors to the Doubletree Guest Suites Nashville Airport, making them feel right at home. Just two miles from Nashville International Airport and minutes from downtown, the Doubletree is ideally located for the business or leisure traveler.

Adding Up Accommodations and Amenities

Each of the Doubletree's 138 spacious guest suites features a separate living room and bedroom. The living rooms are luxuriously appointed with a sleeper sofa, desk, refrigerator, and microwave. Each suite also is equipped with two televisions, complimentary wireless Internet service, a coffeemaker, an iron and ironing board, and a hairdryer.

In addition, the hotel has a state-of-the-art fitness center with cardiovascular equipment and free weights, as well as an outdoor swimming pool and a heated indoor swimming pool.

After exercising, guests can relax and enjoy a meal prepared by an award-winning chef at the Doubletree's Bistro Restaurant or just unwind at the casual Bistro Lounge.

For the business traveler, the Doubletree offers a complimentary business center open 24 hours a day. More than 2,600 square feet of meeting space can accommodate small groups or up to 70 people in a theater setting. Spacious boardroom conference suites, each with an attached comfortable sitting area, are ideal for private conferences or meetings.

The friendly, attentive staff of the Doubletree Guest Suites Nashville Airport distinguishes it from other hotels. The hotel's entire team makes service its first priority. In fact, the Doubletree Guest Suites Nashville Airport ranked among the top five of 150 Doubletree properties for customer loyalty in 2005.

Location, Location, Location

With a long-standing reputation as the capital of country music, Nashville now boasts a music scene that has blossomed well beyond the one genre. Today Nashville is fondly known as "Music City USA."

The Doubletree Guest Suites Nashville Airport is well-situated for guests to take in all that the exciting city has to offer—not only music and entertainment but also sports, shopping, dining, and culture. The Country Music Hall of Fame, the Grand Ole Opry, and Gaylord Opryland Resort & Convention Center are all just minutes from the hotel. The Hermitage, President Andrew Jackson's historic home, is also nearby. Nashville Zoo is a delight for visitors of all ages. Terrific shopping and downtown dining are just a short drive away. Sports fans will find Titans Stadium and the Gaylord Entertainment Center equally close; nature lovers can hike on nearby trails or tour the city's botanical gardens.

Southern Hospitality, Doubletree-Style

People come to Nashville for the music, mild climate, thriving business environment, and quality of life. They stay at the Doubletree Guest Suites Nashville Airport for its convenient location, amenities, and, of course, its signature chocolate-chip cookies. When it comes to gracious service and sincere warmth, Doubletree Guest Suites Nashville Airport truly embodies southern hospitality.

This page, all photos: The Doubletree Guest Suites Nashville Airport strives to meet the needs of every guest. The hotel offers ample space and excellent catering services for stylish events and gatherings or business meetings. Guests can also make use of a high-tech business center, a fully equipped gym, and two sparkling swimming pools.

Tourism and Hospitality | 197

Gaylord Opryland Resort & Convention Center

Boosting Nashville's popularity among business travelers, conventioneers, and tourists, this enormous resort and convention center—the largest nongaming hotel in the world—lies in the cradle of country music and captures the heart of true southern class.

Above left: The Gaylord Opryland Resort & Convention Center covers acres of beautiful indoor gardens, has restaurants and shops aplenty, and is fully outfitted for any kind of business meeting or convention. Above right: The legendary Grand Ole Opry, adjacent to this resort and convention center, stages must-see performances by country music and bluegrass talent.

Whether visiting for business or pleasure, whether locals or out-of-towners, guests at the Gaylord Opryland Resort & Convention Center in Nashville can count on world-class entertainment, business amenities, customer service, and accommodations.

The resort's rooms are undergoing a makeover for a more sophisticated and contemporary look. This multiyear, $45 million enhancement is adding updated appointments to all 2,881 rooms, including the 165 luxurious suites and 741 atrium-view rooms, which overlook nine acres of lush indoor gardens. Each room will have dual phone lines and Internet connectivity as well as plush, upgraded bedding, new wall coverings and carpeting, and flat-screen television sets. For meetings and conventions, the resort offers audiovisual services, teleconferencing, a 24-hour support staff, and an on-site, full-service business center.

Gaylord Entertainment (NYSE:GET), a Nashville entertainment and hospitality company, owns and operates the resort and convention center, which comprises five main areas. The Delta is a glass-domed atrium with an 85-foot-high fountain and an indoor river encircling a New Orleans–themed island. The Cascades, an indoor tropical garden, has a four-story cascading waterfall, a revolving lounge, and the resort's main registration lobby. The indoor Garden Conservatory has romantic paths and park benches tucked into dense foliage. The Convention Center has 600,000 square feet of exhibit halls, conference rooms, ballrooms, and flexible space for all manner of conventions and meetings. And the opulent Magnolia, the resort's thematic centerpiece, welcomes guests with a dramatic staircase and beautiful fireplaces.

For recreation, guests can cruise on the indoor Delta River in a Mississippi-style flatboat and, if lucky, glimpse Donny, the resort's 80-pound catfish. They can shop, relax in live-music lounges, or luxuriate at Relâche, the European-inspired spa and salon. For dining, the resort offers award-winning cuisine at the Old Hickory Steakhouse, casual dining at Rachel's, hamburgers and snacks at Rusty's Sports Bar & Grill (with some 20 television screens and stadium seating), and more.

Just outside the complex, guests find shopping, movies, sight-seeing, riverboat cruises on the Cumberland River, the 18-hole Gaylord Springs golf course, and the world-famous Grand Ole Opry, the 4,400-seat country music and bluegrass mecca where the world's longest-running live radio show is broadcast.

Gaylord Opryland hosts special events, with headlining comedians, top chefs, inspirational speakers, and family celebrations such as A Country Christmas and a Celebrity Chef series. Nashville's country singers—from up-and-comers to Grammy Award–winners—also perform.

For business or pleasure, visitors from around the world choose the Gaylord Opryland Resort & Convention Center as their destination resort and a home away from home.

Gaylord Opryland Resort & Convention Center

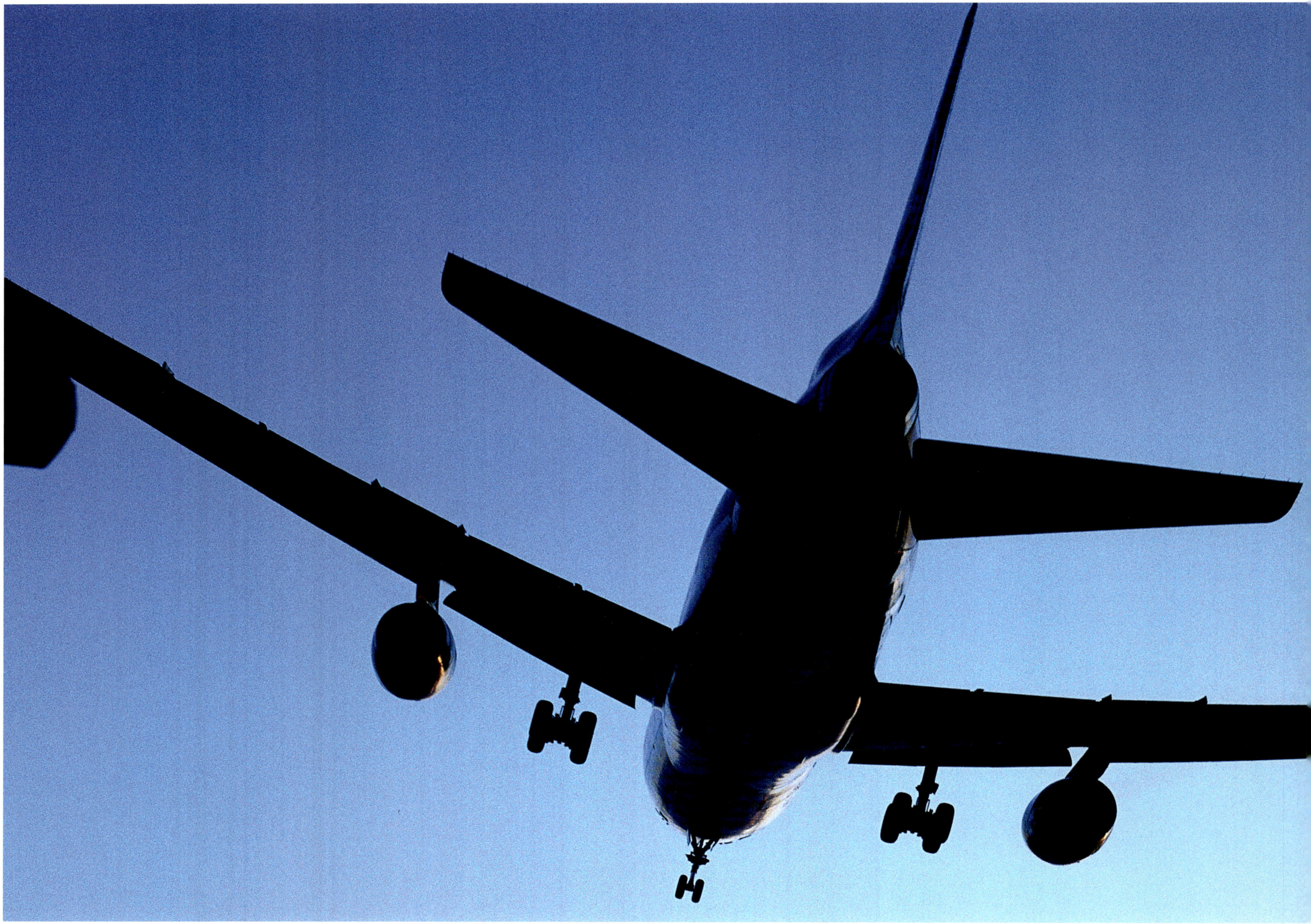

PROFILES OF COMPANIES AND ORGANIZATIONS
Transportation Services

Metropolitan Nashville Airport Authority

Operating airports that serve some 89 North American locations, this organization is dedicated to delivering exemplary service and vibrant facilities that are optimally managed and secure, while also pursuing financial efficiency, entrepreneurial innovation, long-term strategic planning, and support for its communities.

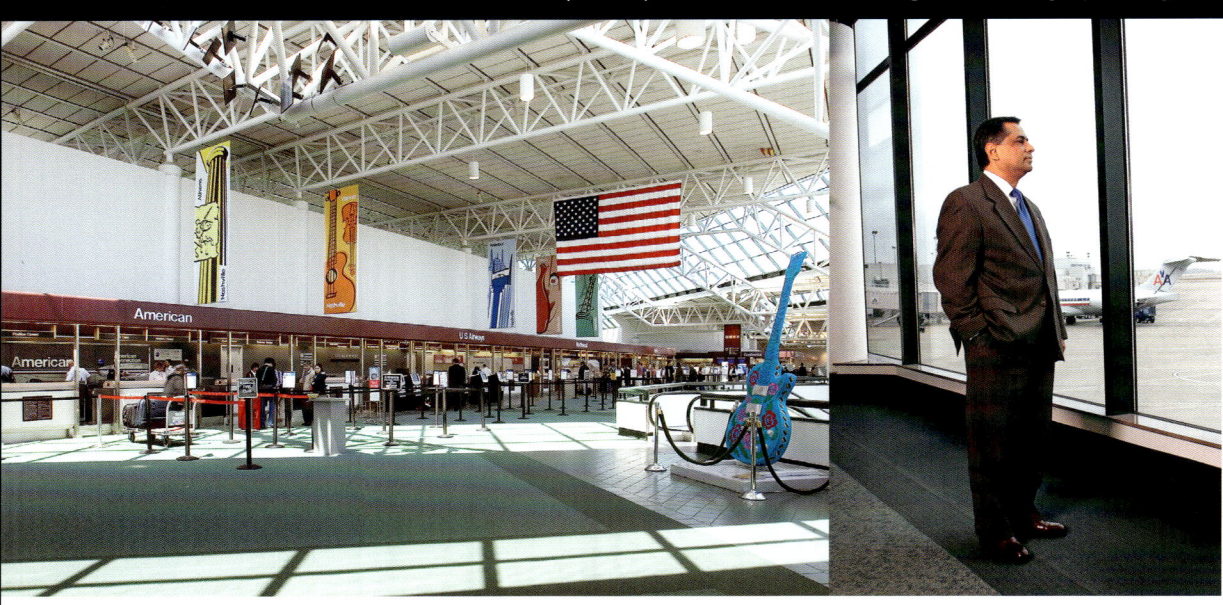

Above left: The Metropolitan Nashville Airport Authority is working on a renovation project for the terminal at Nashville International Airport, projected for completion in 2011. Above right: Nearly 9.5 million passengers per year arrive and depart via the terminal's 61 gates.

In 2002, in the wake of September 11, 2001, the Metropolitan Nashville Airport Authority (MNAA), which owns and operates Nashville International Airport (BNA) and John C. Tune Airport (JWN), a general aviation airport, adopted a new path of productive management through an array of strategic initiatives.

In 2003 the MNAA made history for airports nationwide with the development of a long-term strategic business plan (SBP) that charted a definitive path for the future and included a revised mission statement, key core values, and strategic priorities. Through this process, it was determined that the factors driving the MNAA's economic engine were low costs and exceptional service for customers and airlines. In 2006 the SBP was updated to include a revitalized mission and vision statement that reinforce MNAA's desire to "deliver exemplary customer service by providing premier airport services and facilities."

Through its strategic planning and solid operations, the MNAA also has posted four record financial years, from 2002 to 2006—unprecedented since its inception in 1970.

Financial success also has equated to the MNAA being awarded the Certificate of Achievement for Excellence in Financial Reporting for its Comprehensive Annual Financial Reports (CAFR) for fiscal 1999 through fiscal 2005. Presented by the Government Finance Officers Association of the United States and Canada (GFOA), the award is designed to recognize and encourage excellence in financial reporting by state and local governments.

Because MNAA is attentive to its customers' needs, in 2006 it embarked on a three-phase, five-year terminal renovation project. The 20-year-old terminal will receive an aesthetically pleasing facelift and feature a consolidated security checkpoint flanked by shimmering water walls to ease the stress of travel. Concessions will be completely reconstructed and reconfigured. The terminal transformation is designed to ensure that travelers receive an appealing first impression of Music City.

Community outreach is another integral part of MNAA's culture and has been augmented with the creation of the Small, Minority and Women-owned Business Enterprise (S,M&WBE) Program. This local program exists to enhance opportunities for S,M&WBEs in the performance of contracts, leases, and related business activities of MNAA and complements the federalized Disadvantaged Business Enterprise (DBE) Program. The MNAA also has implemented an informative outreach program entitled "Bridges to Opportunity," which caters to all S,M&WBEs and DBEs to promote, encourage, and stimulate contracting opportunities for firms historically underused in their areas of specialty.

The MNAA is a flourishing example of what can be achieved through a dedicated commitment to strategic planning, operational excellence, and performance management.

✈ **A** **B** International Arrivals

Nashville International Airport (BNA)

Cherbo Publishing Group

Cherbo Publishing Group's business-focused, art book–quality publications, which celebrate the vital spirit of enterprise, are custom books that are used as high-impact economic development tools to enhance reputations, increase profits, and provide global exposure for businesses and organizations.

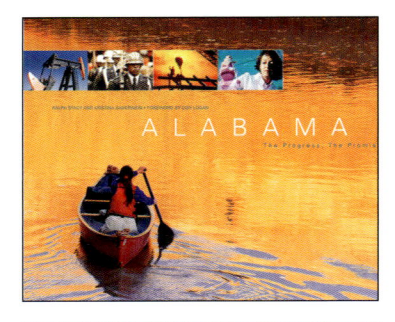

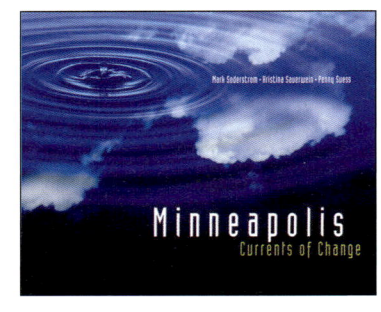

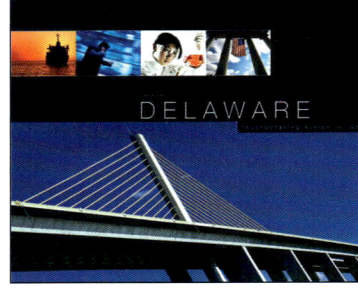

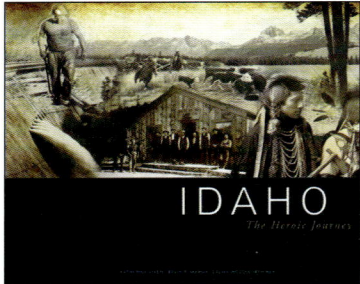

Both pages, all: Cherbo Publishing Group produces custom books for historical, professional, and government organizations. These fine publications promote the economic development of America's cities, regions, and states by chronicling their history—the people, enterprises, industries, and organizations that have made them great.

Jack Cherbo, Cherbo Publishing Group president and CEO, has been breaking new ground in the sponsored publishing business for more than 40 years.

"Previously, the cost of creating a handsome book for business developments or commemorative occasions fell directly on the sponsoring organization," Cherbo says. "My company pioneered an entirely new concept—funding these books through the sale of corporate profiles."

Cherbo honed his leading edge in Chicago, where he owned a top advertising agency before moving into publishing. Armed with a degree in business administration from Northwestern University, a mind that never stopped, and a keen sense of humor, Cherbo set out to succeed—and continues to do just that.

Cherbo Publishing Group (CPG), formerly a wholly owned subsidiary of Jostens, Inc., a Fortune 500 company, has been a privately held corporation since 1993. CPG is North America's leading publisher of quality custom books for commercial, civic, historical, and trade associations. Publications range from hardcover state, regional, and commemorative books to softcover state and regional business reports. The company is headquartered in Encino, California, and operates regional offices in Philadelphia, Minneapolis, and Houston.

About CPG Publications

CPG has created books for some of America's leading organizations, including the U.S. Chamber of Commerce, Empire State Development, California Sesquicentennial Foundation, Chicago O'Hare International Airport, and the Indiana Manufacturers Association. Participants have included ConAgra, Dow Chemical Company, Lucent Technologies, Merck & Company, and BlueCross/BlueShield.

CPG series range from history books to economic development/relocation books and from business reports to publications of special interest. The economic development series spotlights the outstanding economic and quality-of-life advantages of fast-growing cities, counties, regions, or states. The annual business reports provide an economic snapshot of individual cities, regions, or states. The commemorative series marks milestones for corporations, organizations, and professional and trade associations.

To find out how CPG can help you celebrate a special occasion, or for information on how to showcase your company or organization, contact Jack Cherbo at 818-783-0040, extension 26, or visit www.cherbopub.com.

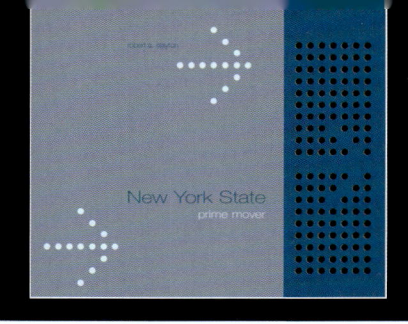

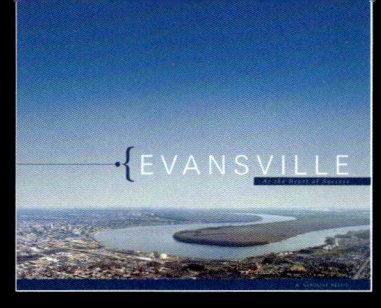

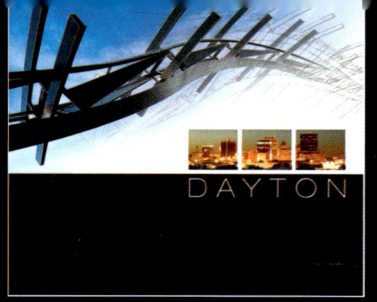

Select CPG Publications

VISIONS OF OPPORTUNITY
City, Regional, and State Series

ALABAMA *The Progress, The Promise*

AMERICA & THE SPIRIT
OF ENTERPRISE
Century of Progress, Future of Promise

CALIFORNIA *Golden Past, Shining Future*

CONNECTICUT *Chartered for Progress*

DELAWARE *Incorporating Vision in Industry*

EVANSVILLE *At the Heart of Success*

FORT WORTH *Where the Best Begins*

GREATER PHOENIX
Expanding Horizons

INDIANA
Crossroads of Industry and Innovation

LUBBOCK, TEXAS
Gem of the South Plains

MICHIGAN *America's Pacesetter*

MILWAUKEE *Midwestern Metropolis*

MISSOURI *Gateway to Enterprise*

NEW YORK STATE *Prime Mover*

NORTH CAROLINA *The State of Minds*

OKLAHOMA *The Center of It All*

SOUTH DAKOTA *Pioneering the Future*

TOLEDO *Access. Opportunity. Edge.*

UPSTATE NEW YORK
Corridor to Progress

WESTCHESTER COUNTY, NEW YORK
Headquarters to the World

WEST VIRGINIA *Reaching New Heights*

LEGACY
Commemorative Series

ALBERTA AT 100
Celebrating the Legacy

BUILD IT & THE CROWDS
WILL COME
Seventy-Five Years of Public Assembly

CELEBRATE SAINT PAUL
150 Years of History

DAYTON *On the Wings of Progress*

THE EXHIBITION INDUSTRY
The Power of Commerce

IDAHO *The Heroic Journey*

MINNEAPOLIS *Currents of Change*

NEW YORK STATE ASSOCIATION
OF FIRE CHIEFS
Sizing Up a Century of Service

VISIONS TAKING SHAPE
*Celebrating 50 Years of the Precast/
Prestressed Concrete Industry*

ANNUAL BUSINESS REPORTS

MINNESOTA REPORT *2007*

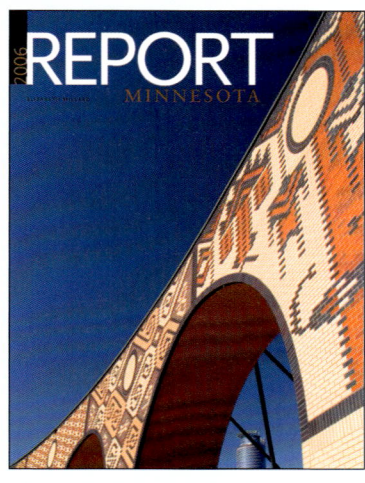

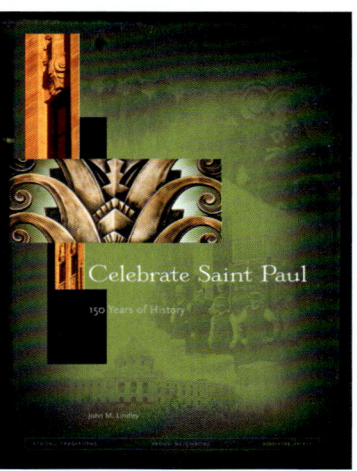

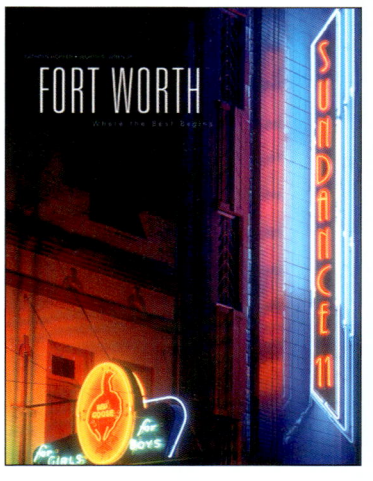

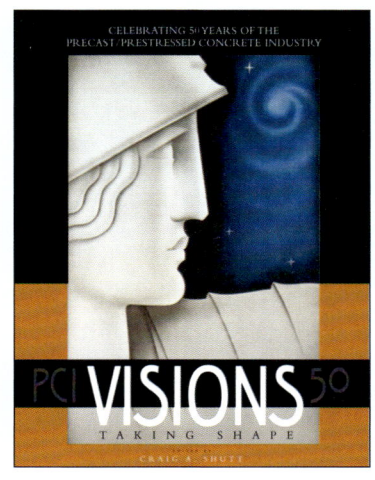

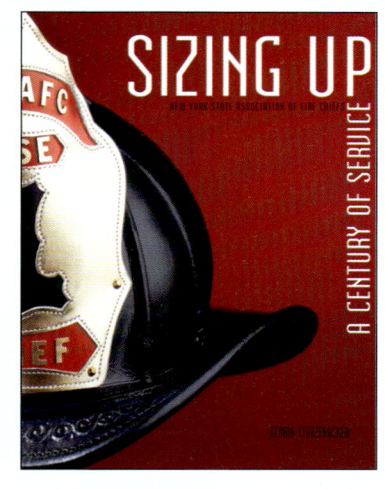

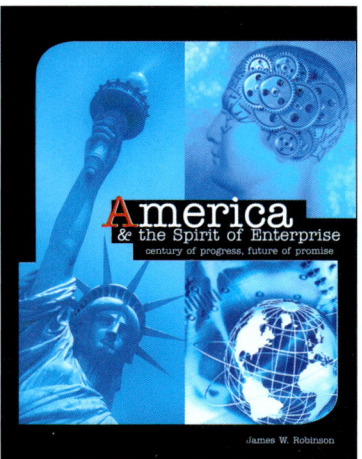

205

BIBLIOGRAPHY

Arik, Murat, and David A. Penn. Jennings A. Jones College of Business, Middle Tennessee State University. "The Health Care Industry in the Nashville MSA: Its Scope and Impact on the Regional Economy." Prepared for Nashville Health Care Council, January 31, 2006. http://www.healthcarecouncil.com/pdf/EconomicStudy2006.pdf (accessed May 17, 2006).

Battelle Technology Partnership Practice and State Science & Technology Institute (SSTI). "Tennessee Bioscience Initiatives," in *Growing the Nation's Biotech Sector: State Bioscience Initiatives 2006*. Prepared for the Biotechnology Industry Organization, 2006. http://wwww.bio.org/local/battelle2006/Tennessee.pdf (accessed May 30, 2006).

BioMimetic Therapeutics. Amendment No. 5 to Form S-1 Registration Statement under the Securities Act of 1933, May 9, 2006. http://www.sec.gov/Archives/edgar/data/1138400/000095013606003622/file001.htm (accessed May 29, 2006).

Capps, Milt. Spotlight: "Dell Inc. Strengthens Healthcare IT Presence with Rebrovick Appointment." *News of Nashville Technology*, July 28, 2005. http://www.technologycouncil.com/photos/File53.html (accessed April 22, 2006).

Cass, Michael. "GEC Wants $7.8 Million Extra Next Year." *The Tennessean*, February 22, 2006. http://www.tennessean.com/apps/pbcs.dll/article?AID=/20060222/NEWS0202/602220402 (accessed May 21, 2006).

Colliers Turley Martin Tucker. "Market Report, Nashville, TN." January 2006. http://www.colliers.com/Content/Repositories/Base/Markets/Nashville/English/Market_Report/PDFs/2005_Year_End_Market_Report.pdf (accessed March 29, 2006).

Colombo, Bettie, Director of Marketing Communications, Asurion. Telephone interview with the author, April 25, 2006.

Country Music Association. "Country Music Wraps 2005 on Strong Note," January 9, 2006. http://www.cmaworld.com/news_publications/pr_common/press_detail.asp?re=498&year=2006 (accessed May 27, 2006).

Designed for Worship: An Architectural History of Nashville's Sacred Spaces. Nashville Public Television. http://www.wnpt.net/worship/styles.html (accessed May 31, 2006).

Duncan, E. Townes, President, Solidus Company. In-person interview with the author, April 17, 2006.

Education USA. "Historically Black American Colleges and Universities." Tennessee State University: Notable Alumni. http://www.petersons.com/blackcolleges/profiles/tennessee_state.asp?sponsor=13.

Farris, Anne. "New Immigrants in New Places: America's Growing 'Global Interior.'" *Carnegie Reporter*, Fall 2005. http://www.carnegie.org/reporter/11/newimmigrants.

Federal Deposit Insurance Corporation. "Deposit Market Share MSA Selection," data on Nashville-Davidson–Murfreesboro, TN Metropolitan Statistical Area as of June 30, 2005 and June 30, 2004. http://www2.fdic.gov/sod/sodMarketBank2.asp (accessed April 25, 2006).

Forgey, Benjamin. "Affordable Housing That's So Nice to Come Home To" (discussing Row 8.9n project). *Washington Post*, February 28, 2004, page C5. http://www.washingtonpost.com/ac2/wp-dyn?pagename=article&contentId= A13890-2004Feb27&notFound=true (accessed March 29, 2006).

Fortune, "Fortune 500: States: Tennessee," April 4, 2006. http://money.cnn.com/magazines/fortune/fortune500/states/T.html (accessed May 17, 2006).

Harlan Howard Songs. http://www.harlanhoward.com/bios/Harlan-Howard.htm (accessed May 31, 2006).

Harris Interactive. "*The Wall Street Journal*/Harris Interactive Business School Survey." http://www.harrisinteractive.com/services/bschools.asp (accessed June 27, 2006).

Inc., "Inc. 500," November 2005. http://www.inc.com/app/inc500/view Company2005.jsp?cmpId=2005016 (accessed May 26, 2006).

Kiplinger's Personal Finance, "The Kiplinger 50," June 2006. http://www.kiplinger.com/personalfinance/features/archives/2006/05/nashville.html.

Krizner, Ken. "2006 America's Hottest Cities: Nashville Is Sweet Music for Expanding Companies." *Expansion Management*, January 26, 2006. http://www.expansionmanagement.com/smo/newsviewer/default.asp?cmd=articledetail&articleid=17012&st=3.

Lawson, Richard. "Nashville Repeats as No. 1." *NashvillePost.com*, January 26, 2006. http://www.nashvillepost.com/news/2006/1/26/nashville_repeats_as_no1. (accessed April 26, 2006).

———. "Weekend Reading: Cautious Bill's Wet Blanket." *NashvillePost.com*, February 17, 2006. http://www.nashvillepost.com/news/2006/2/17/weekend_reading_cautious_bills_wet_blanket (accessed May 27, 2006).

Louisana-Pacific Corporation. "Tennessee Titans' Stadium to Be Named LP Field; LP, Premier Supplier of Building Products, Purchases Naming Rights." Press release, June 6, 2006. http://phx.corporate-ir.net/phoenix.zhtml?c=73030&p=irol-newsArticle&ID=869262&highlight.

Metropolitan Nashville Public Schools. "MNPS Sees Progress, Challenges in AYP Results." http://www.mnps.org/site3.aspx (accessed August 18, 2006).

———. "Tennessee Adequate Yearly Progress Results Show Achievements and Challenges for MNPS." Press Release, August 17, 2006. http://www.mnps.org/site3.aspx; MNPS AYP Results 2005–2006.pdf.

MusicDish e-Journal. "Nashville's Music Industry Worth $6.38 Billion." January 11, 2006. http://www.musicdish.com/mag/?id=10794.

Naipaul, V. S. *A Turn in the South*. New York: Alfred A. Knopf, 1989.

Nashville Area Chamber of Commerce. "2005 Citizens Panel Report Card." http://www.nashvillechamber.com/education/0405report.pdf (accessed July 3, 2006).

Nashville Capital Network. "Nashville Capital Network's Angel Investor Group Invests in Pathfinder Therapeutics." http://www.nashvillecapital.com/news.php?viewStory=37 (accessed July 17, 2006).

Nashville Civic Design Center. *Nashville Downtown Living Initiative*. August 2003. http://www.civicdesigncenter.org/downloads/DowntownLiving.pdf.

Nashville Sports Council. "Our Economic Impact." http://www.nashvillesports.com/nsc/impact.html (accessed May 27, 2006).

Nashville State Community College. "NSCC/Sage Partnership." http://www.nscc.edu/industry/sage.html (accessed July 2, 2006).

———. "Workforce Development." http://www.workforce.nscc.edu/about.htm (accessed July 2, 2006).

National Association of Realtors. Current Report, "Median Sales Price of Existing Single-Family Homes for Metropolitan Areas." Nashville-Davidson–Murfreesboro. http://www.realtor.org/Research.nsf/Pages/MetroPrice.

Pack, Todd. "Health Care Worth $18B Here." *The Tennessean*, February 15, 2006. http://www.tennessean.com/apps/pbcs.dll/article?AID=2006602150432.

BIBLIOGRAPHY

Pinnacle Financial Partners. "Pinnacle Financial Reports Record Earnings." April 24, 2006. http://www.sec.gov/Archives/edgar/data/1115055/000104953506000010/pressrelease.htm (accessed April 24, 2006).

Pitkin, Ron, President, Cumberland House Publishing. E-mail to the author, April 27, 2006.

Raines, Patrick, and LaTanya Brown, Belmont University, College of Business Administration. "The Economic Impact of the Music Industry in the Nashville-Davidson–Murfreesboro MSA." Prepared for Nashville Area Chamber of Commerce, January 2006. http://www.nashvillechamber.com/president/musicindustryimpactstudy.pdf (accessed May 13, 2006).

Riley, Claudette. "Purcell, Garcia Back Reforms to Lift Metro Graduation Rate." *The Tennessean*, May 19, 2006. http://www.tennessean.com/apps/pbcs.dll/article?AID=/20060519/NEWS04/605190411/-1/PHOTO0204 (accessed July 2, 2006).

Smith, Barry, President, Eakin Partners. (Information on first quarter 2006 vacancy rates.) Telephone interview with the author [n.d.].

Tennessee Department of Education. "Davidson County Report Card 2005." http://www.k-12.state.tn.us/rptcrd05/systempf.asp?S=190 (accessed July 2, 2006).

———. "2004 Tennessee No Child Left Behind at-a-Glance Report: Davidson County." http://www2.state.tn.us/k-12/aypglancedist2004.asp?DN=190&Yr=2004 (accessed July 7, 2006).

———. "2005 NCLB Results: Davidson County." http://www2.state.tn.us/k-12/aypglancedist2005.asp?DN=190&Yr=2005 (accessed July 2, 2006).

Travel + Leisure, "America's Favorite Cities," March 22, 2004. http://www.travelandleisure.com/afc/pressrelease.cfm.

U.S. Census Bureau. *1997 Economic Census: Finance and Insurance, Nashville, TN MSA*. http://www.census.gov/epcd/ec97/metro5/M5360_52.HTM#N522 (accessed May 22, 2006).

———. *1997 Economic Census: Manufacturing, Nashville, TN MSA*. http://www.census.gov/epcd/ec97/metro5/M5360_31.HTM#N336 (accessed May 22, 2006).

———. *2002 Economic Census: Real Estate and Rental and Leasing, Nashville-Davidson–Murfreesboro, TN, Metropolitan Statistical Area*. http://www.census.gov/econ/census02/data/metro3/M3498053.htm (accessed March 13, 2006).

———. *2002 MSA Business Patterns (NAICS)*. http://censtats.census.gov/cgi-bin/msanaic/msasel.pl (accessed March 30, 2006).

U.S. News & World Report. "America's Best Colleges 2006." http://www.usnews.com/usnews/edu/college/rankings/rankindex_brief.php (accessed July 2, 2006).

Vanderbilt University, Office of the Chancellor. "Reaching Out to a Larger Community: Engaging in a New Way." http://www.vanderbilt.edu/chancellor/fiveyears/reachingout.html (accessed July 2, 2006).

———. "Vanderbilt's Achievements during Joe B. Wyatt's Chancellorship." http://www.vanderbilt.edu/chancellorsearch/wyatt3.html (accessed July 2, 2006).

Ward, Getahn. "Midstate Housing Remains in Demand." *The Tennessean*, February 13, 2006. http://www.tennessean.com/apps/pbcs.dll/article?AID=/20060213/BUSINESS01/602130331 (accessed March 12, 2006).

Whitehouse, Ken. "Nashville Chamber Issues Grade on Public Schools." NashvillePost.com, February 1, 2006. http://www.nashvillepost.com/news/2006/2/1/nashville_chamber_issues_grade_on_public_schools (accessed July 2, 2006).

Wright, Tina, Director of Media Relations, Country Music Hall of Fame and Museum. E-mail to the author regarding 2005 attendance numbers, May 22, 2006.

WSM Radio. "The History of WSM." http://www.wsmonline.com/page.asp?Page=52 (accessed April 25, 2006).

In addition, the Web sites of the following companies and organizations were consulted:

Advocat, American General Life and Accident Insurance Company, American Homepatient, American Retirement Corporation, American Sentinel University, America Service Group, AmSurg Corporation, A. O. Smith Water Products Company, Avondale Partners, Caremark Rx, the Carl Van Vechten Gallery at Fisk University, Community Health Systems, Emdeon Corporation, Fisk University, Gaylord Entertainment Company, Gen Cap America, Greater Nashville Association of Realtors, Gresham Smith and Partners, Harpeth Capital, HCA, Healthcare Realty Trust, HealthSpring, Healthstream, Healthways, Iasis Healthcare, KIPP: Knowledge Is Power Program, LifePoint Hospitals, MedicSight, Metropolitan Government of Nashville and Davidson County, Nashville Area Chamber of Commerce, Nashville Ballet, Nashville Capital Network, Nashville Children's Theatre, Nashville Convention & Visitors Bureau, Nashville Downtown Partnership, Nashville Greenways, Nashville Opera, Nashville Predators, Nashville Public Library, Nashville Sports Council, Nashville Symphony, National Health Investors, National Healthcare Corporation, National Health Realty, National Hockey League, Neal and Harwell, Nissan North America, North America Administrators, Pathfinder Therapeutics, Petra Capital Partners, Psychiatric Solutions, Renal Care Group, R. H. Boyd Publishing Corporation, Richland Ventures, Symbion, Synaxis Group, Tennessee Biotechnology Association, Tennessee Board of Regents, Tennessee Department of Labor & Workforce Development, Tennessee Performing Arts Center, Tennessee Small Business Development Center, Tennessee State University, Tennessee Titans, U.S. Army Corps of Engineers, Vanguard Health Systems, and Vought Aircraft Industries.

INDEX

A

ACCRA *Cost of Living Index*, 12
Acetadote, 57
Alexander, Lamar, 38
Alex S. Palmer & Company, 86
Allen, Rogan, 81
Altman, Robert, 71
American Association of Architects, 49
American General Life and Accident Insurance Company, 45, 118–19
American Hometown Publishing, 65
American International Group (AIG), 45
American Profile, 65
American Sentinel University, 32
AmSouth Bank, 42, 126
AmSurg, 56
Antioch, 12
A. O. Smith Water Products Company, 63
Area 2, 82
Arena Football League, 24
Arista Nashville, 77
Ashland City, 63
AstraZeneca, 58
Asurion Corporation, 45
Athens of the South, 11, 31, 38
Atkins, Chet, 77
Atlanta, 42, 91
Atlantic Coast Conference, 76
Atmos Energy, 99
Avondale Partners, 43

B

Bank of America, 42
Barthco International, 69
Bass, Berry and Sims, 46
Batten & Shaw, 89
Beacon Technologies, 65
BearingPoint, 49
Belle Meade, 12, 81, 82
Belle Meade Plantation, 20
BellSouth Tennessee, 49, 95
BellSouth Tower, 86
Belmont University, 34, 66, 72, 74
Berry Field, 91
Bicentennial Mall State Park, 19
Billboard, 79
BioMimetic Therapeutics, 57
Birmingham, 42, 54, 55
Blackbird Studio, 79
BNA, 91, 92
BNA Records, 77
Borders Group, 66
Boult, Cummings, Conners & Berry, 46
Boyd, Richard Henry, 65
Bradley, Owen, 77
Brasfield & Gorrie, 83, 172–73
Brentwood, 58, 69, 82
Bridgestone Americas Holding, Inc., 142–43
Bridgestone Corporation, 62
Brookside Properties, 86
Brown, H. Jackson, Jr., 65

C

California, 56
Cannon County, 96
Capitol Nashville Records, 77
Caremark Rx, 55, 95
Carl Van Vechten Gallery, 23
Carnegie Hall, 24
Caterpillar Financial Services Corporation, 43, 112–13
Cathedral of the Incarnation, 20
Cavalry Bancorp, 42
Census Bureau, 86
Centennial Park, 19, 20
Center of Business and Economic Research, 61
Central Parking Corporation, 168–69
Cezanne, Paul, 23
Charlotte, 42
Cheek family, 20
Cheekwood Botanical Garden and Museum of Art, 20
Chicago, 91
Christ Church Epsicopal, 20
churches, 20
Church of Christ, 32
Church Street, 83, 84
Cinram, 66
Citizen's Panel for a Community Report Card, 36
Civil War, 23, 36
Civitas Bank Group, 42
Clarcor, 63
Cline, Patsy, 72
CMA Awards, 76
CMA Music Festival, 17. *See also* Fan Fare
College of Health Sciences and Nursing, 34, 35. *See also* Belmont University
Colliers Turley Martin Tucker, 89

Comcast, 95
Comdata® Corporation, 116–17
Community Education
    Partners, 38
Community Health Systems,
    Inc., 52, 136–37
Construction Enterprises, 89
Consumers Insurance Group,
    Inc., 45, 124–25
Cookeville, 63
Cool Springs, 62, 85, 86
Cool Spings Life Sciences
    Center, 57
Country Music Association
    (CMA), 17, 76
Country Music Hall of Fame and
    Museum, 23, 76, 82
Country Music Marathon, 76
Country Weekly, 79
Crescent Resources, 86
CroFab, 58
CSX, 94
Cumberland apartment tower, 83
Cumberland Emerging
    Technologies Life Sciences
    Center, 57
Cumberland House Publishing,
    65

Cumberland Pharmaceuticals, 57
Cumberland River, 19, 66, 84,
    85, 94
Cummins Filtration, 63, 146–47
Curb, Mike, 77
Curb Records, 77
CytoFab, 58

D
Davidson County, 82
Dean of Nashville Songwriters,
    27
Dell Computer, 65, 95
Dickson, 62
Dickson County, 23
Digital Dog, 65
Direct General Corporation, 45
DirecTV, 95
Dish TV, 95
Disney, 77
Distinguished Hospital—Clinical
    Excellence Award, 52
Distinguished Hospital—Patient
    Safety and Cardiac Care
    Excellence, 52
Dixie Chicks, 79
Doubletree Guest Suites
    Nashville Airport, 196–97

Downtown Loop, 93
Downtown Presbyterian
    Church, 20
DreamWorks Nashville, 77

E
Eakin Partners, 83
Earl Swensson Associates, Inc.,
    49, 182
East Corridor, 93
East Nashville, 20, 23, 85
Echostar, 95
Education Networks of America
    (ENA), 38
Edwards, Edwin, 46
Egyptian Revival, 20
Electric Membership
    Corporation, 96
Electrolux Home Products, 63
Emdeon Business Services
    (EBS), 56
Emdeon Corporation, 56
EMI, 77
Ensworth School, 38
Epic Records, 77
Equitable Securities
    Corporation, 41, 43
Expansion Management, 11

F
Fan Fare, 17
Farmer's Market, 85
Favorite Recipes Press, 65
Film House, 79
Firestone Tire plant, 62
First Horizon National
    Corporation, 45
First Tennessee, 110–11
Fisk Jubilee Singers, 34, 72
Fisk University, 23, 34
Five Points, 85
Forbes, 11, 69
Ford Motor Company, 62
foreign trade zone (FTZ), 66
Forest Hills, 82
Franklin, 42, 43, 49, 56, 57, 63
Franklin American Mortgage
    Company, 43, 122–23
Fresenius, 54
Frist, Thomas F., Jr., 54
Frist, Thomas F., Sr., 54
Frist Center for the Visual
    Arts, 23
Frito-Lay, 26

G
Gallatin, 66

INDEX

Gap, 66
Gardena, 62
Gateway, 65
Gaylord Entertainment Center, 23, 24, 74, 75, 76
Gaylord Opryland Resort & Convention Center, 49, 76, 198
GEM 21S, 57
Gen Cap America, 43
General Motors, 62
Georgia, 42
Germany, 62
Ghertner & Company, 86
Giarratana, Tony, 83, 84
Gibson Guitar Corp., 64
Gideons International, 64
Gordon, Joel, 54
Gospel Music Association, 72
Gothic Revival, 20
Gould Turner Group, P.C., 174–75
Grand Ole Opry, 23, 76
Great Performances at Vanderbilt, 24
Greek Revival, 20
Green Hills, 81, 82
Greenwood, Lee, 77
Gresham, Batey M., Jr., 49

Gresham, Smith and Partners, 49
Gulch area, 84

H

Hardaway Construction Corporation, 89
Hard Rock Cafe, 72
Harpeth Capital, 43
Harpeth Hall, 38
Hartmann, Inc., 148
Hartford of the South, 41
Hastings Architecture Associates, 83
Healthcare Realty Trust, 85
HealthGrades, 52
HealthSouth, 54
Healthways, 56
Hermitage, 20
H. G. Hill Realty Company, 86
Highways, 89
Hoffa, Jimmy, 46
Holland Group, The, 164–65
Hospital Affiliates International, (HAI), 54
Hospital Corporation of America (HCA), 26, 35, 52, 55, 130–33
Houston Oilers, 24
Howard, Harlan, 27

Hume-Fogg Academic, 37

I

Iasis Healthcare, 54
immigrants, 15
India, 56
Ingram, E. Bronson, 32
Ingram Barge Company, 94
Ingram Book Group, 66, 69
Ingram Entertainment Holdings, 69
Ingram Industries, 69
Interstate Highway System, 93
Iroquois Steeplechase, 76
Italy, 62

J

Jackson, Andrew, 20
Japan, 62
J. C. Bradford & Company, 41, 43
John C. Tune Airport, 92
Journal Communications, 65
J. Percy Priest (Lake), 19
Jubilee Hall, 34

K

Kay, John, 72

Kelly, R., 79
Kentucky, 52
Kid Rock, 72
Kiplinger's Personal Finance, 11
KIPP Academy Nashville, 37
Koreans, 15
KPMG Consulting, 49
KraftCPAs, 46
Kristofferson, Kris, 77
Kurds, 15

L

Laotians, 15
Lattimore Black Morgan & Cain, 46
La Vergne, 62, 63, 65, 66, 69
Lay's, 26
Lebanon, 42, 65, 93
Life and Casualty Tower, 84
LifeFlight, 52
LifeMasters Supported Self-Care, 56
LifePoint Hospitals, 54
Life's Little Instruction Book, 65
LifeWay Christian Resources, 64, 156–57
Lipscomb University, 32, 35
London, 58

Los Angeles, 12, 62, 64, 91
Louisiana, 46
Louisiana-Pacific Corporation, 26, 62
LP Field, 23, 24, 75, 76
Lyric Street Records, 77

M
Madison Square Garden, 76
Mahle International, 62
Mahle Tennex North America, 62
Mamma Mia!, 24
Mars Petcare U.S., 152–53
Martin Luther King (High School), 37
Maury County, 99
McGraw, Tim, 77
Meharry Medical College, 32, 52
Mercury, 26, 77
Metropolitan Nashville Airport Authority, 92, 202
Metropolitan Nashville General Hospital, 52
Metro Transit Authority, 93
Mexicans, 15
Middle East, 15
Middle Tennessee Electric, 96

Middle Tennessee State University, 15, 35
Mike Curb College of Entertainment & Music Business, 34. *See also* Belmont University
Milwaukee Brewers, 76
Mitchell, John, 46
MJM Architects, 176–77
M. Lee Smith Publishers, 65
Modern Red SchoolHouse Institute, 38
Monroe Carell Jr. Children's Hospital, 49, 52
Montgomery Bell Academy, 38
Mother Church, 23, 76. *See also* Ryman Auditorium
Movin' Out, 24
Murfreesboro, 35, 45, 62
Music City Bowl, 76
Music City USA, 11, 15, 71
Music Row, 77, 79
Music Row magazine, 79
Music Square East and West, 77

N
Naipaul, V. S., 71
NASCAR, 76

Nasdaq, 42
Nashville Area Chamber of Commerce, 12, 26, 36, 72
Nashville Arena, 23
Nashville Ballet, 24
Nashville Capital Network, 44
Nashville Children's Theater, 24
Nashville City Center, 49
Nashville/Davidson County, 82
Nashville Downtown Living Initiative, 20
Nashville Economic Market, 11, 23
Nashville Electric Service, 96
Nashville Gas, 99
Nashville Gas and Light Company, 99
Nashville Greenways, 19
Nashville Health Care Council, 15, 51
Nashville International Airport, 49, 63, 91, 92, 95
Nashville Kats, 24
Nashville Metros, 24
Nashville Opera, 24
Nashville Predators, 24, 75, 76
Nashville Scene, 12
Nashville Sounds, 24, 76

Nashville Sounds baseball park, 82
Nashville Sports Council, 76
Nashville Stadium, 23
Nashville State Community College, 35, 66
Nashville SuperSpeedway, 24, 76
Nashville Symphony, 23
Nashville Technology Council, 66
National Cancer Institute Comprehensive Cancer Center, 52
National Enquirer, 79
National Football League, 24, 75
National Healthcare Corporation, 85
National Health Realty, 85
National Hockey League, 24, 75, 76
National Life and Accident Insurance Company, 45, 76
National Register of Historic Places, 20
National Sick and Accident Insurance Company, 45
Naxos, 72
Neal, James F., 46

INDEX

Neal & Harwell, 46
neoclassicism, 20
neo-Romanesque, 20
New Jersey, 56
New York, 91
New York City, 12
Nissan Motor Co., 86
Nissan North America, 26, 49, 61, 62
No Child Left Behind, 36
North American Administrators, 45
North Carolina, 42, 86, 99

O
Oak Hill, 82
Odom's Tennessee Pride Sausage, Inc., 144–45
Oh Boy Records, 77
O'Keeffe, Georgia, 23
Opryland hotel, 74, 76
Osburn-Hessey Logistics, 69
Oshkosh B'Gosh, 66
Overton, John, 23

P
Parthenon, 20
Partnership 2010, 26
Pathfinders Therapeutics, 32
Percy Warner Park, 76
Performance Food Group, 66
Petra Capital Partners, 44
Picasso, Pablo, 23
Piedmont Gas Company, 99
Pinnacle Financial Partners, 42
Portland (Tennessee), 62
Prine, John, 77
Producers, The, 24
Protherics, 58
Providence Publishing Corporation, 65
Psychiatric Solutions, 54
Public Square, 82
Publishing Group of America, 65

Q
Quality Industries, Inc., 149
Quanta Computer Corporation, 65

R
Radiology Alliance, 138
Radnor Yard, 94
Randstad USA, 166–67
RCA, 26
RCR Building Corporation, 89
Rebrovick, Linda, 49
REITs, 85, 86
R. H. Boyd Publishing Corporation, 65, 158–59
Richland Ventures, 44
Riverfront Park, 93
Red Hot Chili Peppers, 79
Renal Care Group, 54
Renoir, Pierre-Auguste, 23
Rimes, LeAnn, 77
Robertson County, 23, 63
Ross Bryan Associates, Inc.—Consulting Engineers, 180–81
Route 840, 93
Row 8.9n, 85
Rudolph, Wilma, 35
Rutherford, 11, 36
Rutherford County, 35, 96, 99
Rutledge Hill Press, 65
Ryman Auditorium, 23, 76, 83

S
Sage Group, 35
Saint Thomas Health Services, 52, 134–35
Saint Thomas Hospital, 52
Salix Ventures, 44
Saturn, 61, 62
Schermerhorn, Kenneth, 23
Schermerhorn Symphony Center, 23, 82
Shelby Street Pedestrian Bridge, 76, 82
Shirley Zeitlin and Company, Realtors®, 184
Signature Tower, 84
Skate Park at Wave Country, 19
Skyline Medical Center, 52
Smashmouth, 79
Smyrna, 62
Snider, Todd, 77
SoBro, 84
Solidus Company, 44
Somalis, 15
Sony BMG, 77
Sony Music, 26
South Americans, 15
Southeast Conference, 76
Spheris, 56
Springfield, 63
Spring Hill, 62
Steppenwolf, 72
Stieglitz, Alfred, 23
Street Dixon Rick Architecture, PLC, 178–79
Strickland, William, 20

Sudanese, 15
Sumner, 11
Sumner County, 82
SunTrust Bank–Nashville, 42, 83, 114–15
SunTrust Plaza, 83
Surgical Care Affiliates, 54, 56
Swensson, Earl, 49
Symbion, 56
Synaxis Group, 45

T
Taiwan, 65
Teamsters Union, 46
Teksid Aluminum Foundry, 62
Tennessee, 11, 35, 52, 62
Tennessee Commerce Bancorp, 42
Tennessee Credit Union, The, 120–21
Tennessee Department of Labor and Workforce Development, 12
Tennessee Performing Arts Center, 23, 24
Tennessee State Capitol, 19
Tennessee State Penitentiary, 62
Tennessee State University, 35
Tennessee Titans, 24, 75, 76
Tennessee Valley Authority (TVA), 96
Texas, 99
Thais, 15
Third Coast, 11
Thomas Nelson, 64, 65, 66
Titan Town, 11
T-Mobile, 95
Toulouse-Lautrec, Henri, 23
Tractor Supply Company, 192–93
Travel + Leisure, 11
Travellers Rest Plantation and Museum, 23
Trevecca Nazarene University, 34, 106
Triad Hospitals, 54
Triple A baseball, 24
TriStarHealth Systems, 52
12th Avenue South, 84
2005-06 Adequate Yearly Progress (AYP) report, 36

U
Unipres, 62
United Methodist Publishing House, The, 64, 160
United Parcel Service, 66
United Soccer Leagues, 24
Universal Amphitheater, 64
Universal CityWalk, 64
Universal Music Group, 77
University of Tennessee, 61, 65
University School of Nashville, 38
U.S. Army Corps of Engineers, 94
USA Today, 64
U.S. Department of Commerce, 66
U.S. News & World Report, 31, 35, 52
Utah, 58

V
Vanderbilt, Cornelius, 32
Vanderbilt-Ingram Cancer Center, 32, 52
Vanderbilt University, 31, 34, 44, 66, 104–05
Vanderbilt University Medical Center, 52, 58
Viridian condo tower, 83, 84
Visteon Corporation, 62
Voight Aircraft Industries, 63

W
Waller Lansden Dortch and Davis, 46
Wall Street of the South, 41
Warner Bros. Nashville, 77
Warner Music Group, 77
West End Summit, 86
Whirlpool Corporation, 63
Whitland/West End/Richland, 82
Wildhorse Saloon, 72
Williams, Hank, Sr., 72
Williamson, 36
Williamson County, 11, 23, 62, 63, 82, 86, 96, 99
Wilson, 11
Wilson Bank & Trust, 42
Wilson County, 23, 82, 96
Wilson, Gretchen, 79
Winfrey, Oprah, 35
WorkForce and Community Development Center, 35
WSM (radio station), 76

Y
Young Buck, 72
YMCA of Middle Tennessee, 188–89

PHOTO CREDITS

Page ii: © Evan Whisenant
Page v: © Robert Catalano
Page vi, left: © Bob Carey
Page vi, right: © Andrea Pistolesi/ The Image Bank/Getty Images
Page vii: © Carl Tashian
Page viii: © Dean Dixon/ America 24-7/Getty Images
Page x: © Andy Sacks/Stone/ Getty Images
Page xi, left: © Michael Huff
Page xi, right: © Yosuke Kitazawa
Page xiii: © James Lemass
Page xiv, left: © Blake Wylie
Page xiv, right: © Randy Blaylock
Page xv: © Paul Van Hoy II
Page xvii: © Lise Gagne
Page xviii: © James Lemass
Page xx: © Paul Van Hoy II
Page 2, left: © George D. Lepp/ Corbis
Page 2, right: Courtesy, Library of Congress
Page 3: © Hulton Archive/ Getty Images
Page 4: Courtesy, Library of Congress
Page 5, left: Louise Dahl-Wolfe (American, 1895-1989), William Edmondson with Schoolteacher, n.d., Gelatin silverprint, Gift of the Artist © 1989 Center for Creative Photography, Arizona Board of Regents
Page 5, right: © Dave G. Houser/ Corbis
Page 6: © Bettmann/Corbis
Page 7: © Kenn Stilger/Heavenly Perspective Photography
Page 8: © Paul Van Hoy II
Page 10: © Honey Salvation/Alamy
Page 11: © Paul Van Hoy II
Page 12, left: © AP Photo/ Mark Humphrey
Page 13: © Joe Weaver
Page 14, 15: © Kevin Dodge/Corbis
Page 16, left: © Paul Van Hoy II
Page 16, 17: © Deb Parsons
Page 17: © Rick Murray
Page 18, left: © James Lemass
Page 18, 19: © Kenn Stilger/ Heavenly Perspective Photography
Page 19: © Brent Moore
Page 20, left: © James Lemass
Page 20, right: © James Lemass
Page 21, top: © Jeff Dalzell
Page 21, bottom: © James Lemass
Page 22, left: © Aaron Grayum
Page 22, right: © Paul Van Hoy II
Page 23, top right: © Alan Poizner
Page 23, bottom right: © Erika Sherman
Page 24, left: © Michael Davis

Page 24, right: © Rachel Pennington
Page 25, left: Courtesy, Nashville Children's Theatre. Photo by Dan Brewer
Page 25, right: © Stephen Dunn/ Getty Images
Page 26, 27: © Holly Westcott
Page 27, right: © Christoph Wilhelm/zefa/Corbis
Page 28: © Paul Van Hoy II
Page 30: © Jack Hollingsworth/ Getty Images
Page 31: © Ali Husain
Page 32: Courtesy, Vanderbilt University. Photo by Neil Brake
Page 33, left: Courtesy, Vanderbilt University
Page 33, right: © William Crook
Page 34, left: © Bill Steber
Page 34, right: Courtesy, Belmont University. Photo by J. Michael Krouskop
Page 35, left: Courtesy, MTSU Photographic Services
Page 35, right: Courtesy, Nashville State Community College. Photo by Sue Portanova
Page 36, 37: © Dennis MacDonald/age fotostock
Page 37: Courtesy, Metropolitan Nashville Public Schools
Page 38: © Tom Stewart/Corbis
Page 39: © Paul Thomas/The Image Bank/Getty Images
Page 40: © C. Willhelm/Photex/ zefa/Corbis
Page 41, top: Courtesy, The Tennessee Credit Union
Page 41, bottom: © Masterfile
Page 42, left: © Michael Davis
Page 42, right: © Kathleen Finlay/ Masterfile
Page 43, left: © Masterfile
Page 43, right: © Paul Van Hoy II
Page 44, left: © blackred
Page 44, right: © MTPA Stock
Page 45, left: © Getty Images
Page 45, right: © LWA/ Sharie Kennedy/zefa/Corbis
Page 46: © Bettmann/Corbis
Page 47: Courtesy, Bass, Berry & Sims PLC. Photo by Jeff Frazier
Page 48: © Raoul Minsart/Masterfile
Page 49, left: © Tim Mantoani/ Masterfile
Page 49, right: Courtesy, Vanderbilt Children's Hospital
Page 50: Courtesy, Vanderbilt University. Photo by Neil Brake
Page 51: Courtesy, Vanderbilt University. Photo by Neil Brake
Page 52: © Masterfile
Page 53, left: Courtesy, Skyline Medical Center

PHOTO CREDITS

Page 53, right: © Hellen King/Corbis
Page 54: Courtesy, Meharry Medical College
Page 55, left: © Bernard van Berg/Getty Images
Page 55, right: © Jose Luis Pelaez, Inc./Corbis
Page 56, 57: Courtesy, Cumberland Emerging Technologies, Inc.
Page 57, top right: © Corbis
Page 57, bottom right: © ER Productions/Corbis
Page 58, left: © Joe McDonald/Corbis
Page 58, right: © LWA-JDC/Corbis
Page 59: © Andrei Tchernov
Page 60: Courtesy, Nissan North America, Inc.
Page 61: © Car Culture/Corbis
Page 62, left: Courtesy, Electrolux Major Appliances
Page 62, right: © Chad Breece
Page 63, left: Courtesy, Vought Aircraft Industries, Inc.
Page 63, right: Photo: Bosch
Page 64, left: © John M. Setzler, Jr.
Page 64, right: © BC Moller/Taxi/Getty Images
Page 65: © Seth Wenig/Reuters/Corbis
Page 66: © MedioImages/Alamy

Page 67, left: © Masterfile
Page 67, right: © Alicia Gipson
Page 68: © Ron Wurtzer/Getty Images
Page 69: © Yang Liu/Corbis
Page 70: © James Lemass
Page 71: © Tony Hatton
Page 72, left: © Joanna Spock Dean
Page 72, left: © James Lemass
Page 73: © Edward Pond/Masterfile
Page 74, left: © John P. Ford
Page 74, 75: © James Lemass
Page 75, right: © Michael Davis
Page 76: © Darrell Ingham/Getty Images
Page 77, left: © John P. Ford
Page 77, center: © Leo Reynolds
Page 77, right: © Teresa Cook
Page 78: © James Lemass
Page 79: © James Lemass
Page 80: © Paul Van Hoy II
Page 81: Courtesy, Rogan Allen Builders
Page 82, left: © Curtis V. Palmer
Page 82, right: © Kerry Woo
Page 83: © Brian Siskind
Page 84, left: Courtesy, G&G Advertising
Page 84, right: © Michael Davis
Page 85: © Paul Lithgow

Page 86, left: Courtesy, Nissan North America, Inc.
Page 86, right: © Michael Davis
Page 87: Courtesy, Williamson County Convention & Visitors Bureau
Page 88: Courtesy, Paradigm Productions, LLC
Page 89, left: © Amanda Rogers
Page 89, right: Courtesy, Batten & Shaw, Inc.
Page 90: © Markus Moellenberg/zefa/Corbis
Page 91: © Michael Davis
Page 92, left: © Philip R. Cloutier
Page 92, 93: © Michael Davis
Page 93, right: © Michael Davis
Page 94, left: © J. Niles Clement
Page 94, right: © James Lemass
Page 95, left: © Corbis
Page 95, right: © Flying Colours/Getty Images
Page 96: © Brian Siskind
Page 97: © Paul Van Hoy II
Page 98: Courtesy, Tennessee Valley Authority
Page 98, 99: © Creatas
Page 99, right: © Tomas Kraus
Page 100: © Arne Thaysen
Page 102: © James McQuillan
Page 107: © Corbis
Page 108: © age fotostock

Page 127: © José Luis Gutiérrez
Page 128: © Mario Beauregard/Corbis
Page 139: © Jason Woodcock
Page 140: © Alvaro Heinzen
Page 150: © GK Hart/Vikki Hart/The Image Bank/Getty Images
Page 154: © Ron Watts/Corbis
Page 161: © Jennifer Trenchard
Page 162: © Photodisc
Page 170: © Richard Gerstner
Page 183: © Alessandro Terni
Page 185: © Jonathan Werve
Page 186: © Corbis
Page 190: © Corbis
Page 194: © age fotostock
Page 198: © Richard Gerstner
Page 199: © James Lemass
Page 200: © Perry Mastrovito/Corbis
Page 203: © Joshua Sage Newman for st8mnt.com

cherbo publishing group, inc.

TYPOGRAPHY
Principal faces used: Univers, designed by Adrian Frutiger in 1957;
Helvetica, designed by Matthew Carter, Edouard Hoffmann,
and Max Miedinger in 1959

HARDWARE
Macintosh G5 desktops, digital color laser printing with Xerox Docucolor 12, digital
imaging with Creo EverSmart Supreme

SOFTWARE
QuarkXPress, Adobe Illustrator, Adobe Photoshop, Adobe Acrobat, Microsoft Word,
Eye-One Pro by Gretagmacbeth, Creo Oxygen, FlightCheck

PAPER
Text Paper: #80 Luna Matte

Bound in Rainbow® recycled content papers from
Ecological Fibers, Inc.

Dust Jacket: #100 Sterling-Litho Gloss